Conscientization
AND THE Cultivation
OF Conscience

# Narrative, Dialogue, and the Political Production of Meaning

Michael Peters & Peter McLaren
*Series Editors*

Vol. 3

---

The Education and Struggle series is part of the Peter Lang Education list.
Every volume is peer reviewed and meets
the highest quality standards for content and production.

---

PETER LANG
New York • Bern • Frankfurt • Berlin
Brussels • Vienna • Oxford • Warsaw

Keqi (David) Liu

# Conscientization AND THE Cultivation OF Conscience

PETER LANG
New York • Bern • Frankfurt • Berlin
Brussels • Vienna • Oxford • Warsaw

Library of Congress Cataloging-in-Publication Data
Liu, Keqi.
Conscientization and the cultivation of conscience / Keqi (David) Liu.
pages cm. — (Education and struggle; Vol. 3)
Includes bibliographical references.
1. Conscience. 2. Freire, Paulo, 1921–1997. I. Title.
BJ1471.L53  170—dc23  2013042401
ISBN 978-1-4331-2542-3 (hardcover)
ISBN 978-1-4331-2541-6 (paperback)
ISBN 978-1-4539-1257-7 (e-book)
ISSN 2168-6432

Bibliographic information published by **Die Deutsche Nationalbibliothek**.
**Die Deutsche Nationalbibliothek** lists this publication in the "Deutsche Nationalbibliografie"; detailed bibliographic data are available on the Internet at http://dnb.d-nb.de/.

© 2014 Peter Lang Publishing, Inc., New York
29 Broadway, 18th floor, New York, NY 10006
www.peterlang.com

All rights reserved.
Reprint or reproduction, even partially, in all forms such as microfilm, xerography, microfiche, microcard, and offset strictly prohibited.

# Table of Contents

Preface and Acknowledgments ................................................. vii

Introduction ........................................................................ 1
Chapter One: Paulo Freire: Life, Work, and Theory............................. 7
Chapter Two: The Key Elements of Conscientization........................... 31
Chapter Three: Conscience and its Relationship With Consciousness ........... 51
Chapter Four: The Dynamism of the Work of Conscience...................... 73
Chapter Five: The Cultivation of Conscience.................................... 93
Chapter Six: The Integration of the Cultivation of Conscience
    Into Conscientization........................................................ 121
Chapter Seven: Conscientization: Educational Necessity and
    Cultural Significance ...................................................... 145
Chapter Eight: The Pedagogical Possibilities of Conscientization............... 169

Conclusion ....................................................................... 183
References ....................................................................... 185

# Preface and Acknowledgments

My preoccupation with human suffering has evoked a deep interest in, and concern for, humanity—the goodness, worthiness, and dignity of being "human." There is also a similar curiosity about the individual and collective loss of humanity and the unnecessary human suffering of others, all without which there could be no discourse of humanity.

My interest has been shaped by my birth and 39-year upbringing in China and fueled by my observation of the historic events that have unfolded in my homeland, from Mao's cultural revolution, through Deng's reform and open policies, to the introduction of the market system for economic growth. Problems arising from these significant events created an environment that led many of my generation to question the purpose and the outcomes of the measures taken by successive governments in China: What was the revolution about? Why did the socialist system fail to live out its essence as theorized? In particular, in light of the subsequent corruption and injustice and the increasingly widening gap between rich and poor within China, the question must be posed: What was the use of Mao's revolution? Did millions of people die in vain attempting to set up a socialist system?

The prospect of addressing the concerns and questions I held in a more substantive way arrived in 2006 during my time as a Master of Education postgraduate student at the University of Canterbury in Aotearoa/New Zealand. In reading

Paulo Freire's (1972a) seminal work, *Pedagogy of the Oppressed*, I found a theoretical and dialogical platform from which to consider the nature of human suffering. Such reading prompted a reconsideration of the scope of Freire's notion of conscientization, which he defined in *Pedagogy of Indignation* (2004) as "the building of critical awareness and conscience" (p. 66). This redefinition not only provides a stimulus for better understanding of the root causes of human suffering and dehumanization or the loss of humanity but also brings full effect to humanization, an effective approach to address dehumanizing problems. Ignited by such a critical reading, I started my doctoral thesis, researching how the cultivation of conscience could be incorporated into conscientization.

After four years of hard work, three key tasks were completed: a determination of the notion of conscience that has internal coherence with the process of conscientization, an examination of how to cultivate conscience, and a determination of how to integrate the cultivation of conscience into conscientization. My doctoral study confirmed that conscientization, as an educational initiative, can readily and sustainably maintain both self and social empowerment when it is deeply rooted in the praxis of changing the world. While the cultivation of critical consciousness tackles systemic and ideological crises, the cultivation of conscience addresses problems of human consciousness such as insatiable human desire represented in varying forms of egoism, ambition, lust, greed, and so on. With the benefit of rigorous feedback on my doctoral thesis via the examination process, I now feel my work is ready to appear in book form.

I wish to take this opportunity to make some acknowledgments. I must express my gratitude to Professor Peter Roberts, Dr. Baljit Kaur, Dr. Helen Hayward, and Dr. Deb Hill for their genuine care and enlightening support. I am truly appreciative of Professor Graham Hingangaroa Smith's and Dr. Kariane Westrheim's thorough engagement with my work. Finally, I am very grateful to Professor Peter McLaren and Professor Michael Peters for supporting the inclusion of my book in their "Education and Struggle" series.

# Introduction

The root causes of unnecessary human suffering have been interpreted in two broad ways. Some who have pondered these matters relate human suffering to human nature; others seek an explanation in an oppressive social system and its hegemonic ideology. In terms of the former, the belief is that human beings possess "selfish genes" from which emerge different moral dilemmas; for the latter, human beings are by nature "good," and it is the state of societal conditions that determines whether this disposition remains or is reconfigured. Acts of dehumanization—injustice, oppression, exploitation, and alienation—can be overcome or mediated through social change.

It seems that one explanation of the origins of human suffering exaggerates human self-interest and ignores the influence of social factors while the other acts in the reverse. In reality, however, both social system and human nature problems coexist. The latter problems are better conceived as human consciousness problems, which are far more complex. Social change aided by social and cultural criticism might more readily meet social system and ideological crises; however, it is not easy to satisfy insatiable human desire represented in varying forms of egoism, ambition, lust, and greed. To attend to human consciousness problems requires something different. It necessitates transcendence through the cultivation of conscience. This suggests that the cultivation of conscience is imperative, though it is often ignored in current sociocultural discourses dominated by empiricism, social constructionism, postmodernism, and, in particular, neo-liberalism. The enigma, nevertheless, is that human basic needs and biological desires are simultaneously bound up together in and by social, political, and economic systems and ideology as much as they are by each other. This reality demands a holistic approach that is able to address social system problems and human consciousness problems at the same time.

Freire's (2004, p. 66) redefinition of conscientization as "the building of critical awareness and conscience" offers a possible breakthrough by mediating this dynamic in a particular way. While we can employ social critique and cultural criticism or subversion as an integral part of social change to tackle hegemonic ideology or cultural domination and oppression, we can employ transcendence through the cultivation of conscience to attend to various manifestations of human desire. This is evident through Freire's equal appropriation of Marx's materialist and historical concern of worldliness and Christian transcendency. Accordingly, a down-to-earth implementation of humanization necessitates an important project, the integration of the cultivation of conscience into the practice of conscientization.

Although Freire alluded to conscience in his earlier work, he focused more overtly on this basic component of conscientization in *Pedagogy of Indignation*, published posthumously in 2004. Within Freire's work and that of Freirean scholars, there is extensive coverage regarding the importance of developing critical consciousness, but there is a lack of systematic investigation into the cultivation of conscience and how the latter is crucial to conscientization as a distinctive process of human development. This poses a problem of how the cultivation of conscience can be incorporated into the process of conscientization. Within this broad framing or research problem lie related questions: What is conscience? What notion of conscience has internal coherence with the process of conscientization? What are the conditions for the work of conscience? How can conscience be cultivated? How can the cultivation of conscience be incorporated into the process of conscientization? Also, having addressed these questions, we might ask how conscientization can be usefully applied to current sociocultural, historical contexts and pedagogical practices.

In this book, in order to address these questions, philosophy, literature, and education are combined and treated as a trinity. While a number of philosophical traditions and literary works from various perspectives are drawn on to reinforce and illustrate particular theoretical points, the educational field is taken as a practical arena for action.

The argument starts with a comprehensive study of Freire's life, work, and theory to illuminate why he, as Giroux (1985) commented, has offered the language of not only critique but also possibility. Against this backdrop, a number of the indispensable elements of conscientization are closely and critically examined. Since the development of the concept is also enhanced by those commentators, two comments are highlighted. One is that, as Roberts (1996) contended, the dialogical nature and relation of conscientization should be understood as the multiplication of consciousnesses through meaningful communication. The other is that conscientization, as an integral part of transformative praxis, has an internal relation to humanization (Smith, 1999; Torres, 1994).

The origin and the historical development of conscience are investigated with reference to Despland's (1987) mapping. In order to scope the notion more fully, comments on conscience are reviewed by such figures as Cicero, Bonaventure, Aquinas, Montaigne, Descartes, Butler, Rousseau, and Kant. Considering that conscientization is about the cultivation of critical consciousness and conscience, an etymological study of consciousness and conscience is followed by investigating Arnold's (1994) interpretation of Hellenism and Hebraism and Engelberg's (1972) research on the conscience–consciousness problem.

The examination of the dialectical relation between consciousness and conscience focuses on the conflict and unity between the two concepts. The conflict between consciousness and conscience is traced back to Locke (1959). It became irresolvable when Nietzsche (1966, 2000) stressed free will—unobstructed consciousness of life—and rejected conscience as the herd conscience. Conrad's (1995) novel, *Heart of Darkness*, is employed to show what is wrong with Nietzsche's point; that is, a human being cannot even interpret his or her own consciousness if he or she has no conscience, and a human being lives in horror if he or she has no morality. This makes Hegel's (1971) understanding of conscience more compelling: Conscience, sitting at the highest state of the development of consciousness, acts as a unifying moral agent.

The importance of conscience to morality is reconsidered in a secular or unreligious discourse by first examining Marx and Engels's (1972) view, in which he locates materialism as the foundation of morality, and then Schopenhauer's (2010) view, in which he takes compassion as the basis of morality. Drawing on May's (1983) phenomenological study on conscience, it is argued that conscience can still serve as the basis of morality. According to May, Kant outlined the basic component of conscience: consciousness of maintaining the self's inner harmony by honoring and preserving humanity in one's dignity and personality. However, Kant's notion of conscience still stays at an egoistic level; in fact, conscience, the reflexive consciousness of humanity, not only maintains inner harmony for the self individually but also helps preserve social justice for community collectively (May, 1983). This understanding, compatible with Freire's ethical ideal of humanization, justifies and validates the cultivation of conscience.

The discussion of the work of conscience starts with Arendt's (1978) view that conscience only visits the soul of those who have moral concerns. This sheds light on Mencius's (2003) call: to be moral by setting one's mind on high principles. In this context, Feng's (1960) analysis of "the four spheres of living" is introduced to explain that to live in a moral sphere requires transcendence, because human beings are more likely to be attracted by utilitarian concerns. Here the investigation of the notion of transcendence turns back to Socrates's (Plato, 1955) concept of the good. However, Hume's (1992) challenge of Plato's idea of reason and Kant's (1956, 1998) critique of Hume's empiricism bring to the fore how to approach transcendence. According to contemporary studies, particularly in Damasio's (1994) work, emotion can play a positive and constructive role in motivating the use of reason. This links transcendence to works of love.

As Murdoch (2001) argued, love should be a central concept of philosophy but has been ignored and rejected by philosophy for a long time. Her concept of love of the good provides a departure point for achieving transcendence. According to Murdoch, because love keeps returning surreptitiously to self-indulgence, and because true vision generates right deeds, the object of love should be fixed on *the* good rather than *a* good. However, if people do not love life, love of the good will become empty (Fromm, 1957, 1964). Hence, Fromm's analysis of how modern men and women are seriously alienated and how society is morally decayed is drawn on to illustrate the importance of the concept of *biophilia* (love of life).

As Fromm (1957) pointed out, communication, lying at the center of human existence, forms the basis of love. In Freire's (1972a) phrase, love is at the same time dialogue. This brings prominence to dialogue. Buber's (2002, 1959) study of the "I–Thou" relation and the dialogical principle are highlighted to overcome the serious antagonism between the self and the other as exposed in Heidegger's (1996) *Being and Time*. However, as Levinas (1969) argued, Buber fails to answer the following: Who is this Thou and where is this Thou? Levinas's study of the infinity of the other is thus utilized to show that any other is Thou and conscience welcomes the other. Afterward, Bohm's (1985, 1994, 2004) new mode of mind as the constructive effect of dialogue and a number of preconditions mapped out by Freire (1972a) for undertaking genuine dialogue are also brought into discussion. Dostoevsky's (1866) *Crime and Punishment* and Hesse's (2008) *Siddhartha* are employed to elaborate how love and dialogue can perform a transcendent role in particular life situations.

Nevertheless, love and dialogue might become fragile in front of social injustice. This necessitates integrating the cultivation of conscience into conscientization. Guided by Freire's dialectical meetings with both Marx and Christ, to cherish Marx's revolutionary spirit but to view the revolution as an act of love, the distinctive and irreplaceable functions and roles that both the cultivation of critical consciousness and the cultivation of conscience should perform are further identified and specified.

The cultivation of critical consciousness serves as a sociological goad to awaken people's awareness of a just place in society (Bourdieu, 1984, 1990) and then to fight for it. In addition, it sharpens people's historical awareness of creating a historical place through history-making, as Freire often emphasizes. Here Lu Xun's (1972) novel, *The True Story of Ah Q*, is utilized to illustrate how hard it is for the oppressed to make history; and Westrheim's (2009) research is drawn on to show how education can play a revolutionary role in empowering the oppressed without turning them into the victims of social change.

Only conscience can make an effective connection between concrete life situations and actual demands of moral principles and thus generate ethical responsibility and moral deeds. Therefore, the cultivation of conscience not only maintains the building of moral character, as Aristotle (1976) and Buber (2002) suggested, but it also enhances a universal human ethic, as Freire (1998a) claimed. It thus lends itself more readily to the realization of the ethical ideal of humanization.

The argument then progresses to the educational necessity of conscientization, justified by analyzing the dominance of neo-liberalism in current sociocultural contexts and its detrimental impact upon human life. In terms of cultural work, Foucault's and Lyotard's cultural criticism of oppression and hegemony is utilized to illuminate the richness, depth, and strength of Freire's conscientization. Since conscientization has significant implications for all engaged in the educative act, the theoretical soundness of conscientization is discussed and the potentialities for carrying it out in concrete educational discourses are demonstrated. The whole argument is concluded by locating this philosophical enquiry in an open and dialogical system and directing it toward more meaningful, colorful, and fruitful praxis of changing the world.

The book consists of eight chapters. Structurally, it can be viewed as three main parts. Part 1 (Chapters 1 and 2) provides background material for the book. In Chapter 1, a brief biography of Freire is set within the Brazilian sociocultural and historical contexts in which he was brought up and worked. This is followed by a preliminary discussion of his theory of critical pedagogy, including how others have responded to his work. In Chapter 2, a foundational understanding of the essential elements that characterize conscientization is framed with a view to exploring their potential internal coherence with Freire's ethical ideal of humanization.

Part 2 (Chapters 3, 4, 5, and 6) focuses on the notion of conscience, how to cultivate conscience, and how to incorporate the cultivation of conscience into conscientization. Chapter 3 explores the notion of conscience and its dialectical relationship with consciousness. From here it is envisaged that the most relevant and appropriate notion of conscience for the enactment of conscientization can be determined. Chapter 4 considers the moral importance of conscience in terms of maintaining humanity and what prompts conscience to work. The discussion is developed further into why the employment of transcendence is necessary for the cultivation of conscience and what way is proper for approaching transcendence. Chapter 5 focuses on why love and dialogue can be an alternative for transcendence and how they perform an effective role in cultivating conscience. Chapter 6 deals with the integration of the cultivation of conscience into conscientization and the new features that conscientization has gained from this integration. The chapter also serves the need of transitioning the argument from the theoretical discussion to the practical realm of application.

Part 3 (Chapters 7 and 8) contemplates the application aspect of carrying out conscientization with its new element, the cultivation of conscience. Chapter 7 determines the implications of conscientization as a form of action or conscious resistance to the dehumanizing features in contemporary sociocultural contexts. Chapter 8 then highlights the possibilities of how conscientization can be applied within educational pedagogies and practice.

CHAPTER ONE

# Paulo Freire: Life, Work, and Theory

The essence of Freire's radical, critical, and revolutionary theory of liberation is the idea of becoming a subject through education for conscientization. A better command of Freire's conceptualization of conscientization is required for a holistic and critical reading of his life experience and theory of critical pedagogy.

## A Biography of Paulo Freire

There are many remarkable moments in the life story behind Freire's educational theory of liberation. As Torres (1998b, p. 1) said, "If you scratch a theory, you would find a biography." This biography starts with a brief sketch of the historical and social contexts in which Freire decoded their limit-situations.

### The Historical and Sociocultural Contexts in Which Freire Lived

Culturally and historically, Brazil is identified with the blend of African lifestyle and Indian customs with Roman Catholicism. It has "a sexually permissive but sexist culture founded on patriarchy, slavery and class oppression" (Taylor, 1993, p. 16).

Economically, the production relations in the region where Freire lived were primarily semifeudal; *campesinos*' or peasants' access to land was controlled by the rural landowning class, who had a close relationship historically with the national indigenous bourgeoisie in the southeast, the Sao Paulo area (Mayo, 1999). This kind of production relations produced a severely divided society characterized by widespread poverty and exploitation and incredible inequality and injustice in the distribution of resources, worsened by natural catastrophes (Roberts, 2000). Taylor (1993) noted the following:

> There are sections of the North-east where the annual income is about $50. About 75 per cent of the population is illiterate. The average daily intake is 1,664 calories. Life expectancy is 28 years for men and 32 for women. Half the population dies before the age of 30. In two villages in the State of Piaui, taken at random, not a single baby lived beyond one year. (p. 17)

The stark picture of poverty remained unchanged from the 1960s to the 1970s in Brazil. It is during this decade that Freire made his first literacy efforts.

The inequitable social and political structures in Brazil exactly mirrored its unhealthy economic situation. According to Freire (1996), the governance of the country became the means or opportunity for the shameless to gather personal wealth from the state first and then to use the state apparatus to protect their illegal gains and interests. As a result, the disadvantaged became poorer and more marginalized while the advantaged become richer and more powerful. Even in the 1990s, authoritarianism and corruption still continued. Freire (1996) attacked the "Collored PC's" and "de-Collored PC's," two powerful groups then in Brazil, as "devastating the country with shameless lack of accountability" (p. 46):

> Both [the Collored PC's and de-Collored PC's] are those who have been growing rich by dishonestly wasting public monies, embezzling public monies for their pockets or billing public works with inflated invoices and other distortions, cheating the society with illegal or showdown business, exploiting the working class by paying little attention to their poverty; and provoking the latter outrageous consumer prices—all corrupt and unspeakable practice of Farias and Collor, who saw them as natural and valid. (Ana Maria Freire in Freire, 1996, p. 217)

Hence, Freire did not conceal his indignation: "They steal, they kill, they violate, they kidnap, and nothing or almost nothing happens. To them, deceit is a virtue, dirty business the model. Shamelessness is the example to follow" (p. 46).

Educationally, Brazil bore the scars of colonial and cultural invasion. The whole university education system was strongly influenced by the French intellectuals; the local university was basically a French academic institution (Taylor,

1993). It did not offer courses in education, so Freire chose to study law, which was a symbol of social status for Freire's family members when they overcame the hardships and joined the middle class again (Taylor, 1993). In terms of literacy, in 1960, Brazil had 34.5 million people, and of this population, only 15.5 million were literate; for example, in 1964, 4 million school-aged children had no schools; 16 million people 14 years and older were illiterate (Taylor, 1993).

To liberate the oppressed with the high level of illiteracy and poverty in Brazil during this given historical period from its particular forms of exploitation and suffering was Freire's central concern and moral response in the first instance (Roberts, 2000).

## A Brief Sketch of Freire's Life

Freire's full name is Paulo Reglus Neves Freire. He was born on December 19, 1921, in Recife in the state of Pernambuco, in northeast Brazil, one of the most impoverished regions in the country (Mayo, 1999). Born into a middle-class family of four children, according to Freire's (1996) own account, he experienced unforgettable affection from his parents in a democratic and harmonious family atmosphere. However, the Great Depression of 1929 in Brazil left him and his family with poignant memories of the gnawing pangs of hunger together with humiliation. Intending to alleviate the hardships the family was facing, when he was 10 years old, his family reluctantly moved to Jaboatao. However, life there became even more difficult. When his father passed away, his mother had to support the whole family with her limited widow's pension (Roberts, 2000). Sharing the life of the poor led Freire to discover how class-consciousness worked. For example, stealing a papaya for a poor working-class boy was theft but merely a prank for a middle-class boy (Freire, 1996). The difficult situations he and his family faced sowed the seeds of change in his young heart:

> I never thought that life was predetermined or that the best thing to do was to accept obstacles as they appeared. On the contrary, even in my very early years I had begun to think that the world needed to be changed; that something wrong with the world could not and should not continue. (Freire, 1996, p. 13)

With supplementary lessons in Portuguese, Freire recovered the lost ground owing to the hamper of hunger at primary school and completed his secondary education (Mayo, 1999). Eventually, Freire obtained a law degree from the University of Recife. In 1944, he married Elza Maia Costa Oliveira, a primary school teacher, who inspired and influenced him greatly and with whom he had three daughters and two sons (Mayo, 1999). Together with Elza, Freire participated in a number of Catholic movements. He was closely involved in the Basic Church Communities through Dom Helder Camara, the Bishop of the Recife (Taylor, 1993). Based on community groups, the pastoral ministry attempted to use biblical studies to address local, personal, and social issues. As this movement developed, its participants came to understand the importance of accepting "the need for a clearer identification with the poor and a theology of liberation relevant to the ordinary" (Taylor, 1993, p. 22).

With help from his social contacts established in the church, Freire was invited to be the first coordinator of the Division of Education and Culture in a "private industrial institute," an organization called Social Service of Industry (SESI) in 1947 (Taylor, 1993, p. 22). Freire (1996, p. 108) recalled the following: "Through my time at SESI, I learned something that I will never forget. That is, how to deal with the tense relationship between practice and theory." His doctoral dissertation in 1959 was a presentation of his main thoughts during this period, such as ideas on education and adult literacy supported by his community education program in SESI for working-class adults, his deep involvement with poor laborers, peasants, and fishermen, and realization of the interest contradictions among different classes (Mayo, 1999). The experience in SESI with the oppressed working-class people had an important influence on the writing of *Pedagogy of the Oppressed*, which Freire wrote in 1972 (Taylor, 1993).

Freire's 10 years of working with SESI were significant in making him a progressive educator (Mayo, 1999). In 1961, Freire's anti-elitist pilot literacy project was a big success: Some 300 workers were able to read within 45 days (Taylor, 1993). Before long, in the same year, Freire took a chair in history and philosophy of education at the University of Recife, later the Federal University of Pernambuco. This position enabled Freire to develop what he called "Culture Circles" (Roberts, 2000, p. 5). In 1963, Freire was appointed the director of Brazil's National Literacy Programme, which was to extend his initial program in 1961 to a national scale (Taylor, 1993). His aim was to establish a close connection between reading the word and knowing the world; hence, political consciousness could be cultivated through critical understanding of reality.

In Brazil, under the legacy of Portuguese colonialism, only those who were literate had the right to vote. Hence, a literacy campaign was to claim the right to vote. If Freire's literacy program carried on, it would have had the power to overthrow the whole electoral base (Taylor, 1993). However, in order to serve the interests of multinational companies and to help the landowning class gain prosperity on a *latifundium* system, on March 31, 1964, Goulart's populist government was toppled by the military coup backed up by multinationals (Mayo, 1999). After that, a military regime was immediately created. Freire, seen as subversive, was arrested, interrogated, and imprisoned, and his literacy program was dismissed abruptly (Mayo, 1999). This led to a poignant experience for Freire of the political nature of education. "In prison," as McLaren (2000a, p. 144) cited Gadotti (1994), "the relationship between education and politics became even clearer to him and confirmed his thesis that social change would have to come from the masses and not from isolated individuals."

After taking refuge in Bolivia, Freire sought exile in Chile. During his five-year stay in Chile, Freire worked for the United Nations Educational, Scientific, and Cultural Organization (UNESCO) and the Chilean Institute for Agrarian Reform. In 1969, Freire received two invitations: one was from Harvard University in the United States and the other the World Council of Churches in Switzerland (Roberts, 2000). Freire's visit to the United States was highly significant, leading to the publication of two articles in *Harvard Educational Review* and the release of an English-language version of *Pedagogy of the Oppressed* in 1970. His work had drawn international attention, and "he became a symbol of the time, fashioned by the rhetoric, the liberalism and the romanticism of the post-1968 era" (Taylor, 1993, p. 30). Freire left the United States for Switzerland in January 1970. He was appointed as a consultant in the Office of Education at Geneva. There, he set up the Institute of Cultural Action, through which he traveled widely and had direct involvement in the Third World's struggles against oppression, mostly in Africa (Roberts, 2000; Taylor, 1993). His experience in Guinea-Bissau was also important for the development of his educational ideas. *Pedagogy in Process: The Letters to Guinea-Bissau,* published in 1978, showed "Freire moving towards a much clearer position about the power relationships between learning, conscientization and freedom" (Taylor, 1993, p. 31). Throughout the 1970s, Freire established social contacts with a variety of international intellectuals and made contributions to adult education programs in a number of developing countries (Mayo, 1999).

In September 1979, Freire found his name included in a general amnesty granted by the Figueredo government in Brazil (Taylor, 1993). In June 1980, after 16 years of exile, Freire returned to his hometown of Recife and took up the position of Professor of Philosophy of Education at a university in Sao Paulo (Taylor, 1993). While he continued to give seminars, lectures, and interviews, he did not publish any notable material in the early 1980s (Roberts, 2000). From the mid-1980s onward, Freire showed great enthusiasm for "talking books" (dialogical books), coauthored with a number of writers and educators, including Ira Shor, Donaldo Macedo, Antonio Faundez, Myles Horton, and Frei Betto (Mayo, 1999; Roberts, 2000).

In 1985, Freire and his wife, Elza, were both awarded the prize of outstanding Christian educators by the Association of Christian Educators in the United

States (Mayo, 1999). In 1986, Elza died. On March 27, 1988, Freire married Ana Maria (Nita) Araujo, an educator, a literacy tutor, and an author in her own right (Taylor, 1993).

According to Mayo (1999), Freire was actively engaged in political work once he returned to Brazil in 1980. He was also a founding member of the Workers' Party, PT, one of the three left-wing parties in Brazil. In 1989, Freire was appointed Secretary of Education in the PT's municipal government of Sao Paulo. Through this faculty, Freire carried out several reforms in both schooling and adult education in the public sector. In May 1991, Freire retired from his post of Education Secretary. As Taylor (1993, p. 33) pointed out, the town hall experience had taught Freire that "his real skills and ambitions lay in being a political educator rather than an educated politician." He took up his post at the university again and returned to teaching and writing.

On May, 2, 1997, Paulo Freire died of a heart attack in Sao Paulo's Albert Einstein Hospital. The last words he left for the ongoing world he loved intensely were these: "I could never think of education without love and that is why I think I am an educator, first of all because I feel love" (Mayo, 1999, p. 17). McLaren (2000a) later commented:

> To a great extent than any other educators of this century, Freire was able to develop a pedagogy of resistance to oppression. More than this, he lived what he taught. His life is the story of courage, hardship, perseverance, and an unyielding belief in the power of love. (p. 147)

This is true. Freire has used his life, his theory, and his practice to add a new meaning to the notion of education.

## An Overview of Freire's Pedagogical Theory

It is hard to grasp the essence of Freire's pedagogical theory of liberating education without a holistic grip on his philosophy, which encompassed ontology, metaphysics, epistemology, and ethics.

### Freire's Philosophy

First and foremost, the Marxist concept of dialectics played a pivotal role in Freire's ontology and metaphysics. As Roberts (2000) pointed out, Freire applied dialectics as his philosophical approach to understanding the world and to analyzing the nature of reality. On the one hand, everything in this world is interrelated. There is an interactive relationship between this human being and that human being, between human beings and nature, and between the objective or material world and the subjective or conscious world. On the other hand, the nature of reality is change and development. Everything in the world, such as human beings, history, culture, truths, and knowledge, is in a process of constant change and development. Therefore, the world and history should be understood and analyzed in a dynamic and dialectical manner. It is change and development that create possibilities to build a better world and thus nurture the root of hope.

The concept of praxis serves as the foundation of Freire's epistemology (Glass, 2001; Roberts, 2000). Freire favored practical knowledge with more stress on its ethical and political judgement. His epistemology went against Plato's "effort to remember or rediscover a forgotten *logos*," so he criticized "Socratic intellectualism," noting that knowledge, defined by Socrates as virtue, contains dialogue but does not "constitute a true pedagogy of knowing" (Freire, 1972b, p. 37). As (Freire, 1972a, p. 73) argued, "only human beings are praxis—the praxis which, as the reflection and action which truly transform reality, is the source of knowledge and creation." Thus, knowledge must have a close and living connection to learners' reality, experience, and concrete existential situations (Freire, 1994a). It is not fixed in an abstracted, static, mystified, and inaccessible ivory tower in the mind but emerges through human practice, action, and interaction with an ever-changing world over time. In the same way, knowledge production, construction, and creation comprise a conscious process of praxis; inside which, but not outside which, knowers become curious, restless, investigative, probing, questioning, creative, and in short, learning subjects (Freire & Shor, 1987).

Praxis is also the foundation of Freire's ethics. Since praxis is Freire's metaphysics of human beings ("only human beings are praxis"), it becomes the foundation of his ethics of humanization. For Freire (1972a, 1994a, 1998a), human beings are necessarily imperfect, unfinished, and incomplete, existing *in* and *with* the world. This is because becoming aware of this kind of unfinishedness defines praxis as a central and ontological feature of all mankind. Therefore, praxis gives meaning to human existence. To be a human being is to live out this human nature of praxis. According to Freire (1972a, 1994a), people know what they are thinking and doing; dialectically, what they are thinking and doing promotes their knowing and understanding. This conscious subject position allows human beings to live as free, social, historical, communicative, thinking, transformative, and creative persons. Thus, to exist or to be, in the last analysis, is to take a subject position in a historical process of changing the world as a praxical being. (For the purposes of the book, I have coined the term *praxical* to refer to a praxis-oriented individual or state.)

Dehumanization is dialectically related to humanization. As Roberts (2000, p. 44) interpreted, dehumanization prevents a person from "engaging in praxis—either through limiting the range of possible actions open to that person, or through inhibiting that person's ability to think critically." Therefore, while humanization is both an ontological and historical vocation based on a collective and ever-evolving praxis for all human beings, dehumanization is a historical reality but not an ontological inevitability (Freire, 1972a). Once a person dehumanizes others, she or he is actually dehumanizing herself or himself (Marx, 1964). Hence, the overall aim of revolution is the emancipation of all human beings, both oppressors and the oppressed.

Furthermore, the status of being *in* and *with* the world determines human character. As Freire (1998a, p. 26) pointed out, people not only present and recognize their being but also "take stock of, compare, evaluate, give value to, decide, break with, [and] dream." That is, although dehumanization is the transgression of human ethics, everybody ontologically is ethically grounded. Therefore, a revolutionary cause takes humanization as its ethical foundation, maintained by love of human beings and the world (Freire, 1972a).

Although two dominant strands, Marxism and liberation theology, are strongly reflected in Freire's works (Mayo, 1997), it is important to note that the construction of Freire's theory of liberating education includes other intellectual traditions, such as liberalism, phenomenology, existentialism, and certain aspects of postmodern and poststructuralist thought (Roberts, 2000). For this reason, Freire is sometimes criticized as an eclectic (Taylor, 1993). However, this is a misreading of Freire's philosophy. As Giroux (1985, p. xvii) remarked, "central to Freire's politics and pedagogy is a philosophical vision of a liberated humanity." The wide range of intellectual resources that Freire draws on is at the service of his lifetime work—the liberation of human beings from oppression and hegemony.

## Freire's Theory of Liberating Education

Freire's dialogical social transformation through education starts from his initial preoccupation with relations of oppression. As Torres (1998a) pointed out, the analysis of the relations of oppression and unyielding ethical concern for *the wretched of the earth* and *the excluded* are not only Freire's departure point of all his political-pedagogic principles but also a main theme throughout his works.

Oppression, like other forms of dehumanization such as exploitation, alienation, authoritarianism, and corruption, emerges from the domination of the ruling class or those dominant groups who hold power (Ollman, 1971). Hence, to

eradicate oppression is believed to lie in revolution, a fundamental change of the dominating social structures. However, according to Gramsci (1971), there are two wars: *a war of maneuver* and *a war of position*. The war of maneuver means to change the state and its coercive apparatus and to establish a new set of power relations by head-on, eye for eye, and gun against gun struggles between the rich ruling class and the poor working class. The war of position, which should precede the seizure of power, is the battle against noncoercive powers and takes the form of a critique of ideological hegemony. As Gramsci argued, ideological hegemony oppresses and enslaves the oppressed through justifying the interests of oppressors and distorting the oppressed people's consciousness of reality, so it requires organic intellectuals of a subaltern group as main agents to fight for industrial workers. Hence, the war of position is "a process of wide-ranging social organization and cultural influence" (Mayo, 1999, p. 38).

Deeply influenced by Gramsci and Mao's revolution with Chinese peasants, Freire started his revolutionary educational project for *campesinos* (peasants) in northeastern Brazil as the site of practice (Mayo, 1999). Based on the Hegelian and Marxist analysis of the dialectical relationship between human consciousness and the material world, Freire stressed the importance of awakening the oppressed people's consciousness through education. His example is illuminating. When a *latifundium* (landowner) was seized by some armed peasants to keep as a hostage, no peasants dared to guard him. In their subconsciousness, the landowners were invincible; their power was magical and their presence was terrifying. Moreover, any acts of opposing their bosses would provoke the peasants into feeling guilty. As Freire (1972a, p. 40) pointed out, "in truth, the boss was 'inside' them." Therefore, dehumanization resides not only in the material conditions of situations but also in the psychological conditions of persons (Glass, 2001).

Citing Sartre, Freire (1972a) argued that if one's consciousness is sleeping, one's world is sleeping at the same time. If the image of the oppressors is deeply rooted in the consciousness of the oppressed, it is impossible to remove oppression. Accordingly, the practice of freedom requires people to engage in a kind of historical, cultural, and political psychoanalysis to decode limit-situations (Glass, 2001). Giroux (1985) commented:

> This is an important point in Freire's work and indicates the ways in which domination is subjectively experienced through its internalization and sedimentation in the very needs of the personality. What is at work here in Freire's thought is an important attempt to examine the psychically repressive aspects of domination and, hence, the possible internal obstacles to self-knowledge and thus to forms of social and self-emancipation. (pp. xix–xx)

Therefore, at the core of critical intervention is a practice of liberation, which starts with an educational process of cultivating people's critical consciousness with an overall aim of changing the world. This practice of liberation is known as conscientization.

The cultivation of critical consciousness must take place on the basis of the human solidarity between teachers and students; "solidarity requires true communication" (Freire, 1972a, p. 50). Freire (1972a) argued as follows:

> Only through communication can human life hold meaning. The teacher's thinking is authenticated only by the authenticity of the students' thinking. The teacher cannot think for his students, nor can he impose his thought on them. Authentic thinking, thinking that is concerned about reality, does not take place in ivory-tower isolation, but only in communication. (p. 50)

In the traditional mode of education, however, there is little communication but an act of depositing. Freire (1972a, p. 46) called this the banking concept of education, "in which the students are the depositories and the teacher is the depositor." In the banking mode of education, knowledge is viewed as something abstract and permanent, so cognizable objects are placed over human beings. Both teachers and students are the slaves of the preservation of dead knowledge or the transferral of information. What is being learned has little to do with what is really happening in daily life; students' consciousness is isolated from the real world. Thus, banking education does not prompt critical intervention between human beings and reality. It forms part of a wider system of oppression.

According to Freire (1972a), in banking education, the natural, humane, empathetic bond between teachers and students is dichotomized. Accepted students' ignorance justifies the knowledgeable teachers' authority while genuine dialogue between teachers and students is rejected. All the aims and functions of education are reduced to domestication. Through domestication, students are transformed into mechanical containers while teachers become dogmatic depositors. Consequently, students' desire and curiosity for enquiry are denied and their minds are caged in the fixed signs of dominance. By means of this kind of domestication, banking education fulfills its *necrophilic* role of serving the interests for the oppressors.

Therefore, Freire (1972a) put forward problem-posing education as an alternative, which is closely associated with addressing domestication by means of liberating human consciousness. He remarked:

> "Problem-posing" education, responding to the essence of consciousness—intentionality—rejects communiqués and embodies communication. It epitomizes the special

characteristic of consciousness: being conscious of, not only as intent on objects but as turned in upon itself in a Jasperian "split"—consciousness as consciousness of consciousness. (p. 52)

Placing much stress on communication, Freire took dialogue as the essence of education for the practice of freedom. He phrased his dialogical approach as "dialogics," which starts with his insightful meditation of the word—"the essence of dialogue itself" (Freire, 1972a, p. 60). He explained:

Within the word we find two dimensions, reflection and action, in such radical interaction that if one is sacrificed—even in part—the other immediately suffers. There is no true word that is not at the same time praxis. Thus, to speak a true word is to transform the world. (Freire, 1972a, p. 60)

Freire's philosophy of language conveys two important messages. One is that if the world is transformed by speaking a true word, dialogue will become an important means for men and women to experience and achieve their significance of being men and women. As Freire (1972a, p. 61) maintained, speaking a true word rather than idle talk is true communication, "an existential necessity." This true communication awakens the human heart and enlivens the human mind by piercing through the recurrence of the same or the dead and mundane consciousness caused by the vindication of the status quo.

The other message is the dialectical relation between the word and praxis. To change the world always goes hand in hand with naming the world. Freire (1972a, p. 60) put forward an equation to illustrate this point: "the word (action + reflection) = work = praxis." In this synthesis of the word, if action is sacrificed, the word falls into verbalism; if reflection is sacrificed, the word falls into activism. A true word realizes its power only in praxis.

However, consciousness of reality is often distorted by the domestication of ideological hegemony; the praxis of speaking a true word is not easy. It necessitates encountering reality or "things" in real situations by means of reading the real world critically. Hence, Freire and Macedo (1987) stressed the inseparable and interactive connection and coherence between reading the word and naming the world. Only this kind of reading can help restore the close correspondence between thought-language and the real world. Otherwise, human communication will become difficult and human existence will suffer.

To speak a true word in dialogue also draws out a number of human virtues and qualities, such as love, humility, bravery, mutual trust, hope, faith in humankind, and critical thinking, rather than their opposites, such as contempt, arrogance, cowardice, suspicion, disappointment, fatalism, and slavish obedience

(Freire, 1972a). Accordingly, dialogics tend to transform conquest into collaboration, division into union, manipulation into organization, and cultural invasion into cultural synthesis. As time goes and circumstances change, this dialogical approach enhanced by praxis will constantly enrich programmatic contents of teaching and learning by generating new themes for dialogue.

Based on the aforementioned language philosophy, Freire (1972a) developed *dialogics* into a democratic, humane, and communicative model of education. By means of speaking a true word, dialogue is conducive to not only generating reciprocal kindness and empathetic understanding but also establishing a good emotional and intellectual rapport between teachers and students. As he noted, "it is a learning situation in which the cognizable object (far from being the end of the cognitive act) intermediates the cognitive actors—teacher on the one hand and students on the other" (p. 53). That is, teachers and students become equal co-investigators and conscious subjects, mediated by the world-knowledge nexus. Thus, the vertical hierarchy of the teacher–student relationship in banking education can be changed by means of a critical and dialogical intervention.

Once the teacher–student relation problem in banking education is addressed, instead of an act of depositing, an act of cognition based on the curiosity of knowing becomes a crucial means to unite teachers and students. Hence, they are able to communicate, interact, and above all, live with each other in their learning movement. The general direction of this movement of enquiry is as follows:

> Problem-posing education, as a human and liberation praxis, posits as fundamental that men [sic] who are subjected to domination must fight for their emancipation. To that end, it enables teachers and students to become subjects of the education process by overcoming authoritarianism and an alienating intellectualism; it also enables men to overcome their false perception of reality. The world—no longer something to be described with deceptive words—becomes the object of that transforming action by men, which result in their humanization. (Freire, 1972a, p. 58)

Therefore, Freire's problem-posing education is a revolutionary cause of turning education into an integral part of humanization through social change. It should not be misunderstood as equivalent to "child-centered," "interactive," "problem-solving," and other ostensibly progressive approaches to education (Roberts, 2000).

## Critical Responses to Freire's Pedagogical Theory

Freire's work has had a tremendous impact on various areas, such as political philosophy, human ethics, critical literacy, linguistics, cultural studies, and theology of liberation. As McLaren (2000b) noted, in North America, liberal progressives draw on Freire's humanism, Marxists and neo-Marxists his conception of revolutionary praxis and his experience of working with revolutionary political regimes, left liberals his critical utopianism, and even conservatives show their grudging respect on his view of ethics. While positive comments are predominant, there are quite a few disagreements and criticisms.

## Freire's Original Contributions

The significance of Freire's critical pedagogy can be best expressed by Giroux's (1985) comment: Freire provides not only the language of critique but also the language of possibility. As Giroux noted, the new sociology of education, which had a strong influence in the 1970s in the United Kingdom and United States, shared the same central question with Freire: As a way of being critical, hopeful and emancipatory, how can education make human life more meaningful than it is or used to be? While the language of crisis and critique of the new sociology of education had fallen into either the discourse of domination or the discourse of despair, Freire's work represented "a theoretically refreshing and politically viable alternative to the current impasse in educational theory and practice worldwide" (Giroux, 1985, p. xi). Hence, the major distinction between the new sociology of education and Freire's critical pedagogy is that the former seems "to start and end with the logic of political, economic, and cultural reproduction," while Freire begins his analysis with "the process of production" (Giroux, 1985, p. xvi). In other words, Freire investigated how human beings "construct their own voices and validate their contradictory experiences within specific historical settings and constraints" in various ways (Giroux, 1985, p. xvi). Accordingly, based on his practice of working with working-class people in Brazil, having integrated knowledge production into social practice, Freire shifted from the discourse of reproduction to the discourse of production and offered the language of possibility.

Freire's language of possibility developed from a combination of "a respect for life," "a struggle against oppressive forces," and "a permanent prophetic vision" based on his theology of liberation (Giroux, 1985, p. xvii). Giroux (1985) continued: "By combining the discourse of critique and possibility, Freire joins history and theology in order to provide the theoretical basis for a radical pedagogy that combines hope, critical reflection, and collective struggle" (p. xviii). Hence, values such as love, hope, respect for life, and liberated humanity, for Freire, are not something given by God but are the necessary preserve of humanity's unyielding permanent struggle against oppression. They are a faith in human praxis and "becoming more" in the process of changing the world. The language of possibility Freire contributed is "a discourse that creates a new starting point by trying to make hope realizable and despair unconvincing" (p. xiii). In other words, Freire provides the oppressed with an inspiration to act rather than a consolation for suffering.

Freire's notion of education includes schooling but goes beyond the limit of schooling. Because any individual is conditioned by specific historical and social conditions and cultural norms, the dynamic of Freire's education is forged in the dialectical relation between individuals and structural constraints. As Giroux (1985) pointed out, certain contradictions and struggles caused by certain structural constraints and ideologies define and mark off human lived realities and the development of history in various societies. It is in this dialectics that power and politics find education as the terrain to give a fundamental expression of desire, language, meaning, and values. Therefore, education, for Freire, relates to "the deeper beliefs about the very nature of what it means to be human, to dream, and to name and struggle for a particular future and way of life"; it represents "both a struggle for meaning and a struggle over power relations" (Giroux, 1985, p. xiii).

Giroux's (1985) following remark pinpoints Freire's original contributions:

> As a referent for change, education represents a form of action that emerges from a joining of the languages of critique and possibility. It represents the need for a passionate commitment by educators to make the political more pedagogical, that is, to make critical reflection and action a fundamental part of a social project that not only engages forms of oppression but also develops a deep and abiding faith in the struggle to humanize life itself. It is the particular nature of this social project that gives Freire's work its theoretical distinction. (pp. xiii–xiv)

In the same light, Mayo (1997, p. 365) commented as follows: "The greatest and most enduring aspect of Freire's work is his emphasis on the political nature of all educational activity." For the oppressors, education domesticates individuals so that they can accept the status quo passively. Dialectically, for the oppressed, Freire's liberating education provides people with "the disposition to engage in a dialectical relationship with knowledge and society," which forms a big part of reading of the world critically (Mayo, 1997, p. 365). This is true; Freire (1998a, 1998c, 1994b, 1985) never thought that education is neutral.

Education cannot be separated from culture. According to Shor (1993), Freire's conception of culture was anthropological: Everyone, not only these few elites but also ordinary people, has and makes culture through their daily experience, such as speech and behavior. Hence, "culture is the action and results of humans in society, the way people interact in their communities, and the addition people make to the world they find" (Shor, 1993, p. 30). There is no such culture as high, popular, and low.

However, culture is, in essence, a form of production. Its process occurs within certain productive relations, determined by historical conditions "with the structuring of different social formations particularly that are related to gender, age, race, and class" (Giroux, 1985, p. xxi). Any form of culture is merely the representation of lived experiences, material artefacts, and social practice from different and unequal power relations. Because of hegemonic power, some people's language, knowledge, and experiences are legitimatized while those of some other people are marginalized and silenced. In this sense, culture, like education, also becomes a terrain of struggle and contradictions to voice different interests and values for different social classes. Freire's cultural politics "represents a theoretical discourse whose underlying interests are fashioned around a struggle against all forms of subjective and objective domination as well as a struggle for forms of knowledge, skills, and social relations that provide the conditions for social and hence self-emancipation" (Giroux, 1985, p. xiii). Therefore, Freire's cultural work, with an acute concern for human existence, is the creation or production and legitimatization of the culture for the oppressed. It can be much more fundamental and broader than any political discourses such as Marxism (Giroux, 1985).

Freire's theory of liberating education also takes deep root in his notion of history making. Freire introduced the existentialist notion of the "being" of human beings into the praxis of history making. This locates and makes sense of human existence in time. There could be no idea of history if there was no conceptualization or contemplation of time. It is hard to understand Freire's concept of history making, another important contribution of his, without an existentialist concern for time.

According to Heidegger (1996), the anthropological notion of time originates from the need of management of human work in the field of agriculture. The sun was the first clock for human beings: When the sun rose, people went to work; when it set, people went to bed. In this way, time has gradually embedded itself into human life, not only framing people's experience but also measuring their length of living. Further, the way a person spends his or her time in life might reveal how that person lived his or her life. In Heidegger's (1996) term, being unfolds itself in time. However, the river of time flows timelessly and infinitely, but human life is short and finite. Once Confucius stood by a river and uttered the following: Time elapses like this river, without stopping for one day and one night (Yang, 1980). Confucius is not only conscious of time passing but also feels anxious that life is lost with the passage of time. Whereas time is like an endless river, life is not. As one day goes by in time, that day is subtracted from a life. Lived years never return and the remaining days become fewer and fewer. Thus, a concern over time is a deep care of the temporality of being (Heidegger, 1996). It is a psychological and ontological backlash to the finiteness of human life against the backdrop of infinite time (Sartre, 1994).

Freire is neither pessimistic nor sad about the finiteness of life. For him, "the trajectory through which we make ourselves conscious is marked by finiteness, by inconclusion, and it characterizes us as historical beings" (Freire, 1997, p. 93). This consciousness of finiteness and unfinishedness opens up "an opportunity" for becoming "immersed in a permanent search"; "here lie also roots of the metaphysical foundation of hope" (Freire, 1997, p. 93). Thus, Freire (1997) stressed that "our historical inclination is not fate, but rather possibility" (p. 100).

If history is seen and lived as possibility, the focus of understanding history is placed on its making process. In this context, historical beings are identical with praxical beings. By the same logic, making history is to change the world and vice versa. Hence, making history is not an abstruse concept in metaphysical abstraction but in everyone's conscious activities in daily life. Moreover, everyone is an essential part of history making and people are the primary source of power and the main agents for making history. As West (1993, p. xiii) commented, Freire's "distinctive talent" is that "he makes what is abstract concrete without sacrificing subtlety"; his "genius" is to explicate in his work and exemplify in his life "the dynamics of this process of how ordinary people can and do make history in how they think, feel, act and love." In particular, when the oppressed people are empowered by education, they are more able to see their historical visions and to start their acts of resistance. They start their history making from addressing their specific problems and suffering in their political, social, and cultural particularities (Freire, 1972a, 1994b, 1998a, 2007). This point is taken up again in Chapter 6.

## The Main Objections

The objections to Freire's theory can be categorized into three main arguments. The first criticism is that Freire's theory of liberating education represents a type of intellectual invasion of indigenous people's cultural identity. The second set of arguments involves a number of objections from a postmodernist perspective. The nature of the third critique is of the inner contradictions between Marxism and Christianity in Freire's theoretical construction.

The first set of objections to Freire is reflected in Bowers's criticism. Bowers has persistently launched attacks against Freire's theory. From his standpoint of maintaining cultural identity, Bowers (1983) criticized the linguistic root of cultural invasion in Freire's pedagogy. He insisted that Freire's educational philosophy is analyzing how education can be liberated from cultural domination in theory; but in practice, his theory is embedded in the Western mindset. This will become culturally hegemonic for those indigenous people in local situations. He argued as follows:

> Freire's pedagogy of liberation was based on cultural assumptions derived from the Western mindset that underpins the more problematic aspects of the modernizing process. By using this pedagogy in non-westernized cultural settings the literacy process contributes to the development of a western mindset with regard to the nature of individualism, the authority of critical reflection, and the progressive nature of change. (Bowers, 1986, p. 148)

Therefore, according to Bowers, Freire equated the Western myth of progress with change and oversimplified the notion of tradition and dialogue.

Furthermore, Bowers (1986) contended that Freire did not develop his theoretical research into his original insights published in the early 1970s. Instead, there is a disappointing repetition of earlier themes and an insufficient analysis of issues such as literacy empowerment and critical reflection. If Freire had furthered his insights into the structural and conceptual sources of alienation and strategies for raising consciousness, he could have made "major contributions to our understanding of a more emancipatory approach to education" (Bowers, 1986, p. 147). Bowers (1986) made a suggestion for how Freire should have developed his theory in much greater depth:

> Particularly by engaging the ideas of Foucault and Ong on the politics of discourse, Shils on the nature of human embeddedness, and Nietzsche, Heidegger, and Vygotsky on the controlling nature of language, he may present us with a less romantic and thus more useful view of the dynamic of emancipation. (p. 148)

In a similar vein, Esteva, Stuchal, and Prakash (in Bowers & Apffel-Marglin, 2005) wrote the following:

> Freire was explicitly interested in the oppressed. His entire life and work were presented as a vocation committed to assuming their views, their interests. Yet, he ignored the plain fact that for the oppressed, the social majorities of the world, education has become one of the most humiliating and disabling components of their oppression, perhaps even very worst. (p. 20)

For them, Freire's pedagogy is the pedagogy for mediators qua liberators. In other words, Freire's pedagogy performs the function of how to undermine class conflict by cultural workers' mediation rather than liberation.

By exploring three books, *Pedagogy of Indignation* by Freire (2004), *Engaging Paulo Freire's Pedagogy of Possibility* by Rossatto (2005), and *Re-Thinking Freire* edited by Bowers and Apffel-Marglin (2005), Jackson (2007) suggested rethinking the extent to which Freire's critical pedagogy can be applied to both educators and the oppressed in the light of globalization and environment crisis. She pointed out the following:

> Despite clinging to pedagogies and practices of emancipation, teachers (in the western world at least) are working within the structure of neoliberalism, with government or centrally determined curricula, audits and managerial controls, and funding regimes, all of which militate against pedagogies as the practice of freedom. Coupled with this, the cult of individualism, reliance on technological advances and hierarchical structuring of "knowledge" make social, collective, and transformative actions increasingly difficult. (p. 206)

Although "Freire was concerned with the world's situation in the context of the neo-liberal political model and economic globalization," he failed to contribute a different but effective way to help individuals engage in the struggle against neo-liberalism and globalization (Jackson, 2007, p. 203). Jackson (2007) argued that in the face of the dominant discourse of neo-liberalism and individualism, little evidence of the power of individuals to effect change is seen; in addition, Freire did not pay enough attention to ecology.

Since these main themes and seminal ideas in Freire's classic works, such as *Pedagogy of the Oppressed* (1972a), *Cultural Action for Freedom* (1970b), and *Education for Critical Consciousness* (1973, the same book published in 1976 with a different name, *Education, the Practice of Freedom*), are deeply influenced by his humanist goals in modernist discourse, they are challenged by critics, such as Ellsworth, Weil, Hill, and others, from postmodernist perspectives.

Based on her classroom experiences of engaging herself in developing an anti-racist course with a diverse group of students, Ellsworth (1989, p. 297) pointed out the following: "If these assumptions, goals, implicit power dynamics, and issues of who produces valid knowledge remains un-theorised and untouched, critical pedagogies will continue to perpetuate relations of domination in their classrooms." According to Ellsworth, the practical difficulties of class discussion and dialogue caused by the power relations between raced, classed, and gendered students and teachers can make Freirean notions, such as "empowerment," "critical reflection," "student voice," and "dialogue," abstract and utopian. As everyone can be someone else's other, depending upon specific historical situations or contexts, "there are no social positions exempt from becoming oppressive to others ... any group—any position—can move into the oppressor role" (p. 322). Briefly, there is a gap between Freire's analysis of oppression and the multilayered and complex nature of oppression in concrete educational discourses. She also raised questions about the nature of knowledge and action for social change.

In the same light, Weiler (1991) contended that Freire's concepts such as humanization, dehumanization, oppression, and liberation seem inadequate for confronting the specifics of the problems of oppression in the postmodern world. However, she cherishes Freire's vision of collective conscientization. For her, Freire's collective conscientization is based on a belief in human capacity to feel, to know, and to change the world with the goals of social justice and empowerment. She only cautions that the realization of the Freirean vision requires a much fuller acknowledgment of differences and conflicts of struggling against oppression in specific situations.

Hill (2001) argued that Foucault's antiparadigmatic notion of care of the self and unconditional self-constitution poses a big challenge to Freire's socialist and Catholic paradigms. Freire's solution to the emancipation of the oppressed was to profess "to combat limiting ideas whilst actually advancing their own variation" (p. 24). If social change takes place as Freire expects, it is more likely to have another replacement of world order and social structures with another new hegemonic ideology to maintain another new system.

Andreotti (2009), from the perspective of both postcolonialism and epistemological pluralism, challenged Freire's certainty of the socialist orientation in terms of social change. She argued that future possibilities are better when open to negotiation.

The third set is best expressed by Walker's critique. Walker (1980) first argued that Freire contradicts himself by combining existentialist Christianity with the idea of Marxist liberation. Second, according to Walker, for Marx, class struggle is initiated by workers rather than by the petit bourgeoisie; however, for Freire, class struggle is initiated by dialogue between the working class and the petit bourgeoisie who commit class suicide. In this context, the petit bourgeoisie become the main agent of revolution. This misapplication of Marx's notion of class struggle will undermine workers' powerful agent role in the revolution. Hence, Walker casts doubt on the liberating potential of Freire's theory.

## A Critical Defense

It is crucial to be open-minded to the critique of Freire's work and theory. As Roberts (2000, p. 98) pointed out, criticisms of Freire's work and theory highlight "the potential dangers educators face in involving themselves in the lives of others." The aforementioned objections do form an essential part in reinventing and advancing Freire's critical pedagogy. However, it is equally important not to distort or compartmentalize Freire's ideas out of context in a simplistic or gratuitously negative manner. For example, Esteva, Stuchal, and Prakash's (in Bowers

& Apffel-Marglin, 2005) criticisms appear self-contradictory and ignore Freire's work and theory. Therefore, some major misunderstandings of Freire's work and theory must not be left unattended. Otherwise, they will devalue Freire's original contributions to educational theory and practice.

Bowers (1986) contended that Freire's pedagogy imposes a Western mindset upon the people in non-Westernized cultural settings. However, this is a misreading of Freire's educational theory and practice. If a mindset is understood as the general attitudes and the typical way in which a person or a certain ethnic group of people think about things, different ways of thinking and different habits of knowing in different cultures can be labeled as mindsets. From Bowers's perspective of preserving cultural identities for different peoples, the idea of a mindset may work for him in terms of identifying certain constant characteristics of thinking in certain ethnic groups.

The idea of a mindset, however, does not fit Freire's pedagogical discourse. It is true that Freire lays bare a number of common features the peasants in northeast Brazil at that time shared in thinking about reality, such as magical consciousness and naïve consciousness, but he does not impose a Western mindset upon them. For Freire, the flowing of the human mind is not constrained by something like a mindset. If there is a mindset, it must be shaped by concrete historical and sociocultural conditions. For example, magical consciousness and naïve consciousness are the reflection of the domination and oppression of the poor peasants in northeast Brazil in the 1950s and the 1960s. They should not be labeled as two static and fixed mindsets.

It is imperative to preserve cultural identities of indigenous peoples and to prevent their human rights from being invaded by imperialists. However, it does not necessarily lead to treating indigenous peoples as dead cultural specimens marked by a certain mindset. According to Freire, magical consciousness and naïve consciousness must be replaced by critical consciousness. Otherwise, the social injustice of exploitation and oppression those peasants experienced then would have been internalized and justified. Freire's approach involves a revolutionary venture: not only to understand reality critically but also to change that reality. This necessitates an empowering approach. Freire takes liberating education as a way out. In his literacy campaign, reading the word starts with reading the real world; his curriculum making is based on his students' everyday realities. This is a cultural revolution. However, it is misread as cultural invasion by Bowers.

More importantly, Freire was a communicator; he did not want to brainwash any indigenous people. All cultures, Western, Eastern, and indigenous, have produced valuable knowledge and technology in the history of human civilization. Any fruit of human civilization brings good to everybody on the planet. For example, a mobile phone is convenient for the Western people; this does not mean it is inconvenient for indigenous people. Everyone can enjoy its convenience. There is no reason to forbid indigenous people to use it. In the same way, indigenous people show earnest respect for nature and desire to maintain a healthy and harmonious relationship between nature and human beings. This helps to protect the eco-environment for the whole planet. Therefore, people in different cultures should communicate with each other for a fruitful mutual exchange. This kind of communication not only creates learning possibilities for everyone on the planet to access the fruit of human civilization but also enhances equality and development of the human race. By the same logic, if the notion of dialogue and critical consciousness, developed in the Western culture, is conducive to the revolutionary cause of fighting for emancipation and freedom for the peasants in Brazil, Freire had every right to apply it to his pedagogical practice there. Bowers accused Freire of imposing a Western mindset on indigenous people. However, imposing a mindset is not communication. Freire strongly opposed the top-down imposition of any theory and thinking mode upon anyone. What he did was to use communication to overcome cultural domination and invasion.

Bowers (1986, p. 148) suggested that Freire should draw on Nietzsche, Heidegger, and Vygotsky to work out "the controlling nature of language." This suggestion is fundamentally problematic and contradictory. On the one hand, Nietzsche and Heidegger are in the same tradition. Nietzsche believed that in the sign system of language, there is no one-to-one correspondence between a word and the thing it refers to (Lackey, 1999). Nevertheless, there is a close correspondence between language and consciousness. In other words, language does not necessarily respond to the real world, but it cannot work when it is separated from human consciousness, its working site. As Lackey (1999) interpreted, for Nietzsche, driven by will to power, those "truth players" use language as an effective means to control human beings' consciousness and to run them as herd animals. However, because language can speak one's mind, both Nietzsche and Heidegger took language as the expression of self-being. For them, language has the potential to help a person break away from the recurrence of the same. In particular, Heidegger (1968) emphasized that the genuine way of experiencing one's essential self-being is to voice one's inner self as a poet. Nonetheless, Buber (2002) criticized Heidegger's point, noting that Heidegger's language philosophy is in an antidialogical tradition of a closed system, which is set in the "I" domain without "Thou." Therefore, Heidegger's poets merely speak monologues. Freire was fully aware that sometimes human existence suffers in mundane idle conversations of everyday life, but he also knew the limitations of Nietzsche and Heidegger's language philosophy. Unlike Nietzsche and Heidegger, Freire planted his language philosophy deeply in dialogue and praxis and declared that to speak a true word is to change the world. As Lankshear (1993) has noted, there is a dialectical relationship between language and freedom in Freire's critical literacy.

On the other hand, the language philosophy of Vygotsky, a Marxist Russian psychologist, does not contradict Freire's ideas. According to Vygotsky (1962), language, human thinking, and the real world are inseparable and dialectically interrelated. He emphasized the significance and the role of dialogue during human encounters. The famous theory, the Zone of Proximal Development (ZPD; Vygotsky, 1978), is a manifestation of Vygotsky's insight into the dialogical nature of language. In fact, Freire told Horton that Vygotsky's language philosophy "influenced" him and Vygotsky's *Thought and Language* (1962) was "a beautiful and fantastic book"—"when I read him for the first time, I became frightened and happy because of the things I was reading" (Horton & Freire, 1990, p. 36). In this context, Bowers's suggestion seems confusing and inappropriate.

Bowers also suggested that Freire draw on Foucault, Ong, Shils, Nietzsche, Heidegger, and Vygotsky to avoid the repetitions and to further the development and strengthen the dynamic of his emancipatory theory. The repetition in Freire's *The Politics of Education* (1985) is true. However, it is important to realize that the themes are repeated with a focus on practice. Freire is not a book philosopher. For him, it is practice that provides theory with a living, inexhaustible, and primary source. Accordingly, from the 1980s onward, Freire devoted most of his time to the research of how his theory could be applied in concrete pedagogical situations in those developing and postcolonial countries. The main body of his work during this period is basically about his critical reflections on his educational practice, in which he engaged together with his colleagues and students.

Jackson was not content with the power of Freire's theory to effect change at an individual level. As a matter of fact, Freire (1972a) never downplayed the role of individual effort, but he always stressed the social nature of this process. Jackson (2007) criticized Freire's neglect of ecology in his work, even though ecology gained tremendous importance at the end of the last century. This criticism seems unfair and untrue. Freire stressed love of life, so he would not ignore ecological problems such as air pollution and global warming caused by capitalist modes of production. Although he did not write specifically on ecology, in *Pedagogy of Indignation*, he clearly argued that there is an urgent need to love rivers, mountains, trees, and fish (Freire, 2004).

Jackson (2007) pointed out that the difficulty of social change increases owing to the complexity and dominance of a neo-liberal political model and economic globalization. This is true. However, she contended that Freire failed to offer a workable way and a new theoretical perspective to help people engage in this context. According to her, this has consequently led to the fact that "working-class" languages "leave speakers disempowered and located within a discourse of lack" (p. 205). It would seem that Jackson is ignorant of Freire's concept of praxis and conscientization. Freire never attempted to develop an effective method or theory which can be applicable to solve all problems in all conditions over time. He simply showed how different theories, perspectives, and methods can be generated through the praxis of decoding social reality and taking actions to change it. Moreover, neo-liberal political and economic practice is not undertaken by one person. It is a social practice. To counter it also requires a social practice. Jackson feels that Freire's way of decoding the dehumanization brought about by neo-liberalism and globalization is not sufficient and that there must be an effective way to help people cope with the increasingly difficult situation as she describes. If she feels this way, she can find a better way than Freire for addressing the situation.

In any case, "those who have an important stake in the meaning of Freire's life and work" will continue to debate how Freire's politics and pedagogy should be interpreted and applied (McLaren, 2000b, p. 13). Under such circumstances, Freire's work and theory should be treated fairly in a right attitude. It is meaningless to turn the study of Freire's work and theory into biased polemics.

Freire's theoretical world, as McLaren (2000a, p. 155) pointed out, "comprised a 'narrative space' or discursive economy with its own catalogue of terms out of which he could fashion himself as a public intellectual and cultural worker—what he would call a 'pilgrim of the obvious'—whose guiding interest was rooted in overcoming domination and exploitation through a revolutionary educational praxis." As long as dehumanizing practice such as injustices, inequalities, oppression, and hegemony still exist and will continue to exist as a historical fact for a certain amount of historical time, it is of great necessity to carry forward Freire's liberating education without shifting his main shaft of humanization. Further, if these seminal ideas of Freire's work and fundamental principles of his theory can be reinvented rigorously, creatively, and critically in today's and tomorrow's sociocultural and historical conditions, they will continue working as an effective means of human emancipation to disclose the deepest realities people are facing.

CHAPTER TWO

# The Key Elements of Conscientization

Based on the background knowledge offered in the last chapter, three tasks are completed to capture the indispensable elements as well as the richness, depth, and development of the concept of conscientization. First, Freire's own conceptualization of critical consciousness is investigated. Second, since conscientization has been debated worldwide, a number of key commentaries, both positive and negative, are examined. Third, the problems with applying conscientization as a mere method to concrete educational settings are highlighted.

## Conscientization at its Beginning

The original word for conscientization is *conscientizacao* in Portuguese. The term was first used by professors at the Brazilian Institute of Higher Studies and first introduced into the English world by Helder Camara (Roberts, 2000). It found its own way into international educational discourse through the first publication of Freire's (1970a, 1970b) two essays, "Cultural Action and Conscientization" and "The Literacy Process as Cultural Action for Freedom" in *Harvard Educational Review* in 1970. The two essays were reprinted in the same journal in 1998 as a tribute to Freire's life and work in broadening the spaces for democracy and dialogue by promoting education for possibility, solidarity, and freedom (Brizuela &

Soler-Gallart, 1998; Freire, 1998d). The concept is briefly defined in *Pedagogy of the Oppressed* (Freire, 1972a) as "learning to perceive social, political, and economic contradictions, and to take actions against the oppressive elements of reality" (p. 15, translator's note). Thus, at its very beginning, the concept is basically about education for critical consciousness.

### Freire's Conceptualization of Critical Consciousness

As Mackie (1981, pp. 93–94) pointed out, "any research for the sources of Freire's ideas must begin with his own practice." This is also true of Freire's education for critical consciousness. Critical consciousness, developed from the literacy campaigns Freire ran for the peasants in northeast Brazil in the 1950s and 1960s, is distinguished from two less critical forms: magical consciousness and naïve consciousness.

Magical consciousness refers to the state of consciousness that is semi-intransitive in closed structures, so it is difficult to discern social realities. As Freire (1994a, p. 17) pointed out, "In this state, discernment is difficult. Men [sic] confuse their perceptions of the objects and challenges of the environment, and fall prey to magical explanations because they cannot apprehend true causality." Magical consciousness was predominant in Brazilian rural areas at that time. The peasants in those areas, extremely limited by biological necessity under the pressure of survival, had to seek refuge in believing superstitious fatalism. Magical consciousness, marked by superstitious fatalism, stopped the peasants from comprehending reality and the meaning for their being in the world. It made their life groundless.

Predominant in Brazilian urban areas during the transitional period of the infrastructural change or abolition of slavery at the end of the 19th century, naïve consciousness, or transitivity, represents the peasants' state of thinking in those urban areas (Freire, 1994a). It lacks social explanation of social realities and merely stays superficial on appearance. The peasants with this mode of thinking imputed the root causes of reality to individuals rather than the system. Freire (1994a) wrote the following:

> Naïve transitivity ... is characterised by an over-simplification of problems; by a nostalgia for the past; by underestimation of the common man; by a strong tendency to gregariousness; by a lack of interest in investigation, accompanied by an accentuated taste for fanciful explanations; by fragility of argument; by a strongly emotional style; by the practice of polemics rather than dialogue; by magical explanations. (p. 18)

Critical consciousness stands in contrast to both a magical and naïve state of consciousness. It is conceptualized as follows:

The critically transitive consciousness is characterised by depth in the interpretation of problems; by the substitution of causal principles for magical explanations; by the testing of one's "findings" by openness to revision; by the attempt to avoid distortion when perceiving problems and to avoid preconceived notions when analysing them; by refusing to transfer responsibility; by rejecting passive positions; by soundness of argumentation; by the practice of dialogue rather than polemics; by receptivity to the new for reasons beyond mere novelty and by the good sense not to reject the old just because it is old by accepting what is valid in both old and new. Critical transitivity is characteristic of authentically democratic regimes and corresponds to highly permeable, interrogative, restless and dialogical forms of life in contrast to silence and inaction, in contrast to the rigid, militarily authoritarian state presently prevailing in Brazil, a historical retreat which the usurpers of power try to present as a reencounter with democracy. (Freire, 1994a, pp. 18–19)

Here, Freire maps out the main characteristics of critical consciousness. It shows clearly that conscientization originates from overcoming "false consciousness" such as "a semi-intransitive or naïve transitive state of consciousness" (Freire, 1970b, p. 46). Therefore, conscientization is "the process in which men [and women], not as recipients, but as knowing subjects, achieve a deepening awareness both of the socio-cultural reality which shapes their lives and their capacity to transform that reality" (Freire, 1972b, p. 51).

## To Read the Word Is to Read the World

Freire's reading the word together with reading the world builds a pathway to critical consciousness. He took a sample from a literary textbook at random to illustrate how education of literacy is undertaken in a normal way:

> The wing is of the bird.
> Eva saw the grape.
> The cock crows.
> The dog barks.
> Mary likes animals.
>
> If you hammer a nail, be careful not to smash your finger.
>
> Peter did not know how to read. Peter was ashamed. One day, Peter went to school and registered for a night course. Peter's teacher was very good. Peter knows how to read now. Look at Peter's face. Peter is smiling. He is a happy man. He already has a good job. Everyone ought to follow his example. (Freire, 1972b, pp. 24–25)

According to Freire, this type of teaching literacy only focuses on students' cognitive development. It is basically about the logical or rational structure of language and knowledge, the causal relationship between the careless use of a hammer and the possibility of smashing one's finger, and the naïve and pretentious relationship between knowing how to read and write and getting good jobs. This type of teaching and learning has little to do with what is really happening in students' life world.

By contrast, Freire's reading the word together with reading the world contributes a new mode of learning and thinking: There is no separation between human consciousness and the real world. He took "The Colour of Water," a lesson from *You Live as You Can,* a small textbook published by a Uruguayan team in 1968, to show how learning contents are closely related to historical and sociocultural reality:

*The colour of water*

Water? Water? What is water used for?
'Yes, yes, we saw it (in the picture).'
'Oh, my native village, so far away … '
'Do you remember that village?'

'The stream where I grew up, called Dead Friar … you know, I grew up there, a childhood moving from one place to another … the colour of the water brings back good memories, beautiful memories.'

'What is the water used for?'

'It is used for washing. We used it to wash clothes, and the animals in the fields used to go there to drink, and we washed our clothes there, too.'

'Did you use the water for drinking?'

'Yes, when we were at the stream and had no other water to drink, we drank from the stream. I remember once in 1945 a plague of locusts came from somewhere, and we had to fish them out of the water … I was small, but I remember taking out the locusts like this, with my two hands—and I had no others. I remember how hot the water was when there was a drought and the stream was almost dry … the water was dirty, muddy and hot, with all kinds of things in it. But we had to drink it or die of thirst.' (Freire, 1972b, pp. 45–46)

Although this passage is merely a personal narrative, Freire chose it as an example to illustrate how literacy texts can be written based on those lived experiences such as "the stream where I grew up," the plague of locusts in 1945, and the drought. It suggests that the cultivation of critical consciousness must take a prolife stance—to put human logic—reasoning and thinking skills—at the service of life. As Freire (1972a, p. 81) remarked, "all authentic education investigates thinking." The consciousness of human life and existence will make education more authentic. In this sense, Freire's reading the word and reading the world nexus does make a contribution to the educational studies of thinking, in particular, critical thinking.

Like Freire, Peters (2007) also pointed out that there is no issue more central to education than thinking. According to Peters (2007), the discussion of critical thinking in the Western educational discourse, predominately, still resonates with a Cartesian and Kantian rationalist structure and focuses more on the inner process of mental activity. As he argued, "the contemporary tendency reinforced by first generation cognitive psychology is to treat thinking a-historically and a-culturally as though physiology, brain structure and human evolution are all there is to say about thinking is worthwhile or educationally significant" (pp. 350–351).

In the same light, Mason (2007) reviewed the writings of those who have an important stake in constructing the education of critical thinking such as Robert Ennis, Richard Paul, John McPeck, Harvey Siegel, Jane Roland Martin, and others. According to Mason, although some other thinkers such as Walters and Phelan influenced by Martin suggest that critical thinking responds to the practical realm rather than solely the realm of reason, the aim of critical thinking still remains the same: personal cognitive development based on certain thinking skills and disciplines of knowledge. If there is something new, it is merely to use practical wisdom to substitute logical argumentation and analysis. Each of those thinkers tends to stress one or two main characteristics of the following:

- The skills of critical reasoning (such as the ability to assess reasons properly);
- A disposition, in the sense of: a critical attitude (scepticism, the tendency to ask probing questions) and the commitment to give expression to this attitude, or a moral orientation which motivates critical thinking;
- Substantial knowledge of particular content, whether of: concepts in critical thinking (such as necessary and sufficient conditions), or of a particular discipline, in which one is then capable of critical thought. (Mason, 2007, pp. 343–344)

Considering the reality in this educational discourse of building critical thinking, Freire's methodology of reading the word together with the world is instructive and informative. Although it is naïve to equate Freire's way of teaching literacy with the whole scope of either the cultivation of critical consciousness as Freire maintains or thinking historically and culturally as Peters suggests, to read the word is to read the world can be a stepping stone to the development of critical consciousness. It at least gives a starting point and opens up a new space for thinking historically and culturally.

## Critical Responses to Conscientization

As one of the most influential educational terms in current time, conscientization has provoked both positive and negative commentaries. It merits noting that the communication triggered by them does advance the development of the notion of conscientization.

### The Criticisms and the Defenses

The earliest criticism of conscientization can be traced back to Berger's comment. A few years after the publication of Freire's two essays in *Harvard Educational Review* in 1970, Berger (1976) put forward his critique against conscientization in the discussion of the economic and political development in both developed and developing countries. He argued that conscientization as "consciousness-raising," the cognitive preparation for revolutionary action, "implies philosophical error and political irony" (p. 137). "Because all of us are, in principle, equally endowed when it comes to having consciousness," there is no such thing as "consciousness-raising" (p. 151). He elaborated this point as follows:

> Put simply, no one is "more conscious" than anyone else; different individuals are conscious of different things. Therefore there is no such phenomenon as conscientizacao, unless one is receiving someone who has just been hit over the head. All of us are moving around on the same level, trying to make sense of the universe and doing our best to cope with the necessities of living. No one is in a position to "raise" anyone else; some of us try to convince others that our modus operandi makes more sense than theirs [does]. Such efforts may or may not be laudable, but they are, in principle, transactions between equals. (p. 143)

Therefore, "since every consciousness is immediate to reality," it would be "cognitive imperialism" for a higher class vanguard to raise the consciousness of the lower class without understanding their own situation better than the lower class themselves (p. 142). Freire is merely a missionary with arrogance; conscientization is a kind of conversion based on the benevolent assumption of "I want to save you" because "I know the truth" (p. 142). Berger favors freeing objectivity gaining from value judgment and prefers cognitive respect to ethno-centrism in the process of seeking truth.

However, Berger (1976) ignores the complexity of the workings of consciousness. Harris's defense of conscientization is compelling. According to Harris (1979), consciousness and the real world are inseparable, but the domestication through banking education under ideological hegemony distorts and separates reality from the oppressed people's consciousness. Hence, critical intervention enables the oppressed "to gain undistorted knowledge by interacting with the world in terms of their own interests," to unveil the disguise and mystification of oppression, and to examine the world in the way that is different from domestication sponsored by domination (p. 176). Therefore, conscientization helps the oppressed people understand their own situation properly and to perceive their own world as it really stands.

Harris's (1979) defense captured the point. Freire noted the following:

> The French 'prise de conscience,' to take consciousness of, is a normal way of being a human being. Conscientization is something which goes beyond the 'prise de conscience.' It is something which is starting from the ability of getting, of taking the 'prise de conscience,' something which implies to analyse. It is a kind of reading the world rigorously or almost rigorously. It is the way of reading how society works. It is the way to understand better the problem of interests, the question of power, how to get power, and what it means not to have power. Finally, conscientizing implies a deeper reading of reality, [and] the common sense goes beyond the common sense. (Freire in Torres, 1994, p. 430)

Accordingly, conscientization "implies further the critical insertion of the conscientized person into a demythologized reality" (Freire, 1970a, p. 46). It is hard for people to "integrate themselves into a transitional society, marked by intense change and contradictions … without an increasingly critical consciousness" (Freire, 1994a, pp. 15–16). As Freire (1993b, p. 109) told Torres in their conversation, "conscientization is the deepening of the coming of consciousness. There can be no conscientization without coming first to consciousness, but not all coming to consciousness extends necessarily into conscientization."

Conscientization is not a mission of raising the consciousness of a lower class by a "higher" class educator in an arrogant way. Freire favored Mao's two masses principles: "One is the actual needs of the masses rather than what we fancy they need, and the other is the wishes of the masses, who must make up their own minds instead of our making up their minds for them" (Mao cited in Freire, 1972a, p. 67). (Although Mao took himself as the representative of the will of masses in his later years and to some extent betrayed the masses principles, in theory, his two principles carry weight for how to approach the oppressed people.) Freire's purpose for utilizing Mao's masses principles is clear: Cultural workers must link themselves with the oppressed, and any forms of top-down prescription and imposition must be rejected. For example, Horton told Freire that once there was a man pulling out a pistol and threatening him to tell him what to do. The man said, "Goddamn you, if you don't tell us I'm going to kill you!" Horton replied, "No, go ahead and shoot if you want to, but I'm not going to tell you" (Horton & Freire, 1990, pp. 126–127). Both Horton and Freire agreed to let others make up their own minds and not to be experts in terms of leadership. The following explains more:

> Man [sic] has become free from the external bonds that would prevent him from doing and thinking as he sees fit. He would be free to act according to his own will, if he knew what he wanted, thought, and felt. But he does not know. He conforms to anonymous authorities and adopts a self which is not his. The more he does this, the more powerless he feels, the more is he forced to conform. In spite of a veneer of optimism and initiative, modern man is overcome by a profound feeling of powerless which makes him gaze toward approaching catastrophe as though he were paralyzed. (Fromm in Freire, 1994a, pp. 6–7)

The man who threatened Horton really did not know what to do. Horton told Freire, "I was tempted then to become an instant expert, right on the spot! But I knew that if I did that, all would be lost and then all the rest of them would start asking me what to do" (Horton & Freire, 1990, p. 126). Hence, pretending to be an expert with "a veneer of optimism and initiative" can only make the oppressed become even more powerless, dependent, and conformed to "anonymous authorities," as quoted earlier. It will lead to slavery rather than freedom. This is why Horton and Freire encourage an educator or a cultural worker to be a translator of the oppressed people's problems and dreams so that she or he can help them know and voice what they want, think, and feel, in short, to be the masters and mistresses of themselves. It is clear that Freire has a profound concern for human freedom. He not only shows cognitive respect for the people in a lower class but also wants people to become the subjects of their own thinking and actions. Berger's criticism is merely a misreading of Freire.

Bowers (1986) also criticizes conscientization. As he argued, "even though Freire stresses that reflection must involve a dialogical relation with others, it remains ultimately a capacity exercised by the individual-like intentionality" (p. 150). For him, Freire imposes existentialist-humanist individualism upon the oppressed people.

Freire is truly influenced by humanist existentialism. However, he is not a humanist existentialist. Existentialist-humanist individualism reflects poignant anxiety of how self-being is deeply interwoven with the worldliness and is torn apart by society. The following quotation from *The Fall*, a novel by Camus (2006), an influential humanist-existentialist writer, offers an effective illustration:

In sackcloth and ashes, slowly tearing out my hair, my face ploughed with scratches, but sharp-eyed, I stand before the whole of humankind, going over my shameful actions, ever-conscious of the effect I am having and saying: "I was the lowest of the low." Then, imperceptibly, my speech slips from "I" to "we." When I get to the point of saying: "This is what we are," the switch has been made and I can tell them some home truths. Of course, I am like them: we are in the same boat. But I have one superiority over them, which is that I know, and that gives me the right to speak. You see the advantage, I am sure. The more I accuse myself, the more I have the right to judge you. Better still: I incite you to judge yourself, which relieves me by that much more. (pp. 87–88)

For Camus, the transition from being able to see "I" in a miserable condition to being able to see "we are in the same boat" does not put the viewer in a superior position. The superiority or advantage is that "I" am conscious of this knowledge and able to accuse the fall and the immersion of "myself" in the worldliness on conscience. Through this passage, Camus draws a vivid picture of how hard it is in consciousness to fight a way out for self-being from the agonizing worldliness. It is clear that in existentialist-humanism discourse, conscience of the self-being is highlighted.

Freire's understanding of the worldliness, however, cannot be categorized into existentialist-humanist individualism. The following remark speaks evidently for Freire's (1994a) understanding of self:

If an erroneous solipsism claims that only the Ego exists and that its consciousness embraces everything (since it is an absurdity to think of a reality external to it), the a-critical, mechanistic, grossly materialistic objectivism, according to which reality transforms itself, without any action on the part of men and women (who are mere objects of transformation) is equally in error. (p. 146)

Nonetheless, it is equally important to note that Freire does not reject the notion of self. He states clearly that "by making it possible for men [sic] to enter the historical process as responsible subjects, conscientization enrols them in the search for self-affirmation" (Freire, 1972a, p. 16). For him, the self is affirmed in the historical process of being responsible subjects.

Freire indeed pays much attention to the social and historical aspects of self. However, his understanding of the social and historical aspects of self is different from both Heidegger's and Camus's worldliness. He does not exaggerate the worldliness as an intangible and inescapable web that always produces stress and pressure to threaten individuals' self-being. For him, the worldliness is not abstract, it represents itself in concrete forms of social realities, which not only can generate different themes for dialogue but also can be changed. To be more precise, Freire sees the core of the worldliness as human relations. If there is the most invincible armor for self, given that human beings are ontologically social, self-being will be suffocated in that armor.

In this context, there is an ontological and natural bond between self and others. If self does not keep a harmonious relation with others, self-being will inevitably suffer. The best way to protect self-being from falling in the worldliness is a profound love of human beings and the world. For Freire (1970b, p. 46), to achieve "communion with the people" is "one of the fundamental characteristics of cultural action for freedom"; and what is more, "authentic communion implies communication between men [sic], mediated by the world." Hence, Freire does not think the world is a "hell" for the self-being. Rather, it is a necessary mediation for dialogue. Dialogue and love uplift the unity between self and others; they can address the dilemma between "I" and "they." Here Freire differentiates himself from existentialist-humanist individualists.

More importantly, Freire does not use existentialist-humanist individualism to develop his theory of conscientization, and conscientization does not necessarily end up with "a capacity exercised by the individual-like intentionality." Roberts's comments are a key to understanding this point. According to Roberts (1996, 2000), for Freire, human beings' being (onto)-formation is more self-conscious than self-constituting, so *I* or *self* is actually *we*, relationally and socially constituted. Knowing the self is often provoked and deepened by knowing others. *I think* is actually *we think*. Further, as Roberts (2000, p. 151) argued, dialogue, a key element in conscientization, is never "simply a collection of individual consciousness." Rather, it must be understood as the movement of "*consciousnesses*," socially and culturally constituted and reconstituted "through purposeful communication" (p. 152, emphasis added). By the same logic, the conscientized self is also in "the *synthesis* of a dialogical relation" (p. 151, emphasis added). If this character of dialogue is ignored, conscientization is no longer itself.

If the aforementioned constitutes theoretical arguments in favor of Freire's standing point, Smith's (1999) reflection on Maori people's day-to-day practice of fighting against cultural oppression, economic exploitation, and political domination provides strong evidence to show the shortcomings of Bowers's comments. According to Smith, "from the point of view of indigenous peoples, Paulo Freire is to be regarded as one of the most (if not *the* most) important liberation thinkers of the twentieth century" (p. 35). He pointed out the following:

> Most Maori (and this was certainly my own experience) came to Freire after they were well involved in resistance and struggle. The point is that for many Maori, Freire's writings provided support, direction, validity and confirmation of what they were already doing. Thus Freire's manifesto, *Pedagogy of the Oppressed*, provided a theoretical

reinforcement for and an intellectualisation of the struggles which for the most part were already happening on the ground. (p. 36)

Therefore, it would seem that Bowers failed to capture Freire's (1994a) claim that "humanism is to make dialogue live" and "there is no such thing as dialogical manipulation or conquest" (p. 115). Bowers's comments serve to further confuse Freire's conceptualization of critical consciousness. He may mistakenly "impose" individualism in the tradition of existentialist-humanism upon Freire's dialogical and socially interactive dynamic of conscientization.

## Conscientization, a Humanizing Pedagogy

Torres (1994) conducted a comparative study of both Hegel and Freire's dialectics of consciousness and came to an important revelation: Conscientization is a humanizing pedagogy. As he argued, "the logical structure of Hegel's dialectics" has deeply influenced Freire's critical pedagogy, in particular, the dialectic in *Pedagogy of the Oppressed* (p. 432). That is, conscientization is Freire's reinvention or *Aufhebung* of Hegel's dialectics of human consciousness. (*Aufhebung*, a Hegelian term, is translated into English as "sublation." The term refers to the negation of negations: a triple act or movement of negating, preserving, and superseding.) In this context, Hegel's analysis of human consciousness in the light of Torres's study paves the way to understanding why conscientization is a humanizing pedagogy.

For Hegel (1971), there are two possibilities of consciousness: It can be *in itself* or it can be *for another self,* which results from the situation of a subject concerning an object. This situation brings about two movements: first, the movement of the subject, knowledge, or concept; and second, the movement of the object or the object of knowledge. Hegel sees "concept" as the object "in itself" while the object is the object for another not for itself. This agrees with Hegel's idealist viewpoint: The objects of the world only come back to their spiritual home when they find their subjects or to be known. This requires the work of consciousness. Hence, consciousness by itself is an active process. When human beings are driven by the need or desire to contact or examine the world of objects or nature, they enter into the relations of both a conceptual field and an objectual field. Since the notion or perception of an object is not identical to a thing-in-itself, the truth about this thing-in-itself cannot be found in consciousness or in the appearance of this object. It finds its real essence in the opposition of the appearance. For Hegel, to know this opposition requires the negation of all negations. That is, "truth" comes to consciousness through a process of the negation.

According to Hegel (1971), the truth or the work of negativity in consciousness occurs in the unity of self-consciousness. As he put it, "self-consciousness is reflection out of the bare being that belongs to the world of sense and perception, and is essentially the return out of otherness" (p. 219). However, this reflection of being and return to the self are all driven by desire. Without desire, self-consciousness cannot stand out. Thus, "self-consciousness is the state of desire in general"; it is not a sensible, speculative consciousness but a practical consciousness motivated by satisfying a desire (p. 220).

Desire, a key concept in Hegel's philosophy of consciousness, is closely related to his understanding of life. For Hegel (1971), life is an undivided unity like the whole of the mind; the unity of life forms the fluent condition of the mobility of the self. That is, in life, self-consciousness experiences need (desire) and freedom (satisfaction of need or desire). However, an object always appears independently of self-consciousness. Consequently, there is always a tension between desire and an object used to satisfy desire. This tension makes life psychologically unbalanced and thus drives each self, psychologically, to try to restore the balance.

Hegel (1971) examined three aspects with regard to the relationship between self-consciousness (the ego) and its craving (desire): *the for itself*, true independence; *the in itself*, simple and universal fluidity or life itself; and the *other*, the successive configurations that objects or consciousnesses assume, which are different from the initial self-consciousness. A negation process does not only occur in consciousness but also in objects themselves. The ego obtains satisfaction when the object fulfils its negation in it. This suggests that objects and consciousness are independent. This independence allows self-consciousness to attain the satisfaction of its desire in another self. That is, self-consciousness exists in itself and for itself, but dialectically, it also exists for another self because of the need of being acknowledged or recognized.

According to Hegel (1971), for the sake of recognition, self-consciousness has a double effect in a duplicated movement: one is to lose itself, to behave as the object of craving; the other is to see itself in the other, to behave as the subject. However, while one desire wants the other desire to be for itself and affirms its own universal recognition, the other does the same, trying to continue to be for itself. Hence, they mutually oppose one another. This struggle of opposed consciousness is a life and death battle. In terms of the object of desire, even one human being can be an object of the other, or vice versa. As Torres (1994) noted, "Hegel foresaw that the subject would not only appropriate things (basic property) but it was trying to appropriate subjects as well (the struggle of opposed consciousnesses)" (p. 437). This kind of appropriation of other subjects brings about a battle between *opposed consciousnesses*. Hegel (1971) wrote the following:

> The relation of both self-consciousnesses is in this way so constituted that they prove themselves and each other through a life and death struggle. They must enter into

this struggle, for they must bring their certainty of themselves, the certainty of being for themselves, to the level of objective truth, and make this a fact both in case of the other and in their own case as well. (pp. 232–233)

In this sense, for Hegel (1971), being a person is to obtain freedom and recognition by risking life. On the one hand, everyone tries to kill others because the other is not as valuable as he is to himself. Accordingly, there could be only one victor in the battle for recognition and freedom. On the other hand, if each individual tends toward the death of others or if all the contenders die, no one survives to recognize the winning victor as a master, so negation takes an abstract form in self-consciousness. Thus, the struggle for life, for self-consciousness, and specifically for the recognized self-consciousness, ends up with two important types of consciousness. One is self-consciousness that assumes the role of the subject known by history as the master while the other assumes the role of the object known as the slave, or the servant, or the bondsman. While the master consciousness is to be for itself, the slave consciousness is dependent or to be for the other.

Hegel's (1971) analysis of the master–slave relationship might initiate the notion of alienation. In the master–slave relationship, the master mediates himself through another consciousness. To put it simply, the master lives on or gets everything in need by enslaving his slaves' consciousness. Therefore, the master lives independently of nature or things. By contrast, the slave, because of fear of death, toils in the field and serves at home; his work is formative and educative, so he can satiate his desires qua self-consciousness through work or labor, thereby freeing himself from nature or things and obtaining the truth of being a human. In this case, the master faces the problem of alienation and needs liberation.

Hegel (1971) believed that "SPIRIT knowing spirit is consciousness of itself; and is to itself in the form of objectivity" (p. 696). Therefore, he offered a spiritual approach of negation as liberation toward freedom: self-consciousness "retreats from its object," negates itself, gives itself to "Absolute Spirit," or takes "God as Light" (p. 699). Hegel wrote the following:

> This revel of heaving life [or totality of life] must, however, assume the character of distinctive self-existence, and give enduring subsistence to its fleeting shapes. Immediate being, in which it places itself over against its own consciousness, is itself the negative destructive agency which dissolves its distinctions. It is thus in truth the Self; and spirit therefore passes on to know itself in the form of self. Pure Light scatters its simplicity as infinity of separate forms, and presents itself as an offering to self-existence, that the individual may take sustainment to itself from its substance. (pp. 700–701)

Although Hegel's (1971, pp. 228–240) dialectics and negations are happening in the mind, his analysis of self consciousness in "lordship and bondage" offers an explanation of how oppression occurs in the struggle of opposed consciousnesses. This left a strong impact on Freire. As Torres (1994, p. 443) commented, "In Hegel, Freire finds the sources of an analysis of the situation of oppression, and elaborates it in relation to pedagogic practice."

However, Freire did not take Hegel's idealist approach of negation. While Hegel analyzed "the originating intersubjective genesis of oppression," Freire examined "the social development of the mechanism of oppression as the forms of subordination of consciousness," in a word: "thingification" (Torres, 1994, p. 443). Accordingly, conscientization is "a contradictory individual and social process, embedded in concrete political and social conditions (tensions, contradictions, uncertainties), of a given society or community" (Torres, 1994, p. 444). It becomes a political, historical, and educational synthesis, which forms a dynamic of social change and cultural actions for freedom. This is a new affirmation of restoring the loss of humanity of both the oppressed and the oppressor. Torres (1994) noted the following:

> Conscientization, being not only inter-subjective and causal knowledge or recognition, but also option and commitment, allows the oppressed to launch themselves forward toward a future of human beings seeking to share, unconditionally, the communal truth. Therefore, only one humanizing pedagogy exists: that of the oppressed, which restores at once the humanity of both the oppressed and the oppressor. (p. 440)

In this context, conscientization essentially bears an inseparable, coherent, and internal relation with humanization.

If humanization and conscientization are dialectically interconnected, conscientization will take the role of carrying out the ethical ideal of humanization in concrete pedagogical situations. While humanization gives guidelines, power, and meaning to the practice of education for conscientization, conscientization, as a practical approach, makes maintaining and restoring humanity possible. In Smith's (1999) concise terms, it is an organic part of "transformative praxis on the way to 'humanization'" (p. 37). Therefore, it is inappropriate for a person who intends to empower, conscientize, transform, and humanize others because it runs the risk of dehumanization. Nonetheless, it is certain that people can find themselves empowered, conscientized, transformed, and humanized in the praxical process of conscientization.

## The Methodical Applications of Conscientization

Conscientization not only has been hotly debated in a theoretical realm but also has been widely applied to many practical areas such as the social work, the world peace movement, the struggle for cultural identity, the clinical practice in psychology and health science, the biblical interpretation, the religious education, the feminist research, the postcolonial studies, and the political science of anti-oppression. However, conscientization is also simplified as a mere method in many cases. For example, in the entry of "Paulo Freire" in *Fifty Modern Thinkers on Education* (Apple, Gandin, & Hypolito, 2001), conscientization is interpreted as a method: "In concrete terms, his method of 'conscientization' with adults in literacy programme was basically constituted by a process of coding/decoding linguistic and social meanings, organized through a number of steps" (Apple et al., 2001, pp. 131–132). Smith (1976) published a book about how to carry out conscientization as distinctive clear-cut cognitive developmental stages. Elias (1994) took conscientization as Paulo Freire's method. Here Smith and Elias's treatment of conscientization is investigated to show why treating conscientization as a mere method is a problem.

## Smith's Three-Stage Model

Smith (1976) took Freire's conscientization as a necessary process for developing individual consciousness. Drawing on his experience with Ecuadorian farmers, he translated Freire's analysis of the characteristics of the three types of consciousness into three distinctive stages: magical, naïve, and critical. Smith classified each stage according to different answers to three questions: "What are the most dehumanizing problems in your life?" "What are causes and consequences of these problems?" "What can be done to solve those problems?" (p. 42).

The first question is for naming, the second for reflecting, and the third for actions. For Smith (1976), the peasants with magical consciousness usually use God's will, bad luck, and ill fate to account for why they are impoverished, and they accept their tough social conditions passively. If the peasants are able to make connections between individuals' problems and system problems, their stage of consciousness is classified as naïve. If the peasants are able to blame the system for individuals' problems, but if they choose to make use of the system to overcome the difficulties in their personal life, they are still classified as having naïve consciousness. This is because they have no intention to transform the system. Peasants with an aim to transform the system are classified as having critical consciousness. With this state of mind, the peasants have an increasingly strong self-esteem and also show sympathy for other peers' sufferings. According to Smith, these peasants believe in the possibilities to achieve their self-actualization through identifying and changing different oppressive structures. Based on these three stages of the peasants' consciousness, Smith worked out a linear clear-cut sequential path for the development of consciousness. For him, "one does not begin as critical and become magical, nor move from magical to critical, nor move freely between the three stages. Development is a progression from magical to naïve to critical" (p. 79).

The essence of Smith's stages model is best expressed in Alschuler's (1976) Foreword:

> We needed to define *conscientizacao* ... more concretely than Freire's abstruse philosophizing. We reasoned that if we could create an operational definition of *conscientizacao*, in other words, a way of measuring it, we would have reached a clear understanding of the term. And, we would have a method of accurately gauging the level of consciousness in situations before and after efforts to raise consciousness. (pp. vi–vii)

Smith and Alschuler abandoned the philosophical part of conscientization because it is "abstruse." Accordingly, they treated consciousness as a gadget that could be gauged. In fairness to Smith, and also to Elias later on, at the very beginning, Freire's building of critical consciousness had something to do with magical consciousness and naïve consciousness. However, in Freire's case, magical consciousness was reflected in the minds of the peasants in rural areas in northeast Brazil, while naïve consciousness was in the minds of the peasants in urban areas. The method Freire developed for cultivating critical consciences was Freire's praxical response to the situation in which he found himself. In other words, Freire's method was born out of his critical understanding of the Brazilian sociocultural contexts at that time. This suggests that it is concrete sociocultural context that determines what sort of method a conscientizer is going to use. What matters is specific sociocultural context rather than a concrete method. Further, human subjectivity is formed in multiple ways and complicated by contradictory discourses. Any linear, undialectical, and mechanical method of applying Freire's way of developing the peasants' critical consciousness in northeastern Brazil is inadequate for addressing the complexity, interlayers and multilayers, and specifics of oppression in other different sociocultural discourses. Therefore, to remove Freire's philosophy from conscientization and to reduce conscientization to a mere method in a dogmatic and contextless way is to paralyze or put an end to conscientization (see further, Roberts, 2000).

## Elias's Approach

Elias (1994, p. 17) identified conscientization as "the Paulo Freire Method." He showed his point by drawing on not only Freire's ideas such as adult literacy training, postliteracy training, and political education, the cultivation of critical consciousness described in such books as *Education for Critical Consciousness* (Freire, 1994a) and *Literacy: Reading the Word and the World* (Freire & Macedo, 1987), but also in Freire's educational experience in African countries.

Elias (1994) divided his discussion of Freire's method into three parts. The first part is about the method of adult literacy training. It covers three stages: the study of the context, the selection of words from the discovered vocabulary, and the actual literacy training. This part consists of the motivation sessions, the development of teaching materials, and decodification, the literacy training. According to Elias, Freire's word formation, from basic sounds and letters, has power to generate or suggest other words for the students. Particularly, to speak their own words from their own living contexts has the "capacity to generate in people the ability to confront the social, cultural, and political reality in which they live" (p. 19). For instance, the words they are going to learn are always presented together with pictures showing the real objects in their real-life world. Thus learning often occurs in a "culture circle" rather than merely in a class.

The second part is about postliteracy or political education, which is implemented in Chile. The first stage of this part is an investigation of themes. It involves an interdisciplinary team that could dig more deeply into "generative themes that reflect the aspirations of the people" (Elias, 1994, p. 22). The second stage is codification of themes. It is a process of concretizing various representations, familiar with learners' own situations, into certain generative themes for discussion. The last stage is a postliteracy process. It is about dialogues and discussions based on the previous codified themes between the coordinators of the groups and the people in these groups. Dialogue, as Freire suggested, extends onto newspapers, magazine articles, and books.

Elias's third part is about the refinements based on the Pop Culture Notebooks. They shed light on political nature, a great turning point in both a literacy training phase and a postliteracy phase. In the literacy training phase, apart from the integration of reading into writing, Freire's literacy education has reached a much higher and broader level of promoting national reconstruction. Freire noted the following:

> You did not learn to read by memorizing by heart "ba-be-bi-bo-bu," by simply repeating "ta-te-ti-to-tu." While you learned to read and write, you comrades, discussed the national reconstruction, production, health, unity, discipline, and the work of our People in the national reconstruction. (Freire in Elias, 1994, p. 25)

In the postliteracy phase, the second Pop Culture Notebook presents Freire's political literacy training to its full length:

> In the colonial days, our work was not free. We worked for the interests of the colonialists, who exploited us. They took over our lands and our work force and became rich at our expense. The richer they became, the poorer we became. They were the exploiting minority. We were the exploited majority. Today, we are independent. We no longer work for a minority. We work to create a fair society. We still have much to do.
>
> When we speak today about national reconstruction to create a new society, we are talking about a really different society, a society in which the social relations of production will no longer be those of exploitation, but of equality and collaboration between everyone. (Freire in Elias, 1994, pp. 26–28)

Elias's account effectively pinpoints how Freire successfully applied conscientization into the adult literacy in northern Brazil, Chile, and some African countries. However, conscientization can be applied not only to literacy but also to other knowledge subjects such as history, geography, math, physics, and chemistry. Further, the application of conscientization is not conscientization itself. Having been trapped by the myth of method, Elias mistakes Freire's way of adult literacy as conscientization in itself and misrepresents it as Freire's method.

The ultimate aim of conscientization is to open up one's mind and thus to enlarge her or his world. Thus, the soul of conscientization, the method of all methods, is praxis—the dialectical and dynamic synthesis of subjectivity and objectivity. Since any sociocultural context can neither be renewed nor be copied, conscientization simply manifests its free and liberating spirit through generating new and different methods from a critical and creative study of concrete sociocultural contexts. Therefore, to reduce conscientization as a mere method is the representative of the fetish of method as Aronowitz (1993) criticized. It will either narrow down students' mental horizon or bring about another way of domestication of their thinking.

## A Number of Indispensable Elements of Conscientization Recapitulated

In order to avoid unnecessary misunderstandings and misuse of the concept of conscientization as a dogmatic three-stage model or have it reduced to a mere method for developing critical thinking skills in Western educational discourse while its essentials are left out, a number of key elements in the process of conscientization must be recapitulated.

Critical reflection upon situationality with political will and historical responsibility is the departure point of conscientization. The key theme Freire proposed in his *Pedagogy of the Oppressed* (1972a) and reverberated throughout his life can be defined as "education for liberation and for political and social responsibility" (Torres, 1998a, p. 8). As Torres (1998a, p. 9) argued, "the intimate unity between education and conscientization" does unveil "the intimate connection between politics and education." Therefore, it is crucial to realize that conscientization aims at integrating the cognitive development of critical consciousness of everyday realities in concrete historical-cultural contexts into the development of political consciousness of social justice.

Praxis is the epistemological foundation of conscientization. According to Freire (1994a), conscientization is only manifested in the process of concrete praxis; it can never be confined to the mere activity of the consciousness through a psychological or idealist subjectivist road, and it cannot be arrived at by a mechanical objectivist way. The former downplays the value of action while the latter denies the meaning of reflection. As "a constant clarification of what remains hidden with us while we move about the world," conscientization "should continue whenever and wherever the transformed reality assumes a new face" (Freire, 1985, p. 107). Here Smith's (1999) comment is helpful again: "Conscientization, resistance, and transformative praxis" are embedded in a holistic, interactive, and dialectical process of "becoming more human" (p. 39). This whole process represents itself as an ongoing dynamic cycle of transformation rather than a linear, uni-directional, instrumental, and hierarchical progression. As he argued, "individuals do not 'enter' the transforming cycle; they are always in it" (p. 39). Thus, transformative praxis embraces both unconscious daily life participation of social transformation and conscious political and cultural resistance. This understanding can be taken as an antidote to a dogmatic, mechanical, and rigid reading and application of Freire's conscientization.

Dialogue, as an effective approach, enhances the interactive dynamic of conscientization. As mentioned earlier, for Freire, being able to engage in the practice of dialogue is a manifestation of critical consciousness. From an educational perspective, the program content of problem-posing education is "dialogical par excellence" because it is "constituted and organized by the students' view of the world" (Freire, 1972a, p. 81). The task of the dialogical teacher is to investigate "the thematic universe" of students and then to "re-present" what she or he receives from students to students "not as a lecture, but as a problem" (Freire, 1972a, p. 81). Without dialogue, the problem-posing concept of education—the cultivation of critical consciousness—cannot happen. In the same light, revolutionary social change necessitates a dialogical approach. An individual can never change a given society, and dialogue furthers a collective process of changing the world. Hence, conscientization is fundamentally dialogical.

Authentic democracy is the working regimes of conscientization. Glass (2001) commented as follows:

Since situations are permeated with defining axes of power and authority that establish standards and norms in favour of some rather than others, liberation entails a people's struggle to be, to feel, to know, and to speak for themselves. "The more the people become themselves, the better the democracy (Horton & Freire, 1990)." (p. 19)

Glass (2001) continued: Conscientization, as a practice of freedom, captures "the complex ontological, epistemological, and ethical-political features of education" (p. 19); thereby, political actions, knowledge creation, cultural formation, and linguistic practices are all relevant to self-formation in concrete situations and thus necessarily central to revolutionary social change.

It must be noted that the concept of conscientization does not remain static at its earliest stage. Rather, it undergoes development as Freire's educational practice and research advance. As Torres (1998a, p. 9) commented, "Freire developed his notion of education for conscientization in many of his works, throughout his life." In *Pedagogy of Indignation,* Freire (2004) redefined conscientization as "the building of critical awareness and conscience" (p. 66) or "the development of critical awareness and conscience" (p. 110). However, because this definition only appeared posthumously in 2004, both Freire and Freirean scholars have written more about the cultivation of critical consciousness than about the cultivation of conscience. If Freire is not read closely and holistically enough, this important component of conscientization will be ignored. My own reading is an example. In *Pedagogy of the Heart,* Freire (1997, p. 45) stated that he could not "be indifferent to the pain of those who go hungry" and impute their miserable situation to "the result of God's will." Every time I thought of this, I had a sense that there might be something deeper within conscientization, which actually drove Freire to conscientize the reality of the world. In fact, when I first learned the term conscientization, I had a feeling that conscientization might have something to do with conscience. However, my "hunch" was not proven "valid" until 2008, when I came across Roberts's (2007, p. 513) interpretation that conscientization, as its name suggests, "involves the cultivation of not just a certain kind of critical awareness but of conscience." This conveys an important message that a study of conscience, of how to cultivate conscience, and of how to incorporate the cultivation of conscience into conscientization will open up a new avenue not only for developing Freire's conscientization but also for enriching moral education and human ethics.

CHAPTER THREE

# Conscience and its Relationship With Consciousness

If conscientization is defined as the cultivation of critical consciousness and conscience, the project of incorporating the cultivation of conscience into conscientization necessitates a study of both the notion of conscience and its relationship with consciousness. Therefore, the origin and the historical development of conscience are explored for a clear grasp of the notion of conscience, and the conflict and the unity between conscience and consciousness are examined to illuminate how the two concepts are dialectically interconnected. The chapter concludes with the unifying role that conscience plays in the conscience–consciousness relation.

## The Notion of Conscience and its Development

Three articulations of human experience appear to be at the foundation of the Western notion of conscience: (1) the writings of Cicero, (2) the Hebrew Scriptures, and (3) the writings of Paul (Despland, 1987).

Cicero is believed to be the first Western philosopher who coined the word *conscientia* (Despland, 1987). For him, conscience or *conscientia*, as an inner testimony or an internal moral authority on important issues, is usually consciousness of one's deeds: agreeable consciousness of good deeds while disagreeable consciousness of bad deeds (Martyn, 1972). The bite of conscience figuratively refers to disagreeable consciousness of bad deeds. That is, conscience has the great power for bliss or bane; or, one may have a good conscience or a bad one. As Cicero (1991) argued, a bad conscience is from the influence of others and public opinion while a good conscience is often from isolated self-approval. Accordingly, he often speaks of conscience in a rhetorical context but with moralizing intent: to inveigh against human evil, to commend good deeds, and to appeal the assurance one's own worth.

Unlike Cicero, the articulation of conscience in the Hebrew Scriptures has more to do with one's heart. God, as the supreme judge, knows and evaluates one's entire being by performing the function of guiding the human heart. Take the following verse from Psalms (Ps.139:23–24) for example: "Search me, O God, and know my heart! Try me and know my anxieties! And see if there is any wicked way in me, and lead me in the way everlasting!" A similar expression can also be found in Proverbs: "The spirit of man is the lamp of the Lord, searching all his innermost parts" (Prv.20:27). In this sense, according to the prophet Jeremiah, without divine protection and scrutiny, "the heart is deceitful above all things, and desperately corrupt; who can understand it?" (Jer.17:9). Briefly, one can find safety, goodness, and security of one's heart only under God's protection.

In the New Testament, with common moral reflections, Paul uses conscience on a daily basis. For him there is a good conscience as well as a weak and defiled conscience. Take a verse, for instance: "To the pure all things are pure, but to those who are defiled and unbelieving nothing is pure; but even their mind and conscience are defiled" (Titus, 1:15). If read closely, like David, Paul has an unyielding good conscience, not disturbed by feelings of guilt, but he struggles with his physical handicap and particularly, his inner pains. Paul's inner self is bruised by a number of factors, such as his despairing self-humiliation, his own divided will, his bodily disobedience against him, his convictions challenged by adversaries, his feeling of being caught up in a passing age or time, and his feelings of impotence and worthlessness. All of these inner troubles not only interiorize the death of Christ but also reflect a cosmic crisis. However, this kind of eschatological turmoil or despair, for Paul, is a necessary form of suffering one must experience and pass before sharing the new resurrected life with Christ because God likes a contrite or broken heart (Despland, 1987). Paul's feeling of suffering and unrest, to some extent, supports Arendt's (1972, 1978) view that only those who affirm a commitment to applying moral standards but are hindered by a bad conscience will be troubled with remorse, guilt, or shame when they try to regain integrity and wholeness of the self as their need; and bad people will seldom feel regretful.

Influenced by Paul, Church Fathers accept the notion of conscience as an inner voice of divine origin and assume that all human beings have it but only Christians obey it; hence, conscience can lead Christians to obey God rather than humans and to live for a godly purpose rather than worldly reasons (Despland, 1987). For example, Augustine takes conscience as a tribunal in the mind and confirms it as the synthesis of "divine judgment, moral self-evaluation and the troubled forays into the hidden recesses of one's heart," these three notions of conscience initiated by Paul (Despland, 1987, p. 46). In this religious context, martyrdom is accepted with joy because God welcomes self-rejection.

According to Langston (2006), apart from Paul's impacts, Plato's and Aristotle's writings on virtues, practical wisdom, and the weakness of will influenced the conceptualization of the notion of conscience in the medieval ages. The development of the notion of conscience or *conscientia* is closely related to another term, *synderesis*. The two terms used at that time designate two different functions. *Synderesis* basically refers to the faculty being able to know the moral law while *conscientia* is primarily a *habitus* of practical intellect that can apply the moral law to concrete cases.

The clarification of the distinction between *synderesis* and *consceintia* owes to Bonaventure and Aquinas primarily. According to Potts (1980), Bonaventure sees *synderesis* and *consceintia* as interpenetrating one another. Bonaventure locates *synderesis*, spark of conscience, in the *potentia affective* that stimulates a human being to the good, while he places conscience within the rational faculty, or a part of practical reason when connected to the will, emotions, and performance of actions. Hence, there are two parts in conscience. The first part, which is innate and cannot err, is to discover the truth of general practical principles; by contrast, the second part, also innate but erring, is to apply general principles to particular situations. These two distinctive functions from two parts of conscience open up the possibility of developing new general principles through experience so that the contents of *synderesis* can be enriched over time. Although Bonaventure places *synderesis* and *consceintia* in different parts of a human being, he does not isolate the two: Conscience is driven by *synderesis* and also directs *synderesis*.

As Potts (1980) noted, Aquinas advocates an intellectualistic view of the relationship between *synderesis* and *conscientia* and sees conscience as application of knowledge from *synderesis* to activity. Concerning the weakness of will, or the evaluation of the sensible or pleasures from senses dragged by passion, Aquinas tried to link conscience with prudence and virtues. While *synderesis* motivates and orients people to the good, *conscientia* controls, judges, and decides what is good to do. In other words, *conscientia* informs people of what they have or have not done and what they should and should not do, so it functions as a witness and an accuser. For Aquinas, conscience seems to indicate a concomitant of all moral actions rather than merely an occasional voice or an emotional impulse at critical moments.

The authority of conscience had gained its fullest religious legitimacy in the medieval ages. The intellectual clarification of conscience was accompanied by a system of practical guidance of fostering a good conscience. For example, it is an obligation, made by the Fourth Lateran Council in 1215, for all Christians to confess one's own sins and receive the sacrament, which is known as the tribunal of conscience (Despland, 1987). According to Nelson (1981), this system of spiritual direction was under a three-fold heading: conscience, casuistry, and the cure of souls. Provided that moral law is universal and the individual is different from each other, casuistry is just to study the cases of conscience or individual consciences. Therefore, some practical ways of administering souls in a therapeutic way and the education of conscience were involved in the pastoral care and church services. However, in the 12th and 13th centuries, due to urbanization, increasing royal power, and people's awakening national consciousness, particularly in England and France, there was also a shift of meaning from the self's conscience to the social relevance of conscience—such as forming a good and secure society and having a collective and civil conscience of common peace and universal justice (Despland, 1987).

The development of conscience in the modern ages, in particular from the 16th century to the 18th century, was ignited by religious reformers. As Despland (1987, p. 49) pointed out, "in the middle ages conscience was a function: people had more or less of it, and tried more or less to exercise it." However, for the reformers, conscience is a fact of spiritual life: "People had a troubled or joyful one; it became an individual organ—you have your conscience and I have mine, just as each of us has his own stomach. This conscience was said to be infallible and generally philanthropic. It was inviolate" (p. 49).

Impacted by the Protestant Reformation, although conscience was one of the most militant terms at that time, a big change took place when people applied the term: Conscience was more about individuals' human innerness as it met God than its casuistry practices (Despland, 1987). The human relationship with God was individuals' business and people did not need human beings like Church Fathers or pastors to build an indirect bridge between God and them. As Christians, they could know God personally and establish a rapport with God by themselves. Therefore, all the reformers would agree that those who have faith would have good conscience, and accordingly, could walk correctly in the paths of righteousness. According to Wogaman (1994), the medieval burden of being trapped by a guilty conscience was thrown off; the system of the tribunal of conscience was rejected, and Christians were no longer accountable to ecclesiastical authorities. For example, in Calvin's understanding, the enemies who rose up in one's conscience against God's Kingdom and hindered God's decrees only proved that God's throne was not firmly established therein; and conscience could never be confused with "police." This change indicates that the Protestant Reformation gave more subjective assurance to the notion of conscience. As Wogaman (1994) noted, moral aspirations made Christians believe the world could be transformed by conscientious energies. On this background, the scientific revolution started to offer objective certainty and the concept of the individual began to emerge.

From the 16th century to the 18th century in Europe, the notion of conscience also gained rigorous and fresh articulation with its ample philosophical underpinnings. Montaigne is one of the writers who inaugurated the venture and art of writing for oneself the story of an honest and observant conscience. The approach Montaigne took is an inward or introspective self-discovery by self-examination of the role and social relations in which the self is involved (Taylor, 1989). For him, human experience and human likes and dislikes move to the front stage while the dramas of acceptance and rejection at the hands of the biblical God recede in the background (Montaigne, 1958). "God must touch our hearts. Our conscience must amend itself by strengthening of our reason, not by the weakening of our appetites. Sensual pleasures are neither pale nor colourless in themselves because they seem so to dull and bleary eyes" (Montaigne, 1958, p. 249).

Therefore, the means like work or what you do in a day should not be taken as the end of life. Human life per se "is not only the fundamental, but the most noble of your occupations"; to reflect it, to control it, and above all, to accept it, is "the greatest work of all" (Montaigne, 1958, p. 397). He claimed the following:

> Our duty is to compose our character, not to compose books, to win not battles and provinces, but order and tranquillity in our conduct. Our great and glorious masterpiece is to live properly. All other things—to reign, to lay up treasure, to build—are at the best but little aids and additions. (Montaigne, 1958, p. 397)

For Montaigne, then, conscience is a better means to know oneself and one's life more critically, inwardly, and genuinely.

Descartes made a distinction between mind and body and stressed the role of thinking. Thinking could bridge the deep abyss between the material world and the spiritual world and transcend the material finite world, including human beings and human experience (Descarte, 1995). He claimed that, as a thinking being, "God" is the "author of my existence" (Descartes, 1996, p. 86). As Despland (1987) commented, Descartes set the analysis of conscience as the center of his philosophy. Although his conscience was also in turmoil, troubled by the experiential fallibility of human conscience and by the idea of the infinite, he strongly believed that only the goodness of God can amend the fallibility and imperfection of conscience for human experience and connect mortal finite human beings with the infinity ordained by holiness.

In the 18th century, the whole European world was undergoing a number of tremendous changes, such as the industrial revolution and urbanization enhanced by increasingly developed science and technology; yet, the social contradictions then were not lessened but intensified. Traditional moral codes maintained by Christianity were challenged by empiricist ethics. However, this kind of social milieu did not hinder the development of the notion of conscience. Conscience reached its highest level in the 18th century through three key thinkers: Butler, Rousseau, and Kant.

Butler, a British philosopher, saw the world as a moral order. He took conscience as a sentiment of the understanding as well as the foundation for his whole moral system (Cunliffe, 1992). He took human life as in the presence of God and this life as a prelude to a future eternal life. According to Butler (1898), there are various parts to human nature that are arranged hierarchically. Conscience, as the voice of God, sits at the top of this hierarchy to direct human virtue. Thus, conscience is an ideal bridge or merger between self-interest and the common good. However, Butler did not count on the divine authority in asserting the supremacy, the universality, or the reliability of conscience; he took the autonomy of the conscience as a secular organ of knowledge (Cunliffe, 1992). Butler is so influential that even today the *Oxford English Dictionary* (Simpson & Weiner, 1989, p. 754) still follows his definition of conscience as "inward knowledge" and "consciousness of right and wrong."

Rousseau's political philosophy is about the free, conscious, virtuous social interaction among autonomous and independent individuals (Bloom, 1979). According to him, human beings are naturally good and innocently born, but they are socialized in a bad society; in his own words, "God makes all things good, man [sic] meddles with them and they become evil" (Rousseau, 1911, p. 5). Rousseau believed he could derive the norms of political life for autonomous and independent individuals in spite of the fact that society was decaying (Bloom, 1979). For him, education is the only hope for human beings to return to the natural status of being good, and the key to a good education is to isolate a baby from an evil society and to stop the child from being polluted by the outside world. Rousseau wrote *Emile* (1979) to show how to do so. Conscience is also a key theme in the book.

According to Rousseau (1979), to exist is to sense. One's sensibility is incontestably anterior to one's intelligence; that is, people have sentiments before ideas. "Whatever the cause of our being, it has provided for our preservation by giving us sentiments suitable to our nature"; hence, these sentiments, "at least, are innate" (p. 290). Conscience lies at the bottom of these human sentiments, such as "the love of self, the fear of pain, the horror of death, [and] the desire of well-being." Rousseau argued the following:

> There is in the depths of souls, then, an innate principle of justice and virtue according to which, in spite of our own maxims, we judge our actions and those of others as good or bad. It is to this principle that I give the name conscience. (pp. 289–290)

He continued to elaborate on how conscience works:

> But if, as cannot be doubted, man is by his nature sociable, or at least made to become so, he can be so only by means of other innate sentiments relative to his species; for if we consider only physical need, it ought certainly to disperse men instead of bring them together. It is from the moral system formed by this double relation to oneself and to one's fellows that the impulse of conscience is born. To know the good is not to love it; man does not have innate knowledge of it, but as soon as his reason makes him know it, his conscience leads him to love it. It is this sentiment which is innate. (p. 290)

Although human beings are "ignorant and limited but intelligent and free," through conscience, a "divine instinct," an "immortal and celestial voice," and an "infallible judge of good and bad," they are led unto God (Rousseau, 1979, p. 290). For Rousseau (1979), conscience brings excellence to human nature and morality to human actions. As he noted, "I sense nothing in me that raises me above the beasts" without conscience (p. 290). If people lack conscience, they would go astray "from error to error with the aid of an understanding without rule and a reason without principle" (p. 290).

It is clear that, for Rousseau, taking off from social or relational and affective nature, conscience connects itself to reason, its rational character. As Davies (1990) commented, for Rousseau, conscience involves not only "inner conviction" of *conscientia* as to fully accept the underlying moral principle the self shares with others but also "*sentiment interieur*" of one's heart to feel, to know, to understand the good and to live it out with the aid of reason based on self-awareness.

Kant pursued the point of Rousseau's autonomous and independent individuals with theoretical thoroughness. He fought strongly against empiricist ethics prevailed in his time (Paton, 1963). As Kant (1963) remarked, those inner principles of action that one does not see are more important than actions that one sees. Accordingly, Kant attempted to look for the supreme principle of morality, or the categorical imperative, which is of the utmost importance to all who are concerned with the struggle of the good against the evil (Paton, 1963). For him, the good will is the only thing that is good in itself without limitation and condition, so all moral actions from the good will are conscientious (Kant, 1963). In this good will, conscience never errs but works as a conscientious agent. This accounts for why Kant takes conscience based on the good will as the foundation of morality.

According to Kant (1873), everybody has conscience originally within her or him. Hence, conscience is not something that can be acquired or a duty to acquire, and it is not something man and woman can make for them arbitrarily; it is incorporated in their being as "an inward judge which threatens and keeps [them] in awe (reverence combined with fear); and this power which watches over the laws within him" (p. 321). Therefore, no one can escape conscience because it follows her or him like her or his shadow. He noted the following:

> He [sic] may indeed stupefy himself with pleasures and distractions, but cannot avoid now and then coming to himself or awakening, and then he at once perceives its awful voice. In his utmost depravity he may, indeed, pay no attention to it, but he cannot avoid *hearing* it. (p. 321)

For Kant, "this original intellectual and (as a conception of duty) moral capacity, is called conscience" (p. 321)

Therefore, conscience functions as "the consciousness of an internal *tribunal* in man (before which 'his thoughts accuse or excuse one another')" (Kant, 1873, p. 321). It is the business of a person with herself or himself. However, compelled by one's reason, one would find herself or himself to "transact" her or his conscience as if ordered by "another person"; and "the transaction here is the conduct of a *trial (causa)* before a tribunal" (Kant, 1873, p. 321). In this context, the word tribunal, italicized by Kant, is a key to understanding Kant's conscience. Since a tribunal at least involves an accuser and a judge, it will be absurd or contradictory for the same person to accuse and also judge herself or himself. In order to avoid this self-contradiction and to prevent the complaint from losing her or his case all the time, human conscience "must regard *another* than himself [sic] as the judge of his actions" (Kant, 1873, p. 322). Here what matters is who can be this authorized, righteous, and ideal judge for conscience to hold a fair internal tribunal in one's heart.

God is the answer Kant provided. According to him, God knows the human heart; God is all-obliging; in respect of God, "all duties are to be regarded as his commands"; and God possesses all power both in the heaven and on the earth, "which the office of judge necessarily requires," "otherwise he could not give his commands their proper effect" (Kant, 1873, p. 322). Here it is not hard to see the internal logic of Kant's ethics: God's will is always good; conscience follows God, so it can live out the good will.

Nonetheless, Kant (1873, p. 322) does not stop at conceiving conscience "as the subjective principle of a responsibility for one's deeds before God" but goes further with his strong faith that God is actually "contained in every moral self-consciousness … though it be only obscurely." In God one could conceive and pursue "the ideal of holiness in substance" and any sacrifice one makes can be justified as truly "noble and magnanimous" (p. 256).

Duty and practical reason are the two inseparable key elements in Kant's conceptualization of conscience. According to Kant (1991, p. 202), to be bound to "have a conscience would be tantamount to having a duty to recognize duties." However, conscience itself is not duty; what works at the core of conscience, for Kant, is practical reason: "Holding man's duty before him for his acquittal or condemnation in every case that comes under a law" (p. 202). Kant's duty and practical reason can be understood dialectically. As a moral faculty, conscience is a state of consciousness that is itself a duty. As practical reason, conscience informs people to do what they ought to do. Thus, as Kant (1956) argued, conscience actually does duties for God in a subjectively obedient manner.

Kant (1991) believes conscience is innate, but he does not accept that there is an erring conscience. As he pointed out: "*unconscientiousness* is not lack of conscience but rather the propensity to pay no heed to its judgment" (p. 202). Therefore, he claimed that "the duty here is only to *cultivate one's conscience*, to sharpen one's attentiveness to the voice of the inner judge and to use every means to obtain a hearing for it" (p. 202, emphasis added). Here a genealogical source of the cultivation of conscience is obvious.

Kant (1956) voiced his two profound concerns with awe and admiration in the conclusion of *Critique of Practical Reason:* "the starry heavens above" and "the moral law within" (p. 166). While the former makes human beings feel small, unimportant, finite, limited, and meaningless, the latter does the opposite:

> [The moral law] infinitely raises my worth as that of an intelligence by my personality, in which the moral law reveals a life independently of all animality and even of the whole world of sense—at least so far as it may be inferred from the purposive destination assigned to my existence by this law, a destination which is not restricted to the conditions and the limits of this life but reaches into the infinite. (p. 166)

This is fundamental to understanding Kant's conscience. As Taylor (1989) commented, one can feel, at the center of Kant's moral philosophy, that there is an incomparably higher conception of human dignity marked by human uniqueness of being rational as well as being moral.

It must be noted that in the 19th century, religion started to lose its dominance and gradually gave way to science and technology. Consciousness was increasingly emphasized in a secular discourse while conscience appeared to witness its degeneration. The conscience–consciousness problem was thus brought to the fore.

## The Conscience–Consciousness Problem

As Davies (1990) pointed out, the two words, conscience and consciousness, in German, French, English, and some other European languages, are intimately related. Here English is taken as an example. According to the *Oxford English Dictionary* (Simpson & Weiner, 1989), English adapted conscience from Latin "*conscientia*," meaning "privity of knowledge (with another), knowledge within oneself, consciousness, conscience"; and in Middle English, "conscience took the place of the earlier term INWIT in all its senses" (p. 754).

The *Middle English Dictionary* (Kurath & Kuhn, 1952–2001) defines "inwit" as follows:

1. (a) Mind, reason, intellect, comprehension, understanding; (b) **at (bi, in, to) min inwit,** to my way of thinking, to my mind.
2. (a) Soul, Spirit, feeling, disposition; (b) will, intention.
3. (a) The collection of inner faculties; (b), one of five inner faculties; (c) one of outer bodily senses.
4. Inward awareness of right and wrong, conscience; **ben in inwit of,** to have (sin) on one's conscience; **clene inwit,** pure conscience. (Vol. 5, p. 263)

It is clear that "inwit" includes not only "inward awareness of right or wrong, conscience" but also "mind, reason, intellect, comprehension, understanding"; in short, consciousness and feeling. According to Engelberg (1972), "inwit" is defined as "conscience, consciousness" in Skeat and Mayhew's *Concise Dictionary of Middle English*, and Ancrene Riwle made the following distinction: "within ourselves our own conscience, that is, our mind [inwit] reproaching itself with the fire of remorse for sin" (p. 10).

The *Middle English Dictionary* (Kurath & Kuhn, 1952–2001) gives four definitions for "conscience":

1. The mind or heart as the seat of thought, feeling, and desire; attitude of mind, feelings; **gret conscience,** full awareness, **sure conscience,** strong conviction, **putten upon conscience,** to call to mind, remind (sb.); **setten conscience upon,** put one's heart into (a task).
2. The faculty of knowing what is right, esp. with reference to Christian ethics; the moral sense, one's conscience, awareness of right and wrong; consciousness of having done something good or bad.
3. A sense of fairness or justice; scrupulousness, conscientiousness.
4. Tenderness of conscience, solicitude; anxiety. (Vol. 2, pp. 528–530)

The *Oxford English Dictionary* (Simpson & Weiner, 1989) has two main definitions for conscience. The first is "inward knowledge, consciousness; inmost thought, mind" (p. 754). It includes "internal or mental recognition or acknowledgement *of* something"; "knowledge, feeling, sense"; "reasonableness, understanding"; and "heart" (p. 754). The second is "consciousness of right and wrong, moral sense" (p. 754). It is basically about "the internal acknowledgement or recognition of the moral quality of one's motives and actions; the sense of right and wrong as regards things for which one is responsible; the faculty or principle which pronounces upon the moral quality of one's actions or motives, approving the right and condemning the wrong" (p. 754).

The *Oxford English Dictionary* (Simpson & Weiner, 1989) shows that the term consciousness made its first independent appearance in the 17th century. In its early use, consciousness meant "consciousness to oneself"; "internal knowledge or conviction; knowledge as to which one has a testimony within oneself; especially of one's own innocence, guilt, deficiencies, etc." (p. 756). It is obvious that the two terms, conscience and consciousness, were used concurrently at the early stage of the word, consciousness.

This etymological study suggests that conscience and consciousness are close relatives; the word consciousness was originally evolved from conscience, while the word conscience became increasingly associated with its moral sense of good or bad. Although conscience appeared earlier than consciousness, "conscience is something of which one is conscious"; one must have consciousness even to define the state of possessing conscience, without which one cannot know or become conscious of conscience (Engelberg, 1972, p. 12). Therefore, consciousness is a permanent home for conscience to reside. As long as the distance from conscience to consciousness is unknown (Engelberg, 1972), an investigation of the conscience–consciousness problem is necessary. The core of the problem is about the conflict between conscience and consciousness and the attempt to look for the unity between them.

## The Conflict Between Conscience and Consciousness

The conflict between conscience and consciousness in the history of Western philosophy could at least be traced back to the time of Leibniz, Spinoza, and Locke. Locke can be taken as a good example. He is commonly believed to be the father of liberalism and one of the most influential empiricists. He voices a very different view of conscience from the rest of the others as reviewed earlier. According to Locke (1997), conscience urges people to the internal obligation and to check if moral principles are breached. However, this function of preserving the principle is not innate but acquired. Conscience, in effect, is nothing but an opinion or judgment of actions from one's own moral perspective. Thus, this is to say that the moral rectitude of one's deeds is a personal but not a universal judge, because conscience is a matter of practicality, background, and education from knowing moral principles to becoming convinced of moral obligation. In this sense, conscience cannot make the distinction of good and evil but only judge if actions accord with the eternal rule of good and evil. In other words, conscience is a means of measuring and judging the law of nature, good or bad behaviors, but not the law itself. For Locke, what is innate is the "power" to distinguish the good from the bad rather than moral ideas or moral rules about what is good or evil. Hence, conscience could neither guide actions nor reveal eternal moral principles.

From his empirical standpoint, Locke (1997) rejected the notion that knowledge is innate and stressed the identical nature between consciousness and knowledge. For him, the chief sources of knowledge are identified as from the data of the senses: "Consciousness is the perception of what passes in a man's [sic] own mind.... No man's knowledge here can go beyond his experience" (p. 138). Hence, as far as consciousness extends, "that conscious thinking thing, (whatever substance, made up of whether spiritual, or material, simple, or compounded, it matters not)" is "sensible, or conscious of pleasure and pain, capable of happiness or misery, and so is concerned for itself" (p. 307). He gave a clear picture of the extension of consciousness:

> For since consciousness always accompanies thinking, and 'tis that, that makes everyone to be, what he calls *self*: and thereby distinguishes himself from all other thinking things, in this alone consists *personal identity*, i.e. the sameness of a rational being: and as far as this consciousness can be extended backwards to any past action or thought, so far reaches the identity of that *person*; it is the same *self* now it was then; and 'tis by the same *self* with this present one that now reflects on it, that action was done. (Locke, 1996, p. 138)

Therefore, the making of personal identity is merely cast in a continuity of consciousness accompanied by thinking. According to Davies (1990), Locke's consciousness in the aforementioned passage was translated into "conscience" in French. This translation, a cultural exchange, nonetheless, opened a new horizon of understanding conscience and consciousness in relation to self and developed a new habit of using conscience in that time (Davies, 1990).

It bears little doubt that while philosophers such as Kant emphasize conscience, others such as Locke highlight consciousness. Their differences suggest two distinctive foci, which can be elucidated by Arnold's (1994) interpretation of the two notions, "Hebraism" and "Hellenism": "The governing idea of Hellenism is spontaneity of consciousness; that of Hebraism, strictness of conscience" (p. 88). "The uppermost idea with Hebraism" is to find God through "conduct and obedience" by fastening upon the biblical projection of the universal order (p. 88). Therefore, Hebraism cares about the triumph of obedience to God's law over sin, human animality driven by the instincts of lust and flesh. In short, Hebraism pursues righteous acts because of the "Eternal that loveth the righteousness" (Cowling, 1994, p. 209). By contrast, Hellenism is concerned with "the law and science, to use Plato's words, of things as they really are" (Arnold, 1994, p. 94). Hence, Hellenism strives for thinking, "an unclouded clearness of mind, an unimpeded play of thought" (Arnold, 1994, p. 88). As Lipman (1994, p. 216) explained, while Hebraism and the ancient Jews offer the source of righteousness, Hellenism contributes culture for "the study of perfection."

In the Hebraist tradition, people struggle for salvation (Arnold, 1994). In Genesis, knowledge or consciousness may lead human beings to a state of sin. Therefore, the awareness of mortality, sin, or death is a precondition for developing the consciousness of conscience. Adam and Eve's awareness of nakedness is merely the visual manifestation of an encompassing awareness, a new dimension of eyesight, of something to which they were blind before. Hence, the tree of life, opposed to the tree of the knowledge of good and evil in the Garden of Eden, suggests that to see is to look without one's own eyes, completely in one's mental darkness; to live a good life is to live without the self-consciousness of life itself. Accordingly, Hebraists emphasize righteous acts or deeds by following God's commandments. However, the struggle of the Hellenist tradition is to look for perfection through thinking (Arnold, 1994). They fight against the denial of life in the excessive form of a denial of self for the sake of a deity or for the sake of God's kingdom in the other world. Rather, Hellenists appeal to individual freedom and genuine human life in this world; they place stress on consciousness or consciousness of the self.

Hence, salvation is to be saved by God while becoming perfect is an individual spiritual journey without any divine intervention. Although the two concepts appear to be distinct, the two sides share the final aim: transcendence through either salvation or perfection (Arnold, 1994).

It is important to note that prior to the 19th century, different thinkers might not have agreed with each other about conscience or consciousness, but however different their perspectives, they nonetheless could attain inner harmony and unity either through conscience or in consciousness. When it came to the 19th century, the conflict between conscience and consciousness became increasingly acute and represented itself differently. Unlike thinkers in the 18th century, some thinkers and writers such as Kierkegaard and Dostoevsky were undergoing the disunity or multiple levels of the self caused by the contradiction between conscience and consciousness. As Kierkegaard (1954, p. 175) said, "with every increase in the degree of consciousness, in proportion to that increase, the intensity of despair increases: the more consciousness, the more intense the despair." Hence, the despair, related to guilt or mortality, is potentiated in proportion to consciousness, to which self is inescapably committed. Consequently, what is innate is no longer the philanthropic impulse but a demonic conscience of the self reached by means of deep consciousness. What is intrinsic to him is far more painful than what is not. It is clear that the philosopher's inner harmony and unity in relation to self are strongly affected and disturbed.

The conflict between conscience and consciousness becomes insolvable when it comes down to Nietzsche. In order to keep the unity of self, Nietzsche wants no conscience. He cries out "God is dead" and suggests the metaphysics together with morals be dismantled. Therefore, Nietzsche's ethical theory has become the bone of contention and a must study for the conscience–consciousness problem.

Darwin's analysis of conscience is conducive to understanding Nietzsche. Darwin is not a moral philosopher, although his evolution theory has greatly influenced moral philosophy. In *The Descent of Man* (1871), Darwin defined conscience, a moral sense, as follows:

> At the moment of action, man [sic] will no doubt be apt to follow the stronger impulse; and though this may occasionally prompt him to the noblest deeds, it will far more commonly lead him to gratify his own desires at the expense of other men. But after their gratification, when past and weaker impressions are contrasted with the ever-ending social instincts, retribution will surely come. Man will then feel dissatisfaction with himself, and will resolve with more or less force to act differently in the future. This is conscience; for conscience looks backwards and judges past actions, inducing that kind of dissatisfaction, which if weak we call regret, and if severe remorse. (p. 91)

Therefore, Darwin (1871) defined conscience as an after-the-fact reflective social or society-forming instinct, which evolves for the maintenance of safety and social order for a family and community. In other words, as a natural necessity, conscience evolves in human beings to resolve conflicts between competing natural impulses for self-preservation. Therefore, the claim of conscience to moral authority emerges from human beings' reflection on their social instincts shaped by the struggle for survival in conflict situations.

By the same logic, the notion of good or evil also evolves from within a society for the sake of the survival of a tribe or protection of a community. Hence, any deeds "with instinct of sympathy and good-will to his fellows" would be considered as good while any behavior destructive to the general good or welfare of a tribe or community can be regarded as selfish, bad, or evil (Darwin, 1871, p. 90). This accounts for why, "as ye would that men should do to you, do ye to them likewise," as "the golden rule …lies at the foundation of morality" (Darwin, 1871, p. 106).

Nietzsche (1966) goes even further than Darwin. According to him, the morality in an insecure forming society is different from that of a secured formed society. When a society is in its forming process, some dangerous but strong drives, "like an enterprising spirit, foolhardiness, vengefulness, craftiness, rapacity, and the lust to rule," are highly honored because they are socially useful and constantly needed to fight against enemies (p. 113). Therefore, in view of danger to the whole community, these drives or instincts have to be trained and strengthened as much as possible. By contrast, after the structure of society is fixed on the whole and seems secure against external dangers, these great and strong drives or instincts become dangerous to the order of the formed community or society. Since there are no channels to divert strong drives or inclinations, they are gradually abandoned and slandered as immoral. Oddly, however, weak drives and inclinations are translated into "herd conscience" and start to receive moral honors in "herd morality." Nietzsche (1966) argued as follows:

> How much or how little is dangerous to the community, dangerous to equality, in an opinion, in a state or affect, in will, in talent—that now constitutes the moral perspective: here, too, fear is again the mother of morals.
>
> …under very peaceful conditions, the opportunity and necessity for educating one's feelings to severity and hardness is lacking more and more, and every severity, even in justice, begins to disturb the conscience; any high and hard nobility and self-reliance is almost felt to be an insult and arouses mistrust; the "lamb," even more the "sheep" gain in respect. (pp. 113–114)

In this kind of moral climate, correspondingly, good and evil, these two key concepts of ethics are merely created as the normative social means only. "Everything," for example, "high and independent spirituality, the will to stand alone … that elevates an individual above the herd and intimates the neighbour is henceforth called evil"; by contrast, "the fair, modest, submissive, conforming mentality, the mediocrity of desires attain moral designations and honours" (Nietzsche, 1966, pp. 113–114).

Consequently, when the mediocrity could be maintained by the "herd conscience," the criterion of good and bad is confounded. "Good" is not really "good" but "evil" that is "dressed in societal garb purporting to represent a value system of morality that is violated even in its conception" (Engelberg, 1972, p. 97). Thus, Nietzsche (2000) refused to regard conscience as an inner judge of good and evil because "good" conscience is born upon "bad" conscience of the mediocre. Further, in essence, the "herd conscience" can only imitate values but it does not create them (Nietzsche, 2000). For example, an action could be condemned by conscience just because that action has been condemned by most people for a long time.

After identifying herd conscience, Nietzsche furthered his investigation into what makes "herd conscience" to imitate rather than create values in a submissive and meek way. He found out that the nature of language has played a formative role in producing "herd animals" with "herd conscience" through human institutions such as churches (Lackey, 1999). To put it simply, "herd conscience" is cultivated through language. In this respect, it is necessary to examine Nietzsche's philosophy of language.

According to Lackey (1999), Nietzsche's language philosophy is very different from Saussure, whose linguistic theory of what language is constituted has greatly influenced linguistics. For Saussure (1966), language is made up of signifier, signified, and referent; the signifier refers to the spoken word or the written word, the signified the meaning, and the referent the actual object to which the sign (signifier and signified) refers. Language is derived from the essence of things, an encoded, prediscursive referent. There is a natural bond or direct one-to-one correspondence between the sign (the signifier and the signified) and the referent. If there is the real world and apparent world distinction, words will correspond to an atomistic fact in the real world. Tethered to referents or the essence of things, language is continuously in flux with itself.

Nietzsche, however, as Lackey (1999) remarked, rejected this correspondence ideal or the apparent/real-world distinction and denied the existence of that encoded referential world. For Nietzsche, language is not created by any divine force to understand the idealist referent world. Rather, as the most endangered of all animals, human beings are forced to develop language to empower themselves. Thus, language is signs, technically agreed upon and communally accepted, for people to function necessarily in society for the sake of communication (Lackey, 1999). As a complex communication network, language serves not only as a "utilitarian device for survival" but also as "a bridge between human beings" (Nietzsche in Lackey, 1999, pp. 749–750). According to Nietzsche, it is in building these bridges that those concepts or ideas come into being.

If language cannot reflect the referent and the thing-in-itself, consciousness, likewise, as a mere surface and sign world, can never experience or penetrate a final moment of coming to be. This is because "the development of language and the development of consciousness … go hand in hand" (Nietzsche in Lackey, 1999, p. 751). Although Nietzsche prefers consciousness to conscience, he does not take consciousness as an essential feature of human beings. For him, consciousness "does not really belong to man's [sic] individual existence but rather to his social or herd nature"; it "has developed subtlety only insofar as this is required by social or herd utility" (Nietzsche in Lackey, 1999, p. 751).

According to Lackey (1999), Nietzsche believes that language, for the sake of human survival, functions in the form of innocent lies; by means of which, the lordly users with strong desire for power produce willful lies. For him, the biggest lie of all lies is the concept of God and its by-product, metaphysics. The seductive nature of language grants the possibility for the lordly users to employ their rhetoric of redemption to capitalize on people's consciousness, a mere surface and sign world. It also lets the biggest lie of all lies work itself out as the truest of all truths. The weak-willed populace with the feeble feelings is thus tamed as herd animals. Subjects constituted as such will never know themselves. Hence, Nietzsche pointed out the following:

> We are unknown to ourselves, we men of knowledge—and with good reason. We have never sought ourselves …. So we are necessarily strangers to ourselves, for the law 'Each is furthest from himself' applies to all eternity—we are not 'men of knowledge' with respect to ourselves. (Nietzsche in Lackey, 1999, pp. 752–753)

Since the genesis of both language and consciousness is from the sign or symbol world, Nietzsche maintains that most people live in the recurrence of the same in the surface and sign world. This might make human existence to its core bleak and miserable in a withered wasteland.

In this case, as Heidegger (1968) pointed out, what matters for Nietzsche is to find a way to pierce this mundane hollowness and mediocrity of the recurrence of the same. Because human subjective reprojections are subject to the other and "more subtle wills to power which lurks deep in the bowels of language," Nietzsche's alternative is to reconstitute human subjectivity in and through language (Lackey, 1999, pp. 753–754). This necessitates a linguistic turn from Christianity and metaphysics. In order to make this linguistic turn happen, people have to become both a destroyer and a creator at the same time.

As a destroyer of Christianity, one should listen to Zarathustra: "I beseech you, my brothers, remain faithful to the earth, and do not believe those who speak to you of otherworldly hopes!" (Nietzsche, 1968, p. 125) "To have faith," Nietzsche maintains, "means, necessarily, to lack freedom; or to be free means, necessarily, to reject faith" (Nietzsche in Lackey, 1999, p. 738). Nietzsche is committed to freeing individuals from God. As a destroyer of metaphysics or Kant's rationalism, Nietzsche (1999) stressed the Dionysian spirit—to weaken rationality and intensify the energy of will by means of intoxication. Nietzsche (1999) believed that the cosmic unknown, an object of nonsensible intuition qua will, can be experienced through the pleasure, the celebration of life, as well as the escape from pain and suffering of existence, in the form of ecstasy in the Dionysian way, mediated by the body like sexuality and by the mind through art. Hence, being free from all dogmatic fictions, the natural power of human beings can be restored. Meanwhile, human nature, made inimical and subjugated by Christianity, can also be reconciled to humankind.

As a creator, one should voice one's self-being in a new language. Love, too, as Nietzsche advocated, has to be learned (Higgins, 1987). Heidegger (1968) took Hölderlin as an example to elaborate how a poet can experience her or his self-being through writing poems.

For Nietzsche, to become both a destroyer and a creator is to become an "overman" or "superman." As a philosopher of life, Nietzsche's (2000) overman is one who is able to follow what one wills as far as one's life can go, that is, to be able to break away from social constraints imposed by others and to allow human life to naturally grow. Above all, it is to be ready to pay the price of consciousness. According to Engelberg, Nietzsche quoted the following lines from Byron's *Manfred* and called it "immortal":

> Sorrow is knowledge: they who know the most
> Must mourn the deepest o'er the fatal truth,
> The tree of Knowledge is not that of Life.
> (Nietzsche in Engelberg, 1972, p. 41)

"The tree of Knowledge is not that of life"; neither is the tree of life in the Garden of Eden. Like Byron, Nietzsche shifts his focus from mortality or death to life itself. In order to live, mortality or death is the price a human being must pay. The overman is fully aware of this price. He or she must face this reality fearlessly. Accordingly, Nietzsche is not concerned with the fear of death or mortality. He has little concern about transcendence from the finite world to the infinite world. What he cares about is how to stand up persistently from human sufferings and seek adamantly for a solid earthly life without falling into mediocrity with an unyielding willpower. Therefore, the essence of an overman is how to transform inevitable suffering in life into free, natural, and strong vitality of life without concealing inner vision and will.

However, for Nietzsche, morality is a major obstacle to becoming an overman. As Singer (1994) argued, Nietzsche is strongly antimorality in that "morality is the means by which the herd restricts the superior and independent human spirits, from whom alone (Nietzsche thinks) greatness can come, and drags them down to its own level" (p. 19). In this context, Nietzsche's stance of antimorality and rejection of conscience might pose at least three questions: (1) What will happen if one only has a strong will but no conscience? (2) What is the nature of human will? (3) Is conscience really meek and imitating by nature as Nietzsche philosophized?

As Goonetilleke (1995) commented, Conrad takes up the challenge of addressing what will happen if one only has a strong will but no conscience in his novel *Heart of Darkness*. In this novel, Conrad (1995) created a character called Kurtz on the background set in the colonial and slave-trading time in Congo, where and when everything could be done without limits. The whole atmosphere depicted by Conrad is a hot, wild, and desolate place; the reader cannot feel the drive of life but can only see the image of death and tusks cut off elephants as the symbol of wealth. Kurtz is "'perhaps a specimen of the free spirit' who has gone 'Beyond Good and Evil' to answer affirmatively Zarathustra's question: 'can't thou give thyself thine own evil and thy good, hanging thy will above thee as a law?'" (Goonetilleke, 1995, p. 33).

Through the mouthpiece of a Russian, another character in the novel, readers can see Kurtz clearly. As a loyal slave, suppressed by Kurtz, the Russian understands how the "spell" of wilderness alone drives Kurtz to "pitiless breast by the awakening of forgotten and brutal instincts, by the memory of gratified and monstrous passions," and how this "spell" alone beguiles "his unlawful soul beyond the bounds of permitted aspirations" (Conrad, 1995, pp. 135–136). According to the Russian, Kurtz is really free because there is nothing either above or below him; he is also strong so he kicks himself loose of the earth, confounds human beings, and kicks the very earth to pieces. Kurtz's independence and aloneness often make the poor Russian feel that when he stands before Kurtz, he does not know whether he stands on the ground or floats in the air. The Russian says that Kurtz's intelligence is perfectly clear and concentrates upon himself with horrible intensity, but his soul is mad and peace of mind is not for him. Subsequently, the spell of the wilderness and the madness of his soul have driven Kurtz out "to the edge of the forest, to the bush, towards the gleam of fires, the throb of drums, and the drone of weird incantations" (Conrad, 1995, p. 135). The Russian commented as follows:

> No eloquence could have been so withering to one's belief in mankind as his final burst of sincerity. He struggled with himself, too. I saw it,—I heard it. I saw the inconceivable mystery of a soul that knew no restraint, no faith, and no fear, yet struggling blindly with itself. (Conrad, 1995, p. 136)

Accordingly, Kurtz "was hollow at the core" (Conrad, 1995, p. 126). However, his hollowness is safeguarded by human skulls around his dwelling and is filled with the avarice for power, slavery for ruling, and human desires emerged in all their force. To be more exact, Kurtz is hollow because he has no conscience to interpret his own consciousness of himself. When he is dying, he cries out twice: "The horror! The horror!" (Conrad, 1995, p. 139). His cry is no more than a breath. He stands thus naked before horror with a heart of impenetrable darkness. Tragically, it is too late for Kurtz to become aware of the horror he has lived out.

The outcome, as Conrad tried to show, is an impasse if the self is driven by strong will but without conscience. To exaggerate realizing what the self wills, but to take no concern and care of the other, will cause one to end up with the suppression of the other by using her or him as the means.

Schopenhauer's (1966) analysis of will is helpful for addressing the second question. For him, the whole world presents itself as "will." As he argued, "the course of life itself, with all its multifarious dealings, is nothing more than the external clock-face of that internal, original machinery, or the mirror in which everyone's will, which is his core, can uniquely become manifest to his intellect" (Schopenhauer, 2009, p. 243). Thus, the word "will" is a focal point in Schopenhauer's ethics: "For this word indicates that which is the being-in-itself of everything in the world, and is the sole kernel of every phenomenon" (Schopenhauer, 1966, p. 118). The nature of will is in itself egotistical, uncontrolled, blind, malign, and either conscious or unconscious, this kind of will is its own well-being or ill-being based on a self-interested morality (Schopenhauer, 2009).

Engelberg's (1972) study of Edgar Allan Poe is also compelling. According to him, Poe's works show how people struggle with their will. Poe's interest or concern in conscience, reflected in his characters, is not the function as the avenging agent. Rather, Poe illustrates how will drives people either to resist or to succumb in the process of how consciousness becomes conscience through thought. In other words, for Poe, will either succeeds or fails, "it annihilates rather than frees" (Engelberg 1972, p. 127). Engelberg (1972) wrote the following:

> Indeed, will is ultimately not freedom but bondage—bondage to universal guilt. A superfine consciousness destroys itself by producing an equally superfine conscience; the utmost exertion of will becomes a force of the utmost determinism and in Poe, all leads to decay and disintegration. (p. 127)

With regard to the third question, if confined to Nietzsche's logic of "herd conscience," it is difficult to deny that conscience is meek and imitating by nature. However, as Schopenhauer (2009) pointed out, conscience bears a close relationship with the self: "For conscience is in fact just acquaintance with one's own self, arising out of one's own actions and growing ever more intimate" (p. 175). In a similar vein, Lucas cited Thomas Mann's concept of conscience:

> The fact of conscience as a force in life gives both expression and acknowledgement to the discrepancy between things as they are and things as they ought to be, between appearance and essence .... Conscience then is simply the injunction: "Become what

you are; be your essence, develop the essential, living core within you, whatever the disruptive influences of the inner and outer world." (Lucas in Engelberg, 1972, p. 143)

"Become what you are; be your essence, develop the essential, living core within you, whatever the disruptive influences of the inner and outer world." This quotation can be regarded as the declaration of Nietzsche's philosophy of life. However, it is the injunction of conscience for Mann as the sincerity of a genuine self. This indicates that conscience does not necessarily produce mediocrity and stop the self from standing out from averageness as Nietzsche thought. As a matter of fact, conscience is a testimony of individuals' pursuing the good and being good. Particularly in some difficult times, to live out conscience requires a person's strong obligation, extraordinary courage, and an unyieldingly free mind.

## The Unity Between Conscience and Consciousness

In order to illustrate the significance of the unity between conscience and consciousness, it is better to draw on Engelberg's (1972) analysis of two literary texts. One is Goethe's (1989) *The Sorrows of Young Werther*, and the other is Wordsworth's (1970) *The Prelude*. According to Engelberg, Goethe's Werther shows a good example of a "distempered idyll" (p. 58). Werther's despair is due to the fact that his consciousness of reality cannot reconcile with his conscience of the self, his love for Lotte. Death is the only way to escape this torture of despair. Thus, Lotte is more than a symbol of a disappointed and unconsummated love for Werther but an inner world crushed by the outer world of social reality. By contrast, in *The Prelude*, Wordsworth offers a "tempered idyll," an alternative to Werther's distempered idyll (Engelberg, 1972, p. 68). Facing the harsh realities, the lake poet gains his inner tranquillity and harmony between his consciousness of the outer world and his conscience of the inner world by means of listening to nature attentively and lovingly.

In ordinary daily life, the conflict between consciousness of reality and conscience of the self may not necessarily be a life and death problem as in Werther's case, but it is at least a serious matter about the state of being. The problem is that not everyone is a poet like Wordsworth who can create a world for himself through imagination and inspiration. As a matter of fact, efforts in looking for the unity between conscience and consciousness have never stopped. Coleridge (1969) is a good example. As he argued: "consciousness itself … of which all reasoning is the varied modification, is but the Reflex of Conscience" (p. 112). Therefore, conscience and consciousness are dependent upon each other in a holistic manner: "The Head is the Light of the Heart" while "the Heart is the Life of the Head" (p. 523).

Hegel (1974) is deeply concerned with the unity of conscience and consciousness. In the analysis of Socrates's death, he wrote the following: "Knowledge brought about the Fall, but it also contains the principle of Redemption. Thus what to others was only ruin, to Socrates, because it was the principle of knowledge (consciousness), it was also a principle of healing" (p. 447). Hegel (1971) took conscience as a unifying agent of consciousnesses:

> Conscience, then, in its majestic sublimity above any specific law and every content of duty, puts whatever content it pleases into its knowledge and willing. It is moral genius and originality, which knows the inner voice of its immediate knowledge to be a voice divine; and since in such knowledge it directly knows existence as well, it is divine creative power, which contains living force in its very conception. It is in itself, too, divine worship, "Service of God," for its action is the contemplation of this its own proper divinity. (p. 663)

Thus Hegel (1971) maps out a hierarchical declension from conscience to consciousness and places conscience at the highest level of consciousness. Engelberg (1972, p. 94) interpreted it in an inverted order: "Consciousness houses self-identity; self-identity houses selfhood; selfhood houses knowledge of duty; knowledge of duty is the palace over which reigns the self-sufficient conscience." Therefore, conscience is the most important determinant in the dialectics of consciousness and conscience. Consciousness serves the departure point of reaching conscience while conscience directs and leads consciousness upward. From consciousness, the lowest point, to conscience, the highest point, the unity and harmony of conscience and consciousness embody themselves in a knowing process.

However, if people abandon Christianity and believe in Marx's materialism and Nietzsche's claim that God is dead, can conscience still work as the unifying agent of moral individuality? Rather, how can conscience harmonize the relationship between consciousness, selfhood, and the knowledge of duty and thereby elevate the status of the being of a human person? These questions lead the discussion to the next chapter.

CHAPTER FOUR

# The Dynamism of the Work of Conscience

In this chapter, two justifications are made. One is whether conscience still functions as the basis of morality to maintain humanity and why. The other is why conscience as moral intervention is prompted by transcendence to work constantly and freely. The former reconsiders the raison d'être for the cultivation of conscience while the latter clears the way for the cultivation of conscience.

## Conscience, the Basis of Morality, Reconsidered

As discussed in the last chapter, Kant claims conscience as the foundation of morality. However, as Nietzsche contends, "herd conscience" and "herd morality" espoused by Christianity and metaphysics stop people from being strong and shift their attention from the real concrete world to an invisible, intangible, and imaginary world. They are a means of self-negation to level off everyone to averageness and to weakness. In addition to Nietzsche, Kant's conception of conscience has encountered strong objections from other philosophers such as Marx and Schopenhauer. This requires reconsidering the concept of conscience in a secular sense to address the questions posed in the last chapter. Accordingly, the relevant views on morality of Marx and Schopenhauer are examined.

## Marx's Materialist Foundation of Morality

According to Safranski (1990), prior to Hegel, there is a "direct juxtaposition of the individual and the whole: God and man [sic], or man and nature, or man and Being" (p. 307). Most philosophers then tried to answer the question—"What is a human being?"—by identifying the innate qualities or attributes of women and men. They were looking at "humanity" in a universal sense, the common features that could be shown to exist in every individual. By contrast, after Hegel, in particular, after Marx, both an epistemological and a linguistic turn occurred: "A new in-between world was inserted between that duality of 'the individual and the whole': *society* and *society in action*, in other words, history" (p. 307). The old metaphysics of the whole and of being thus gave way to the new metaphysics of society and history; talk of the individual appeared meaningless and useless. Both Hegel and Marx thought that owing to human subjective agency, social and historical necessity would win over natural necessity.

In the German idealist tradition or metaphysics, conceptions such as Spirit, Mind, God, the Absolute, the Infinite, and so on, are treated as ultimately real while the finite and material world, like ordinary humans, animals, plants, and inorganic things, are regarded as a limited and imperfect expression of the spiritual world (Singer, 2010). Unlike the German idealist tradition (including Hegel), Marx takes a materialist approach. He insists that the center of philosophy should be human beings rather than God, and thought and philosophy should start with the finite, material world. As Marx and Engels (1972, p. 48) noted, "life involves before everything else eating, drinking, a habitation, clothing and many other things. The first historical act is thus the production of the means to satisfy these needs, the production of material life itself." However, labor—the work of life engendering life or the productive life—takes place in a human society. Human beings enter into definite social relations of production when they labor or work. It is this sum total of productive relations that constitutes the real basis, the economic structure of society, on which rises a legal and political superstructure and to which correspond definite forms of social consciousness and ideology. Marx and Engels wrote the following:

> In direct contrast to German philosophy, which descends from heaven to earth, here we ascend from earth to heaven. That is to say, we do not set out from what men say, imagine, conceive, nor from men as narrated, thought of, imagined, conceived, in order to arrive at men in the flesh. We set out from real, active men, and on the basis of their real life-process. The phantoms formed in the human brain are also, necessarily, sublimates of their material life-process, which is empirically verifiable and bound to material premises. Morality, religion metaphysics, all the rest of ideology and their corresponding forms of consciousness, thus no longer retain the semblance of

independence. They have no history, no development; but men, developing their material production and their material intercourse, alter, along with their real existence, their thinking and products of their thinking. Life is not determined by consciousness, but consciousness by life. (p. 47)

For Marx and Engels, "consciousness can never be anything else than conscious existence; and the existence of men [sic] is their actual life-process" (p. 47). Morality, too, is built on this materialist foundation.

Marx and Engels (1972) rejected addressing dehumanizing problems from metaphysics of human nature inherent in the human mind and related human crimes and moral issues or sins to the social system. For them, problems such as oppression, exploitation, and inequality have private property as their political and economic basis. In particular, the capitalist mode of production is the root cause of self-alienation (Marx, 1964). Hence, Marx (1977) offers communism as an alternative:

> There is communism as the positive abolition of private property and thus of human self-alienation and therefore the real re-appropriation of the human essence by and for man. This is communism as the complete and conscious return of man [sic], conserving all the riches of previous development for man himself as a social, i.e. human being. Communism as completed naturalism is humanism and as completed humanism is naturalism. It is the genuine solution of the antagonism between man and nature and between man and man. It is the true solution of the struggle between existence and essence, between objectification and self-affirmation, between freedom and necessity, between individual and species. It is the solution to the riddle of history and knows itself to be this solution. (p. 89)

Marx's historical ideal of communism can be read as an epitome declaration of humanism with acute moral concern for humanity. However, as Singer (2010) argued, except for a number of sketchy suggestions, Marx did not give a systematic account of how to approach communism. Among these suggestions, there are two main ideas. One is the proletariat dictatorship and the other is the historical development of productive forces.

In terms of the proletariat dictatorship, there is value in reading the marginal jottings Marx (1977) made when he read Bakunin's *Statism and Anarchy*. He defended himself from Bakunin's strong objections against his proletariat dictatorship:

> *Bakunin:* Universal suffrage by the whole people of representatives and rulers of the State—this is the last word of the Marxists as well as of the democratic school. They are lies behind which lurks the despotism of a governing minority, lies all the more dangerous in that this minority appears as the expression of the so called people's will.

| | |
|---|---|
| *Marx:* | Under collective property, the so called will of people disappears in order to make way for the real will of the co-operative. |
| *Bakunin:* | Result: rule of the great majority of the people by a privileged minority. But, the Marxists say, this minority will consist of workers. Yes, indeed, but of ex-workers, who, once they become only representatives or rulers of the people, cease to be workers. |
| *Marx:* | No more than a manufacturer today ceases to be a capitalist when he becomes a member of the municipal council. |
| *Bakunin:* | And from the heights of the State they begin to look down upon the whole common world of the workers. From that time on they represent not the people but themselves and their own claims to govern the people. Those who can doubt this know nothing at all about human nature. |
| *Marx:* | If Mr. Bakunin were in the know, if only with the position of a manager in a workers' co-operative, he would send all his nightmares about authority to the devil. He should have asked himself: what form can administrative functions assume on the basis of that worker's state, if it pleases him to call it thus? (p. 563) |

However, Bakunin's objections are not a "school boy's asininity," as Marx (p. 561) criticized. According to Singer (2010), the lived experience of the proletariat dictatorship in several different countries bore out Bakunin's objections. Common ownership in the socialist countries such as the Soviet Union failed to eradicate the social problems, such as the alienation of labor, oppression, and inequality in accordance with the change of their economic basis and social conditions—private ownership. The proletariat dictatorship turns out to be a state ruler's absolute dictatorship against the will of individuals. In addition, human consciousness is not as pliable as Marx believed. Human consciousness problems such as egoism, lust, greed, and ambition take different forms in the social system with common ownership. It is important to realize that human beings live in or can be shaped by certain social systems, but ultimately they are not of these systems.

If Stalin's socialism is a distortion or misreading of Marx's proletariat dictatorship, then it is better to look at the other option: the historical development of productive forces. As Singer (2010, p. 115) argued, "Everything Marx says about communism is premised on material abundance." That is, the ultimate determining factor of historical development is the development of productive forces, in particular, technology, which will create proper conditions for human development. If communism will come, it must take this historical path.

Nonetheless, human beings are not robots and machines. The scope of the development of human thinking and feeling cannot equate with the development of history. That is, the development of productive forces or technology cannot substitute full human development. Likewise, human moral life cannot be merely confined to and determined by their economic life and productive labor. The satisfaction of material needs and the freedom in labor do not necessarily lead to intellectual, emotional, and moral appropriation. As a matter of fact, Marx wrote little about the specificity of how morality works and failed to offer some spiritual and moral resources. In this case, to use the materialist concept of history to talk about morality is to simplify human moral life; it will bring about moral mediocrity.

As Singer (2010, p. 131) questioned, no matter how the productivity can be developed, "it will never be possible to satisfy everyone's material desires"; "how could we provide everyone with a house in a secluded position overlooking the sea, but within easy reach of the city?" This hammers home the problem of human consciousness. In many human minds, not only the insatiable urge for consumer goods but also a desire for power and status persist tenaciously. Despite repeated efforts of suppression, these human consciousness problems such as egoism, lust, greed, and ambition tend to surface continuously and take different forms in different societies. "No society, no matter how egalitarian its rhetoric, has succeeded in abolishing the distinction between ruler and ruled" (Singer, 2010, p. 131).

Therefore, human moral life is conditioned or preconditioned by material life but not limited by it. As Feuerbach (1957) argued, hunger and poverty can deprive the cottagers' nutrition of supporting their subsistence of considering morality. This is true; material abundance can better human moral life. However, it is equally crucial to realize that material life is not moral life itself and does not necessarily support moral life. If morality is placed on a materialist foundation, it lacks the power to lift the human spirit and carries the danger of allowing insatiable material desires to lower the status of humanity or destroy it. A girl who prostitutes herself to make a living is different from a girl who does that in order to take drugs. Therefore, it is imperative to look for the foundation for morality elsewhere.

## Schopenhauer's Compassion as Moral Foundation

According to Schopenhauer (2010), the root cause of human suffering results from the fact that one's desire cannot be satisfied; that is, what one wills is limitless but the ability to achieve one's will is limited. Given that human nature has this antimoral or central egoistic incentive, every human being strives for ends of her or his own: Everybody "wills unconditionally to preserve his existence; wills it unconditionally free of pains … wills the greatest possible amount of well-being, and wills every pleasure of which is capable" (Schopenhauer, 2010, p. 202). Therefore, a human being is susceptible to malice or orients the other as a means on the way to attaining her or his own ends, which forms an incentive to harm others. This blind and egoistic will represents itself in such motives as self-interest, malice, jealousy, and spitefulness. These motives are not something that can be further explicated and taught or something dependent on chance. They embody themselves differently in different human beings as something unalterable and inborn. As Engelberg (1972) commented, Schopenhauer's idea of will in some way could resemble Freud's concept of ego.

Schopenhauer values Kant's work highly, but he challenges taking conscience as the foundation of ethics. For him, most human suffering is due to the conflict of human egoistic wills among each other. This blind and egoistic will hinders a person from approaching conscience. Particularly, under the serious threat or pressure of life, nobody would pay attention to such an intellectual morality as Kant advocated but rather suffer in "a universe of merciless necessity" (Safranski, 1990, p. 317). Thus, Schopenhauer (2009) argued, if someone says s/he has conscience, it is no better than the Englishman saying that "I cannot afford to keep a conscience" (p. 187). According to Schopenhauer (2009), "conscience is genuinely composed of: 1/5 fear of human beings, 1/5 fear of gods, 1/5 prejudice, 1/5 vanity, and 1/5 habit" (p. 187).

Schopenhauer (2009) maintained that "conscience is simply the acquaintance with our own unalterable character arising through the mediation of our deeds"; that is, it is "the receptivity to motives of self-interest, malice and compassion" (p. 243). He explained how conscience works:

> It is in the nature of the matter that conscience speaks only afterwards, which is why it is also called verdict-giving conscience. Beforehand it can speak only in a non-genuine way, that is indirectly, as reflection infers from the memory of similar cases to the further disapproval of a merely projected deed. (p. 243)

Therefore, conscience is inadequate for serving as the foundation of ethics. Schopenhauer (2009) takes compassion as the basis of morality: "The wholly immediate sympathy, independent of any other consideration, in the first place towards another's suffering, and hence towards the prevention or removal of this suffering, which is ultimately what all satisfaction and all well-being and happiness consists in" (p. 200). Thus, compassion is more fundamental and reliable than conscience.

However, Schopenhauer's way of placing compassion as the basis of morality is a repetition of Hume. Taking a naturalistic approach, Hume (1992) conceptualized sympathy as the moral basis. He is looking for an impulse that is inborn in human nature but is more powerful than human blind egoistic will. This is to treat morality in a mechanical, dogmatic, and passive way. Hume ignores human praxical agency. His notion of sympathy is insufficient to generate spiritual strength to uplift human moral acts. In the same way, Schopenhauer (2009) insisted that people do not just imagine how others suffer as some other German philosophers interpreted, but they suffer with others together when they see sufferers suffering; they can feel others' pain and distress. However, I would argue, if a person has lost conscience, she or he may gloat over other people's misfortune, being in a state of *schadenfreude* (a German word meaning a feeling of pleasure at the misfortunes of others). This is not to devalue the importance of compassion. It is about not relying on the workings of compassion mechanically.

It is equally important not to downplay Schopenhauer's contribution to moral philosophy. If Kant gives too much credit to reason—the human rational character—and equates emotion with irrationality that makes the soul ill, Schopenhauer offers a positive backlash to amend Kant's limitations. His notion of compassion sheds light on the significance of the affective power of human moral feeling: the acute sentiment of justice and love of kindness.

Further, if Rousseau's analysis of conscience is taken into account, Schopenhauer's idea of compassion can be seen as the emotional part of conscience. Schopenhauer (2009) wrote the following:

> Boundless compassion for all living things is the firmest and surest guarantee of pure moral conduct, and needs no casuistry. Whoever is inspired with it will assuredly injure no one, will wrong no one, will encroach on no one's rights; on the contrary, he will be lenient and patient with everyone, will forgive everyone, will help everyone as much as he can, and all his actions will bear the stamp of justice, philanthropy, and loving-kindness. (p. 223)

In this state of being compassionate, thereupon comes "the absence of all egoistic motivation," which forms "the criterion of an action of moral worth" (p. 197). However, this can be taken as a display of how compassion, as a key motivation trigger, activates conscience to work. Therefore, what matters then is how to extend human natural compassion as such in a world full of sufferings—a task for the cultivation of conscience.

## Conscience: Consciousness of Maintaining Humanity

May's (1983) phenomenological study of conscience is helpful for reconsidering conscience from a secular or unreligious perspective. According to him, conscience maintains the "self's inner harmony" (p. 57). He cited Socrates from Plato:

> It is better for me that my lyre or a chorus I directed should be out of tune and loud with discord, and that multitudes of men should disagree with me rather than that I,

being one, should be out of harmony with myself and contradict me. (Plato in May, 1983, p. 57)

This citation pinpoints the importance of the self's inner harmony to one's existence.

In the conclusion of his article, May (1983) showed how conscience maintains the self's inner harmony by quoting from Kant's (1956) *Critique of Practical Reason:*

> Does not a righteous man hold up his head thanks to the consciousness that he has honoured and preserved humanity in his own person and dignity so that he does not shame himself in his own eyes or have reason to fear the inner scrutiny of self examination? This comfort is not happiness .... But he lives and cannot tolerate seeing himself unworthy of life. (Kant in May, 1983, p. 66)

That is, the duty of all duties for conscience is the awareness of humanity honored and preserved in one's own person and dignity. At the same time, May (1983) warned that an inner comfort (or harmony) that drives people to perform their duty as Kant thought should not stop at an egoistic level of one's own person and dignity. Thus, he remarked, "we are egoistically motivated by conscience not to view our own selves as the end to be served, but to view humanity in our own and other persons as the end to be served" (p. 66).

May (1983) claimed that the aforementioned quotation from Kant contains the essential components of conscience. If so, conscience becomes a matter of consciousness of humanity. As Coleridge remarked, "it is still the great definition of humanity, that we have a conscience ... an element of our being; a conscience unrelenting yet not absolute; which we may stupefy but cannot delude; which we may suspend but cannot annihilate" (Coleridge in Engelberg, 1972, p. 242). In this context, humanity becomes the key word. If humanity is ignored or taken away, the talk of morality will be meaningless or useless. Accordingly, the discussion of conscience turns out to be a discussion of humanity, and the necessity of humanity determines the necessity of conscience or morality. This draws the discussion back to Nietzsche again.

Nietzsche was greatly influenced by Schopenhauer's study of will. Taking off from Schopenhauer's idea that human life is in thorns and shards of suffering, Nietzsche finds out that human will is the manifestation of human life in essence. The suppression of human free will or desire makes human existence lifeless. Therefore, for Nietzsche, as discussed in the last chapter, the best way to overcome human suffering is to become more conscious of different kinds of personal earthly wills, that is, to strengthen, sharpen, and uplift them in an inevitable war of egoistic wills as an "overman." Otherwise, the self will be crushed by the mob of others. As Buber (2002) commented, Nietzsche did not attack humanity but shared the same purpose with Kant: to elevate the being of a human person above animality, an animal state. He only blames morality and conscience for making people herd animals, in short, "un-self man" [sic], and "fundamentally negates life" (Nietzsche, 2000, p. 789). His problem is that he went to another extreme: to abandon morality or to go beyond good and evil. This runs the risk of oppressing and enslaving others and also turns the self into a desolate land of horror and darkness. He failed to see the intrinsic need of morality for not only protecting the well-being of community but also self-development.

As Hamilton (2008) argued, ontologically, human beings are moral beings; nobody can remove morality from the human race:

> Throughout the history of transformation since the Enlightenment—the death of God, the enthronement and subsequent deposing of reason, the breaking of icons and stripping away of illusions, the retreat to individualism, the sexualisation of everyday life, and the shallowness of consumerism—one fact stood firm. At their core, humans remained moral beings. (p. 130)

Even the postmodernists "have not blown away the moral law" but simply "removed the fog of modernist ideology that obscured it" (p. 130). They only want to make free moral decisions and choices for themselves.

Individual freedom, pivotal to human morality, can never be downplayed. Its significance was well expressed by Hayek (2001), as follows:

> Outside the sphere of individual responsibility there is neither goodness nor badness, neither opportunity for moral merit nor the chance of proving one's conviction by sacrificing one's desires to what one thinks right. Only where we ourselves are responsible for our own interests and are free to sacrifice them, has our decision moral value. We are neither entitled to be unselfish at someone else's expense, nor is there any merit in being unselfish if we have no choice. As Milton said: "If every action which is good or evil in man of ripe years were under pittance and prescription and compulsion, what were the virtue but a name, what praise should then be due to well-doing, what gramercy to be sober, just, or continent?"

> Freedom to order our own conduct in the sphere where material circumstances force a choice upon us, and responsibility for the arrangement of our life according to our own conscience, is the air in which alone moral sense grows and in which moral values are daily re-created in the free decision of the individual. Responsibility, not a superior, but to one's conscience, the awareness of a duty not exacted by compulsion, the necessity to decide which of the things one values are to be sacrificed to others, and to bear the consequences of one's own decision, are the very essence of any morals which deserve the name. (pp. 216–217)

If human relations essentially need moral intervention, it is hard to find anything more reliable and more sound than conscience to act as a principal agent to maintain human beings' moral welfare. There are a number of good reasons for claiming conscience as the foundation of morality. First, as Rousseau (1979) explained, conscience connects emotion with reason, makes them work interactively to apply high moral principles into concrete life situations, and thus brings forth conscientious actions. For this reason, conscience directs the human spirit and gives a life-leading force for people to pursue human perfection spiritually. Second, conscience is innately free; nobody can force a person's conscience to work. Third, the consciousness of humanity necessarily includes a concern with social justice, caring for the dignity and the worth of being for both the self and others in particular social discourses. Fourth, conscience performs self-examination not only backward but also forward. Therefore, the self's inner harmony is maintained simultaneously through preserving and honoring the humanity of others. This coheres with Freire's ethical ideal of humanization. It offers a solid ethical foundation for the cultivation of conscience and thus advances and upholds the practice of conscientization.

However, that conscience maintains humanity still stays in principle. What makes conscience work down to earth to maintain humanity for both self and others and how? This warrants further investigation.

## Conscience: The Working Mechanism

The precondition of the work of conscience is to be moral, which requires transcendence as an essential prerequisite. Therefore, the core of the dynamism of conscience involves being moral in a transcendent living sphere and a proper approach to it.

### Being Moral in a Transcendent Living Sphere

According to Arendt (1978), if one's soul or true self is analogous to a house, then "conscience is the anticipation of the fellow who awaits you if and when you come home" (p. 191). Arendt believes that people who are not familiar with the process of silent critical reflection about what they say and do will not mind contradicting themselves by an immoral act or crime, and bad people are not full of regrets. Some blackguards in some underground organizations would use cruelty and bad conscience to establish their status and reputation. Thus, only those who have moral standards and affirm a commitment to applying them will be troubled with remorse, guilt, or shame by a bad conscience, so only for them is there a need and concern about regaining integrity and wholeness of the self (Arendt, 1972). In other words, the precondition of the work of conscience is to be moral. This agrees with the Confucian tradition of taking "to be moral" as the benchmark of being a *Jun Zi*, an intellectual or a gentleman. It is clearly made by Mencius in his dialogue with Prince Dian:

> Prince Dian asked, "What is the business of an intellectual?"
>
> "To set his mind on high principles."
>
> "What do you mean by this?"
>
> "To be moral. It is contrary to benevolence to kill the innocent; it is contrary to rightness to take what one is not entitled to. Where is one's dwelling? In benevolence. Where is one's road? In rightness. To dwell in benevolence and to follow rightness, the sum total of the business of a great person." (Yang, 1960, pp. 315–316)

If the work of conscience takes place in the site of consciousness, then to set one's mind on high principles is to become morally conscious. This can be a departure point for the work of conscience. As Coleridge (1906) remarked, conscience unconditionally commands people to attribute the concrete reality or the actual existence to those moral ideas or principles, without which conscience cannot work or would become groundless and contradictory. In the same light, in discussing some extraordinary qualities sprung from the great heart of those avatars of virtue such as Gandhi, Mandela, and the Dalai Lama, Hamilton (2008) pointed out the following:

> At the source is a goodness of the heart that transcends the everyday decency of others. The presence of goodness to such a degree 'makes the heart so large that [it] embraces the world, so that everything now lies within it.' From such an expanded heart spring several qualities that provide inspiration. The first is a commitment to the highest principles of justice—an unbending opposition to oppression and a commitment to equality. (p. 167)

Thus, a key issue here is how to become committed to these highest moral principles and to act them out in not only a free and spontaneous but also conscious and voluntary manner. Feng You-Lan's notion of "four spheres of living" is relevant for addressing this issue. He is a key figure of neo-Confucianism. According to Feng (1960), humans are different from animals in that when they do something, they usually are conscious and understand what they are doing. This understanding and self-consciousness is what gives significance and meaning to the actions of humans. For Feng, the various significances that thus attach to one's various acts, in their totality, constitute what he would call the "sphere of living" (p. 338). He classified the various spheres of living into four general grades. These four spheres are a hierarchy from the lowest: "the innocent sphere, the utilitarian sphere, the moral sphere, and the transcendent sphere" (p. 338). The innocent sphere could be a primitive stage. In this sphere, a person with little self-consciousness is not able to understand or make sense of what she or he is doing. The utilitarian sphere refers to a state in which a person acts and behaves with strong self-awareness and self-benefit motivation but little moral consideration. Thus, everything she or he is doing has the significance of utility for herself or himself. The moral sphere indicates a state in which a person acts for the benefit of society rather than for her or his own personal profit with a good understanding that an individual is merely a member in a whole society. In this state, whatever she or he does may have moral significance, as Confucianists say, "for the sake of righteousness" (p. 339). Finally, the transcendent sphere means a person is able to understand that over and above the whole of society, there is still a larger whole: the universe. As a human being, she or he is not only a member of a social organization in society but also a member of the universe, in Mencius's term, "a citizen of Heaven" (p. 339). For people in this sphere, everything they do will have significance for the universe. Here Weil's (2002a) interpretation of Lao-Tse's remark—"heaven's net is vast, its meshes are wide; yet nothing gets through"—is convincing: "the union of his [Lao-Tse's] mind with the mysterious wisdom eternally inscribed in the universe" (p. 259).

According to Feng (1960), the former two spheres are "the gifts of nature," while the latter two "the creation of the spirit." These four spheres, especially the latter three, have different requirements for human understanding. "The innocent sphere requires almost no understanding and self-consciousness, whereas the utilitarian and the moral require more, and the transcendent sphere requires the most. The moral sphere is that of moral values, and the transcendent sphere is that of super-moral values" (Feng, 1960, p. 339).

The noble business of philosophy is to provide people with an understanding of the way or the truth of how to become a morally perfect human being, in particular, a sage living in the transcendent sphere (Feng, 1960). As Feng (1960) argued, like other branches of knowledge, philosophy must start with experience, but it is different from other branches; its development ultimately comes to something that can transcend experience. Regarding matters of fact, philosophy, particularly metaphysics, cannot increase human knowledge, but it is "indispensable for the elevation of the mind" (Feng, 1960, p. 337).

Moral actions are not simply mechanical actions that accord with the moral rules, and moral beings do not simply cultivate certain moral habits; one must act out and live out moral principles involved in a certain society with an understanding of them (Feng, 1960). In other words, a human being cannot act morally without an understanding of society. Likewise, a person fails to achieve the transcendent sphere if she or he cannot understand the universe.

In the Chinese cultural tradition, a sage cannot and need not do anything extraordinary such as miracles; "he [sic] does nothing more than most people do, but having high understanding" with a different significance to him "in a state of enlightenment ... while other people do what they do in a state of ignorance" (Feng, 1960, p. 340). Hence, "it is the significance which results from this understanding that constitutes his highest sphere of living" (Feng, 1960, p. 340). If understanding or understanding power is the key to or the only "source of all mysteries" (Feng, 1960, p. 340), then everyone, properly educated by philosophers, has the potential to become a moral person or a sage or a citizen of Heaven. Thus, "the highest achievement of man [sic] living in the transcendent sphere is the identification of himself with the universe, and in this identification, he also transcends the intellect" (Feng, 1960, p. 340). In other words, if the philosopher is in the world of intellect, he or she will be also in the transcendent sphere of living.

However, there is a translation problem here. In the Chinese version, the fourth or highest sphere was translated into "the cosmological sphere" or "the sphere of the universe," but in the English version it was "the transcendent sphere." Although Feng (1960) stated clearly that the moral sphere and the transcendent sphere are "the creation of the spirit," his English version is suspicious of excluding morality from the notion of transcendence. This poses a key question: What is the significance of the transcendent sphere to conscience, the core of morality? It requires a review of the utilitarian sphere.

Predominately, people are more likely to stay utilitarian. This point is best expressed by Bentham (1996) and Mill (1998). According to them, in human beings' public relationships, the preference would often be given to selfish over social interests; and in their private morality, a lesser good would be frequently preferred to a greater good because the former is present and easy to obtain while the latter is distant and hard to reach (Bentham, 1996; Mill, 1998).

Moreover, for the sake of self-interest, one can also make use of obeying moral codes to gain a reputation in order to win over others' trust for selfish purposes. One could also behave morally in a coerced manner or in a habit of following moral codes with the herd animal consciousness, as Nietzsche revealed. However, if the human spirit is taken as the leading life force, if the transcendent sphere is identical with the light of the human spirit, genuine morality will represent itself as listening to one's conscience and acting morally in a free and conscious manner. If one wants to live in a moral sphere, one must at the same time reside in a true transcendent sphere. Otherwise, the gravity of human desire or selfish indulgence will easily pull human beings down from the moral sphere to the utilitarian sphere (Weil, 2002b).

Therefore, a key point here is that any obligatory act is driven and led by spiritual power. Herein the freedom of responsible moral acts resides as well. Kant (1956) gave an example to illustrate this point. If someone's friend falls into the water from a shipwreck, a man could risk his own life to save his friend for the sake of friendship or patriotism. However, both friendship and patriotism cannot make the action a must-do for the man. By contrast, if the man can hear God's call to save the person in the water, he would respond to God without any hesitation and take it as an obligatory duty. God here can be taken as a symbol of the highest spirit of humanity. From friendship to patriotism and to following God, Kant draws a picture of spiritual elevation or moral development. That is, when spirit develops, one's morality develops simultaneously. Dialectically, if the human spirit declines or collapses, morality will follow a downhill spiral; if one does not need to be led to look upward by a spiritual power such as God, eventually, the concept of patriotism as well as friendship will become redundant, and care of the self will be the only pragmatic choice left.

Accordingly, in a transcendent moral sphere, with the deep awareness of the greatness and infiniteness of the universe, with the sharp understanding of human beings' incompleteness, a person can develop a sense of humility and be sympathetic toward the sameness of being in and with the world between "I" and "the other." Thereby, she or he will be able to embrace otherness in the world with an open and broad mind and a large humble heart. Only then can a person follow her or his conscience to transcend the selfish indulgence caused by myopic egoism and present to the world a genuine self with humanity alive and shining. This requires clarifying what on earth transcendence is.

## An Illumination of the Notion of Transcendence

Plato is a foundational and original philosopher of the notion of transcendence in Western philosophy. In Plato's (1955) *The Republic*, Socrates develops two similes: the simile of the sun and the simile of the cave. These two similes actually refer to two worlds: the material one and the spiritual one. The material world is not a problem for people to perceive because most of the things in the material world can be sensed with the five senses. By contrast, the spiritual world is not only metaphysically superior to but also ethically higher than the material world. Values such as justice, love, peace, truth, beauty, and above all, good, are to be found only in the spiritual world. Compared with things in the spiritual world, material things are like shadows, or echoes, or reflections in a mirror. While the body belongs to the material world, the soul has its true home in the spiritual realm.

For Socrates, the division between the two worlds, the material and the spiritual, corresponds to the material and spiritual components within human nature itself. Socrates classifies the human body or an earthly self as part of the material world. The spiritual part, according to Socrates, is not just an accessory but the best and highest part or the essence and identity of human beings. People would normally think human consciousness or mind is nonmaterial and therefore spiritual. However, it is not in Socrates's category of the spiritual world. For him, the human mind consists of two parts: the nonrational and the rational. The nonrational parts of the mind, such as passions, emotions, sensations, pains, and pleasures, still belong to the body, the material world. Only the intellect is spiritual. Just as the world of spirit is naturally superior to the world of matter, reason, too, is naturally superior to passion and feeling.

Socrates privileges reason over emotion or feelings. For him, reason is the highest human faculty, and the body with its unruly passions and impulses should be under the control of reason. Only through power of reason can humans achieve true dignity, true nobility, and true goodness in their lives. Otherwise, when feeling, emotion, and bodily impulses take charge of human lives, pain, evil, suffering, and war could become a human lot. Accordingly, the only solution to the problem of human evil is to allow reason to prevail in people's lives. When reason rules, in the face of self-interest conflicts, people will achieve general agreement and rational concord. Socrates prescribes four presumed elements of goodness in the republic he imagines: wisdom for the philosopher-king to rule out of thought and resourcefulness; courage for the auxiliaries including military, police, and executive duties to protect and administer the community; self discipline for the ruled class; and "justice" in Lee's translation (Plato, 1955, p. 196) or "morality" in Waterfield's translation (Plato, 1993b, p. 133), necessary for these mutually related classes. Socrates tries to prove that if morality cares about the good of all, it is in everyone's best interest to be "just." As Rousseau (1979) remarked, the good and justice will never separate from each other. However, as Thrasymachus challenged, Socrates's "justice" or "morality" is a fraud because it could simply be imposed on the weak by the strong (Plato, 1955).

Socrates uses two similes, the cave and the sun, to interpret the division between the material world and the spiritual world. For Socrates, human beings are prisoners in a dark cave of the material and sensuous world, in other words, the human body. Sometimes some light enters the cave from outside and throws the shadows of objects in the world outside on to the rear wall of the cave. However, imprisoned in the cave and held by material chains, ordinary people can only see the shadows on the wall before them, and they can hear only the echoes rebounding from the wall. They believe these shadows and echoes, or mere appearance, as the real world. Thus, the only reality they know is composed of shadows and echoes while truth and reality can only be found in the spiritual world or in the good.

Socrates cannot explain what the good is, thereupon the simile of the sun comes: "One has grasped by pure thought what the good is in itself, one is at the summit of the intellectual realm, as the man who looked at the sun was of the visual realm" (Plato, 1955, p. 342). In the visible world, the sun is the "source of growth and light, which gives visibility to objects of sense and the power of seeing" or the faculty of sight. In the same way, in the intelligible world, the good is the "source of reality and truth, which gives intelligibility to objects of thought and the power of knowing to the mind" or the faculty of knowledge (Plato, 1955, p. 306). Socrates emphasized the role of the good as the following:

> What gives the objects of knowledge their truth and the knower's mind the power of knowing is the form of the good. It is the cause of knowledge and the truth, and you will be right to think of it as being itself known, and yet as being something other than, and even more splendid than, knowledge and truth, splendid as they are. And just as it was right to think of light and sight as being like the sun, but wrong to think of them as being the sun itself, so here again it is right to think of knowledge and truth as being like the good, but it is wrong to think of either of them as being the good, whose position must be ranked still higher. (Plato, 1955, p. 309)

Socrates privileges reason over emotion, the intelligible world or spiritual world over the material world because, for him, knowledge, truth, and above all, the good reside over there. According to Socrates, the philosopher is the only one who can undertake the ascent to the spiritual world because the philosopher is the one who has dedicated his or her life to reason. For him, the journey out of the cave into the bright true world of sunshine is not a journey of faith, or morality, or even achieving the dream of celebrity, but an intellectual journey, a philosophical quest. In Plato's (1993a) *Phaedo*, Socrates describes the life of the philosopher as practicing for dying and being dead. The life in this world is fatally compromised by material things and the passions of the body; only after death, when the soul and the rational intellect will be released from the body, will the true and best state of being be achieved. As Weil (2002b, p. 11) noted, "to love truth means to endure the void and, as a result, to accept death. Truth is on the side of death." Plato's writings thus set the tone for the theme of transcendence: to escape from the cave of the material, sensuous, and bodily world to pursue the good, the sunshine in the spiritual and intellectual world.

## A Proper Way to Transcendence

While Plato's notion of transcendence is helpful, it is equally important not to leave unattended the limitations of his intellectual approach. Hume's (1992) analysis of passions and critique of Plato's reason deserve attention. He takes reason as an activity to use mental powers to do reasoning. He strongly rejects the reification of reason. For him, reason is not a thing, not a real part of the mind or of the soul as Plato thought. For example, people use mental ability to imagine things, but there is no specific part or department of the mind called "imagination."

Concerning the role of reasoning, Hume (1992) classified reason into two categories: *a priori* or speculative reasoning about relations between ideas such as in logic and mathematics and empirical or practical reasoning about matters of facts such as causal relations or chains among things and events. The former is free from empirical causality. It can be locked into the world of abstract ideas like numbers and propositions. The latter is based on perceptual senses of the material world of empirical facts. Neither kind of reasoning by itself can provide a person with a motive for action:

> It can never in the least concern us to know, that such objects are causes, and such others effects, if both the causes and the effects be indifferent to us. Where the objects themselves do not affect us, their connection can never give them any influence; and it is plain, that as reason is nothing but the discovery of this connection, it cannot be by its means that the objects are able to affect us.
>
> Since reason alone can never produce any action, or give rise to volition, I infer, that the same faculty is as incapable of preventing volition, or of disputing the preference with any passion or emotion …. Nothing can retard the impulse of passion, but a contrary impulse … reason is and ought only to be the slave of the passions, and can never pretend to any other office than to serve and obey them. (Hume, 1992, pp. 414–415)

Therefore, reason alone could never be a motive to action of passions; it could not motivate a person to set goals for action, and it would never oppose passion in the direction of human desires. As Hume (1992) argued, all motivation basically contains beliefs and desires, that is, both a rational part and a nonrational or affective part. In this context, any judgment about a fact could be counted as a belief while any want or preference or desire as a desire. In the province of beliefs, all reasoning about actions, particularly practical reasoning, is reasoning about how to satisfy desires. Actions are chosen in order to satisfy desires; intentional acts are undertaken because they are believed to achieve goals. Therefore, at its source, it is passions, desires, preferences, and the like, that give goals for people to act.

If the whole practical function of reason is to show how to satisfy desires, then how people's lives go, both individually and collectively, will rest crucially on what desires and passions they *happen to have* (Hume, 1992). Therefore, Hume (1992, p. 457) maintained that morality could only be comprehended under the philosophical division of "practical reasoning" and could not be derived from the pure "speculative" function of reason. However, Hume is not as pessimistic as Hobbes. According to Hobbes (1996), human benevolence, compassion, fellow feeling, sympathy for others, and so forth, are at best all weak and unreliable passions. They tend to be swept aside as soon as self-interest is challenged. Hume is not ignorant of the dismal history of human cruelty or the comparative ease with which human groups can descend into conflict. He recognizes that many negative emotions and desires, such as anger, hatred, jealousy, *schadenfreude*, and feeling indifferent to help distant strangers, are directed to one's own welfare. But he insists on the reality of other-directed feelings or positive human passionate nature, like benevolence, compassion, love, and friendliness. They are real feelings and can act against descent into a Hobbesian war of all against all.

Hume (1992) believed that concerns of individuals can extend beyond their narrow self-interest so that they are able to take into account the welfare of their families, friends, and neighbors. For him, sympathy, the affection of humanity, is common to all people because the humanity of one person is the humanity of everyone. Further, sympathy is not a passion but a mechanism of the mind, by which a person comes to reverberate in tune with the sentiments of others (Hume, 1992). This capacity to share the feelings of others is the basis for morality, fellow feeling, and other positive human traits. Thus, sympathy is the chief source of moral distinctions; it enables the welfare of others to get a grip on individuals' motives.

However, there are two major limitations in Hume's (1992) theory. One is that he downplays the role of reason in intervening human motivation. He argued as follows:

> It is not contrary to reason to prefer the destruction of the whole world to the scratching of my finger. It is not contrary to reason for me to choose my total ruin, to prevent the least uneasiness of an Indian or person wholly unknown to me. (p. 416)

He makes a serious mistake to undermine the function of reason as Plato does the same to emotion. As he claims, no feeling, emotion, or passion, is in itself rational or irrational; it just is. This means that passions can stand alone without reason: "Nothing can retard the impulse of passion, but a contrary impulse" as quoted earlier. Feelings can be *unreasonable* only in the derivative (figurative) sense. He fails to see that there is a significant distinction between a person using reason to satisfy her or his desire and a person only living in desires and passions.

The other limitation of Hume is that his sympathy is limited by his empirical or naturalist philosophical approach. Desires and passions set goals for life, as Hume believes, but what kind of passion and desire a person has is determined by *happening to have*. In other words, whether a person's passions and desire are negative or positive is only a matter of chance. This chance is more likely to be controlled by biological factors than social factors. However, in any society, compared with those who have these unruly passions and desires, those people with kind and sympathetic will become fairly weak. An armed person may have more powerful passions and desires than an armless one. Thus, Hume's naturalist perspective of sympathy is highly questionable. It will end up with an unintended outcome: the degradation of the sentiment of justice.

Kant launched his attack against Hume's empirical and naturalist standing point and took passions as the diseases of the soul. He reinforced the notion of transcendence. According to him, a person does not need to go somewhere else to look for transcendence. Kant (1998) believed that everybody has the faculty of reason, and reason in the intelligible human character has a transcendental nature, because it is not limited by causal necessity. Just because of this intelligible character, human beings are innately free to think or will. Hence, humanity manifests itself through being free, autonomous, rational, and morally responsible agents rather than being objectified or treated as things or merely the means to another's end. Along with his categorical imperative, Kant (1963, p. 91) offered "the practical imperative": "act in such a way that you always treat humanity, whether in your own person or in the person of any other, never simply as a means, but always at the same time as an end."

According to Kant (1956), reason and freedom elevate the being of humans above animality and thus are the condition and quality of humanity. In the same light, conscience, a kind of practical reason, allows people to know necessity and consequence in advance and thereby eventually gain freedom in their empirical character. To put it simply, great events take place in the mind. Even living with other people in the empirical world, one can certainly enter the moral and spiritual world and achieve transcendence by doing one's duty based on conscience, the use of practical reason. For Kant, practical reason leads people to these high principles.

Kant was insightful to perceive that the light of the human spirit shines through reason. His criticism against Hume's empirical and naturalist position was compelling. However, it is equally important to realize his limitations. As Hamilton (2008, p. 133) commented, Kant's duty ethics employs "pure reason to determine a universal moral imperative that defines the obligations we ought to comply with." Kant exaggerated the negative and destructive side of passions. He was reluctant to see the positive and constructive side of passions and eventually took passions as the diseases of the soul.

In truth, neither conscience nor practical reason is a mechanical button fixed on everybody's mind, waiting for its users to press. The validity and reliability of Hume's theory of motivation with regard to the role of passions and Schopenhauer's emphasis on affective power of moral feeling have increasingly been proven by contemporary psychological research. For example, from his experiences and experiments with neurological patients affected by brain damage, Damasio (1994) found that the absence of emotion or feeling can break down rationality. As he remarked, from Plato to Descartes, particularly, the Cartesian way, the separation between the body and the mind, and between reason and feeling, is "spectacularly wrong" (p. 250). According to him, a study of the human mind should take an "organismic perspective" (p. 252). The power of reason cannot be appropriated without emotion and feeling. Emotion and feeling, the directing sense of body states, serve an important link or interconnection between the human mind and the survival-oriented regulations and adjustments of the body (Damasio, 1994).

This is not to abandon or downplay the significant functions and roles of reason. Rather, this is to emphasize that human affective power or moral feeling serves the motivation to trigger practical reason or conscience to work in the way Kant claimed. As Blackburn (2001, p. 133) argued, "as Confucius saw long ago, benevolence or concern for humanity is indispensable root of it all … the foundations of moral motivations are not the procedural on a kind of discourse, but the feelings to which we can rise."

It is important to note that either reason or emotion is the means but not the end. Reason and emotion are always dialectically interconnected and interacted; they are also unified in a dynamic process of serving the sole end: the pursuit of human moral perfection, rather, love of the good.

CHAPTER FIVE

# The Cultivation of Conscience

If the work of conscience aims at a transcendent sphere, it must undergo two key approaches: love and dialogue. The cultivation of conscience, similarly, must rely on the transcendent role that love and dialogue assume. This chapter examines how this process occurs.

## The Transcendent Role of Love

An examination of the transcendent role of love focuses on two dialectically interrelated notions: love of the good and love of life.

### Love of the Good

Murdoch is a key philosopher in claiming love of the good. She values highly Socrates's concept of the good, which highlights the significance of human spiritual life. Murdoch is also influenced by Weil's (2002b) point—human beings' fall is due to gravity. To put it simply, if a person is fettered by material gains and bodily pleasure, it is very hard for that person to embrace the light of the spiritual world. Accordingly, Murdoch (2001) warned that it is important not to take *a* central good as *the* good. For example, freedom or happiness is merely *a* good, but not *the* good. Once a good is taken as the good, one's attention will be shifted from spiritual thirsting for *the* absolute good to *a* particular thing or concept. This is like taking the sun as a candle. If this happens, as Weil (2002b, p. 60) argued, "idolatry ... a vital necessity in the cave," will come to "set narrow limits for mind and heart"; the human spirit will stop functioning. Hence, "the image of the Good as a transcendent magnetic centre" is "the least corruptible and most realistic picture for us to use in our reflection upon the moral life" (Murdoch, 2001, p. 73). Willing spiritually the ultimate and highest good brings up human enthusiasm, energy, power, and wisdom together harmoniously toward the goal of human excellence or perfection.

The notion of the good has been contemplated by not only dedicated experts but also ordinary people, both inside and outside religion (Murdoch, 2001). What is more, attention is paid to "not just the planning of particular good actions but an attempt to look right away from the self towards a distant transcendent perfection, a source of uncontaminated energy, a source of new and quite undreamt-of virtue" (Murdoch, 2001, p. 99). The significance of this attempt of turning attention away from the particular is huge because it "may be the thing that helps most when difficulties seem insoluble, and especially when feelings of guilt keep attracting the gaze back towards the self" (Murdoch, 2001, p. 99).

However, philosophy has deviated from this center of morality or ethics and slipped to its periphery or sideline, such as psychology and sociology. From empiricism to utilitarianism, from existentialism to linguistic analysis, owing to its indefinability of the concept of the good, many concepts, such as reason, freedom, history, happiness, courage, will, and self, have consecutively been tried as "a form of belief in an external reality," which speaks to the notion of the good (Murdoch, 2001, p. 46). None of these candidates is found convincing: "They seem to represent in each case the philosopher's admiration for some specialized aspect of human conduct which is much less than the whole of excellence and sometimes dubious in itself" (Murdoch, 2001, p. 99). In this climate, there could be some forms of false transcendence. Modern empiricism is such an example:

> [It is] a transcendence which is in effect simply an exclusion, a relegation of the moral to a shadowy existence in terms of emotive language, imperatives, behaviour patterns, attitudes. "Value" does not belong inside the world of truth functions, the world of science and factual propositions. So it must live somewhere else. It is then attached somehow to human will, a shadow clinging to a shadow. (Murdoch, 2001, p. 57)

Murdoch (2001) continued to argue that Marx's concept of alienation provides an instrument for criticizing the false transcendence. Thus, it is imperative to build up a moral philosophy as the source in generating aesthetic and political views, in which the concept of love "can once again be made central" (Murdoch, 2001, p. 45). However, as Murdoch (2001) argued, love, "a single supreme principle in the united world of the virtues" (p. 56) and "the most obvious as well as the most ancient and traditional claimant," has been "rarely mentioned by our contemporary philosophers" (p. 99).

In truth, there is a natural bond between love and the good. The good has the power to attract the human heart and soul: "Good is the magnetic centre towards which love naturally moves" (Murdoch, 2001, p. 100). Therefore, it is the good that transcends rather than any other alternatives such as will. To be more exact, to love the good performs the function of a transcendent authority to empower human beings to break away from the cave of selfish indulgence:

> When true good is loved, even impurely or by accident, the quality of the love is automatically refined, and when the soul is turned towards Good the highest part of soul is enlivened. Love is the tension between the imperfect soul and the magnetic perfection which is conceived of as lying beyond it. And when we try perfectly to love what is imperfect our love goes to its object via the Good to be thus purified and made unselfish and just. (Murdoch, 2001, p. 100)

When love is even partially refined by the good, it is still "the energy and passion of the soul in its search for Good, the force that joins us to Good and joins us to the world through Good" (Murdoch, 2001, p. 100). Likewise, "attracted by excellence and made for the Good," the existence of love of the good is "the unmistakable sign that we are spiritual creatures" as well as "a reflection of the warmth and the light of the sun" (Murdoch, 2001, p. 100).

However, love, the most powerful of natural forces known to us, also has its limitations. As Murdoch (2001, p. 100) remarked, "love is the general name of the quality of attachment and it is capable of indefinite degradation and is the source of our greatest errors", hence, "false love moves to false good" and "false love embraces false death." In this context, the object of love does matter because love is motivated and attracted by its object and also realizes itself in the movement toward obtaining its object. In short, the object of love gives power and direction to love itself.

Here Kierkegaard's (2009) two kinds of love—spontaneous love (or poets' love) and refined love—should be given due attention. Spontaneous love is driven by human desire, so it is temporary and unreliable. By contrast, refined love led by God is high-minded and eternal. While spontaneous love has a particular preference for a specific person, refined love has the ability to love not only one's self but also one's neighbor. According to Kierkegaard, love starts from people who are nearby. If a person is able to love her or his neighbor, she or he is able to love everybody. Therefore, refined love "has made every human relation between man and man [sic] a relationship of conscience" and it is the highest good, "the sum of the commandments" (Kierkegaard, 2009, p. 139). From a Christian perspective, it is not wrong to say that God is love. Nonetheless, according to Murdoch (2001), refined love and the good should not be identical because love is self-assertive and can produce something bad. Hence, the good is sovereign over love and other concepts.

The intrinsic nature of the good has spirit-leading power, which drives human love to pursue relentlessly the indefinable, unobtainable, and infinite perfection. This does not mean that a person merely waits mechanically for the good automatically to fall upon herself or himself. A human being is very much likely to return to the cave frequently. That is, "returning surreptitiously to the self with consolations of self-pity, resentment, fantasy and despair" will make it difficult "to keep the attention fixed upon the real situation" (Murdoch, 2001, p. 89). Hence, a true transcendence is to look lovingly and attentively beyond the self and to construe freedom as the absence of self-preoccupied fantasies or illusions. Murdoch (2001) remarked as follows:

> It is in the capacity to love, that is, to *see,* that the liberation of the soul from fantasy consists. The freedom which is a proper human goal is the freedom from fantasy; that is the realism of compassion. What I have called fantasy, the proliferation of blinding self-centred aims and images, is itself a powerful system of energy, and most of what is often called "will" or "willing" belongs to this system. What counteracts the system is attention to reality inspired by, consisting of, love. Freedom is not strictly the exercise of the will, but rather the experience of accurate vision which, when this becomes appropriate, occasions action. It is what lies behind and in between actions and prompts them that is important, and it is this area which should be purified. (p. 65)

To love or to see brings "an exercise of justice and realism and really *looking*" (Murdoch, 2001, p. 89). As "true vision occasions right conduct," the more awareness of other people's alienation and differences, the fact seen that another person has similar needs and wishes as demanding as one's own, the harder it will become for a person to treat another person as a thing (Murdoch, 2001, p. 64).

## Love of Life

Fromm (1964), an influential psychologist, developed the notion of *biophilia,* or love of life. As he argued, "If man becomes indifferent to life there is no longer any hope that he can choose the good" (p. 150). This is true. If a person is dumb, indifferent, or insensitive to the tears on a child's face, to the song of a bird, and to the greenness of grass, and is unable to smile sincerely to others, it is impossible for her or him to choose the good and love the good.

From a personal development perspective, according to Fromm (1964), when a person reaches an optimum of maturity of *biophilia*, all these factors such as love of self, love of a neighbor as well as a stranger, independence, freedom, and the ability to overcome narcissism will all come together to form the "syndrome of growth" (p. 113). Freire's (1985) idea of living life intensively helps us understand the nature of love of life:

> The first thing I must say about what I like to do is I like to live!
>
> I am the type of person who loves his life passionately. Of course, some day I will die, but I have the impression that when I die, I will die intensely as well. I will die experimenting with myself intensely. For this reason I am going to die with an immense longing for life, since this is the way I have been living. (p. 195)

Fromm (1964) probed critically and profoundly not only *biophilia* but also regression of love, *necrophilia*, and love of death. He pointed out that, "at the optimum of maturity of necrophilia," (to put it simply, when it comes to its worst condition) factors such as love of death and destruction, incestuous symbiosis, and malignant narcissism will converge to form the "syndrome of decay" (p. 114). Hitler's life illustrates this character (Fromm, 1964). It bears little doubt that without love of life, even when one is not necessarily trapped by necrophilia, her or his own life will become lethargic, colorless, shortened, and diluted.

From a historical and anthropological perspective, Fromm (1964) discovered that there is a deep contradiction inherent in human existence: Human beings are animals but they transcend all other creatures and nature because they are aware of themselves. For Fromm, self-awareness separates human beings from nature and other animals and makes them lonely and frightened strangers in the world. This demands a solution to overcome this sense of separateness, that is, to find harmony and to be at home in the world and "to gain a sense of union, of oneness, of belonging" (Fromm, 1964, p. 117).

There are two solutions to overcome the problem of human separateness in existence. One is archaic and regressive: "to return to where he came from—to nature, to animal life, or to his ancestors" (Fromm, 1964, p. 118). Throughout the development of civilization in human history, this regressive approach has not entirely disappeared. The other is progressive and humanist: "finding a new harmony not by regression but by the full development of all human forces, of the humanity within oneself" (Fromm, 1964, p. 118). The progressive solution was first visualized in a radical form between 1500 BC and 500 BC. During this period, Ikhnaton in Egypt, Moses with the Hebrews, Lao-Tze in China, Buddha in India, Zarathustra in Persia, the philosophers in Greece, and the prophets in Israel, all expressed ideas, in different concepts and symbols, about "the new goal of man [sic], that of becoming fully human and thus regaining his lost harmony" (Fromm, 1964, pp. 118–119). As Fromm (1964, p. 123) warned, it is crucial to take human nature neither as good nor as bad but to treat it as a matter of development: "A realistic view sees both possibilities as real potentialities, and studies the conditions for the development of them."

As Murdoch (2001, p. 45) claimed, love should be taken as a central concept to "speak significantly of Freud and Marx." Fromm's concept of love of life serves well this need. According to Fromm (1957), Freud's evolutionary assumptions of libido are too deterministic to overcome the pathological regression of narcissism. Freud's notion of love, the manifestation of libido, is not the truth of love but only a reaction to the prohibition of sex in the Victorian age and an historical expression of alienation in a capitalist society. Therefore, Freud's psychoanalysis of his patients could have given "a realistic and detailed picture of the fallen men": objectivity and unselfishness is not natural to them; fantasy is a stronger force than reason; "the deep tissue of ambivalent and unconscious motive" lies at the bottom of consciousness; and psyche, "an egocentric system of quasi-mechanical energy ... whose natural attachments are sexual, ambiguous, and hard for the subject to understand and control," is "largely determined by its own individual history" (Murdoch, 2001, p. 50).

As an alternative to Freud's deterministic view of love, Fromm (1957) offered a developmental notion of love. As Fromm argued, "the child's potentialities to love, to be happy, to use his reason, and more specific potentialities like artistic gifts" are "the seeds which grow and become manifest if the proper conditions for their development are given" (p. 89). Otherwise, these potentialities can be stifled if the proper conditions are absent.

Fromm's insights have at least two important implications. One is that Fromm's psychology of development will rectify Hume's (1992) passive, dogmatic, and deterministic passion. As aforementioned, Hume (1992) claimed that nothing can retard or oppose the impulse of passion (for example, selfish desire) except for a contrary but stronger impulse (for example, sympathy). Fromm (1964) believed that when the positive and constructive sides of emotion and feeling have become fully developed, the negative side of these feelings will have no channel; thus they will naturally decline. In the same vein, "hate is a love which has become its opposite, a ruined love" (Kierkegaard, 2009, p. 49). Thus, it is essential to create the proper conditions such as freedom for the development of human potentialities, in particular, love; and to develop the ability and power to love is the only workable and satisfactory answer to the problem of human existence (Fromm, 1957, 1964). As Fromm (1957, p. 20) argued, only love can overcome the isolation and separateness resulting from the contradiction inherent in human existence;

"without love, humanity could not exist for a day." In other words, "love is where you're most virtuous" (Hurka, 2011, p. 144). It not only brings home fellowship to men and women in the world and nature but also preserves their goodness, kindness, and individuality.

The other implication is that "education is identical with helping the child realize his potentialities"; "the opposite of education is manipulation" on the basis of "the absence of faith in the growth of potentiality" (Fromm, 1957, p. 89). If one of the main functions of education is to give students hope and direction in their future life, a key task is to help them identify and develop their own potentialities.

Fromm (1957) further elaborated the fallen society of disintegration caused by Marx's notion of self-alienation. As he pointed out, "the marketing orientation prevails" and "material success is the outstanding value"; therefore, "human love relations follow the same pattern of exchange which governs the commodity and the labour market" (p. 10). In this buying and selling culture, human aesthetic and moral value are pulled down to a mutually favorable exchange; consequently, "modern man [sic] is alienated from himself, from his fellow men, and from nature" (p. 64). Fromm (1957) criticized as follows:

> He has been transformed into a commodity, experiences his life forces as an investment which must bring him the maximum profit obtainable under existing market conditions. Human relations are essentially those of alienated automatons, each basing his security on staying close to the herd, and not being different in thought, feeling and action. While everybody tries to be as close as possible to the rest, everybody remains utterly alone, pervaded by the deep sense of insecurity, anxiety and guilt which always results when human separateness cannot overcome. (p. 64)

In order to escape the emotional and spiritual torture of this insolvable separateness, human "civilization" offered many "palliatives" to help people feel dumb about this "aloneness" (Fromm, 1957, p. 64). At first, "the routine of bureaucratized, mechanical work" is applied to stifle people's consciousness of "their most fundamental human desires" and of "looking for transcendence and unity" (Fromm, 1957, p. 64). Inasmuch as this strict, boring, lifeless, mechanical bureaucratized routine of work alone could not succeed in the suppression, the routine of amusement is employed to overcome human "unconscious despair," and thus the amusement industry starts to work on people's "passive consumption of sounds and sights" (Fromm, 1957, p. 64). However, people satisfy themselves not by the value of products they buy but by the mere action of buying and exchanging new things.

Fromm (1957) continued to portray how superficial modern men and women are becoming:

> Modern man [sic] is actually close to the picture Huxley describes in his *Brave New World*: well fed, well clad, satisfied sexually, yet without self, without any except the most superficial contact with his fellow men, guided by the slogans which Huxley formulated so succinctly, such as: "When the individual feels, the community reels"; or "Never put off till tomorrow the fun you can have today," or as the crowning statement: "Everybody is happy nowadays." (p. 64)

Therefore, happiness is made up by "having fun," which "lies in the satisfaction of consuming and 'taking in' commodities" (p. 64). These commodities for people to consume and swallow include not only sights, food, drinks, cigarettes, lectures, books, movies, and so forth, but also human beings.

The world has thus turned out to be "one great object" like "a big apple, a big bottle, a big breast" for human "appetite" (Fromm, 1957, p. 64). People become "sucklers," "the eternally expectant ones" or hopeful ones, but simultaneously, "the eternally disappointed ones" (Fromm, 1957, p. 64). Even human values and qualities are packaged "on the personality market" for a fair bargain, controlled by the supply and demand of desires and interests of those haves (Fromm, 1957, p. 10). Particularly, "our character is geared to exchange and to receive, to barter and to consume; everything, spiritual as well as material objects, becomes an object of exchange and of consumption" (Fromm, 1957, p. 64). Consequently, the being of human beings is totally commercialized and domesticated; the strong conviction that we love and are loved is equated with "having fun"; the concept of happiness has lost its original meaning. On this artificial wasteland, fallen human beings and fallen society are interdependent on each other. The consciousness of life is dead, the conscience of justice and rightness is dead, the aspiration for the good is dead, the imagination of beauty is dead, and the longing for the sublime is dead.

Under such circumstances, it is imperative to change the attitude of love conditioned by the market society and culture. That is, love should not be objectified through pursuing pleasure-giving commodities, including commercializing human beings. Love must be understood as the faculty and ability rather than the object (Fromm, 1957). On the one hand, the art of love manifests and develops itself in its capacity to love actively, creatively, productively, communicatively, faithfully, hopefully, generously, and unyieldingly. Only can this kind of genuine love awaken the soul and invigorate the spirit and thus bring freedom and vital life force back to human life. On the other hand, love flourishes when human development happens in an environment in which faith in humankind, care, courage, humility, respect, responsibility, communication, concentration, patience, knowledge, objectivity, and reason can live to their full potential. This requires putting the concept of love of people above the superstition in any concept of free market.

In the same light, Freire (1985) disclosed the truth of love with acute and profound historical awareness:

> I feel my incompleteness inside me, at the biological, affective, critical and intellectual levels, an incompleteness pushes me constantly, curiously, and lovingly toward other people and world, searching for solidarity and transcendence of solitude. All this implies wanting to love, a capacity for love that people must create in themselves. This capacity increases to the degree that one loves; it diminishes when one is afraid to love. Of course, in our society it is not easy to love, because we derive much of our happiness from sadness; that is, very often for us to feel happy, others must be sad. Under these circumstances it is difficult to love, but it is necessary to do so. (pp. 197–198)

Freire (1985) maintained that to keep a heart of the child is a precondition for love: "The only way we can stay alive, alert, and be true philosophers is never to let the child within us die"; "society pressures us to kill this child, but we must resist"; if we fail and "kill the child within us, we will kill ourselves" (p. 197). In other words, to preserve an innocent heart of the child perpetually within is to remain youthful and alive in spirit and to love life dearly. Even though we all age, this innocent spiritual child will continue to make us embrace the world sensitively and love people authentically.

Nevertheless, as Fromm (1957, p. 75) argued, "Love is possible only if two persons communicate with each other from the centre of their existence"; this central experience of each other's center of existence is "human reality"; "only here is aliveness, only here is the basis for love." Freire (1972a, p. 62) also noted the following: "Love is at the same time the foundation of dialogue and dialogue itself." In this context, the significance of dialogue comes to the fore.

## The Transcendent Role of Dialogue

An investigation of the transcendent role of dialogue includes the following four sections: the antagonism between the self and the other, the "I–Thou" dialogical principle, the transcendent function of dialogue, and the dialogical effect of dialogue.

### The Antagonism Between the Self and Others

Dialogue has played an important role in the development of human civilization. For example, the most influential ancient texts are nearly all constructed in dialogue: as *Analects* to note down Confucius's dialogues with his students, as Plato's

(1993b) *Republic* and some other writings to account Socrates's dialogues with his interlocutors, and as the New Testament to record Jesus's dialogues with his disciples. However, an ontological study of dialogue as a primal and fundamental way of being or existential phenomenon is fairly recent. Buber is a foundational philosopher in the construction of the dialogical principle based on the "I–Thou" relation. In order to grasp Buber's dialogical principle, it is crucial to understand his analysis of the antagonism between the self and others, particularly seen in Heidegger's philosophy.

Antagonism between the self and others has remained persistently throughout the history of Western philosophy and seems to go to its extreme for some existentialists such as Heidegger (Buber, 2002). Since God is declared dead and others could be the hell to the self, as Buber (2002) commented, Heidegger, in *Being and Time* (1996), tried to work out knowledge in how to deal with one's relationship with her or his self-being.

A key to grasping Heidegger's notion of self-being is Heidegger's notion of "the they." For Heidegger (1996), "the they" is the general, impersonal, faceless, and nameless crowd or mass into which an individual was born or thrown and thereafter became lost and unrecognizable. "The they" gains its existential character from averageness created by being with one another in the world. With this real essence, "the they" tends to level off every possibility of being, to disperse every self, and takes the form of "public" to determine and arrange the interpretation of the world and existence in advance such as what is granted as proper, allowed, and successful, and what is not. Heidegger (1996) wrote as follows:

> This averageness, which prescribes what can and may be ventured, watches over every exception which thrusts itself to the fore. Every priority is noiselessly squashed. Overnight, everything primordial is flattened down as something long since known. Everything gained by a struggle becomes something to be manipulated. Every mystery loses its power. The care of averageness reveals, in turn, an essential tendency of Dasein, which we call the levelling down of all possibilities of being. (p. 119)

Hence, the situation of being is always there, controlled by others or "the they," but not here controlled by the self. "The they," purely negative and destructive of the self, reduces human existence to a uniform of flatness and boredom. On the one hand, "the they" serves the source of "idle talk," "curiosity," and "ambiguity" (Heidegger, 1996, p. 206). On the other hand, in the dominance of "idle talk," "curiosity," and "ambiguity," humans in turn have fallen prey to "the they." To use Sartre's (1994) analogy, once a drop of rain touches the surface of the water, it becomes the water surface immediately; self is like a raindrop and "the they" is like the water surface. This could be the essence of "*Mitda-sein,*" being there in the world as being with others (Heidegger, 1996, p. 112).

Heidegger (1996) also gave an "existential interpretation of conscience": "conscience is the call of care from the uncanniness of being-in-the-world that summons *Da-sein* to its own-most potentiality-for-being-guilty" (p. 266). Correspondingly, "wanting-to-have-a-conscience" is to understand "the summons" (p. 266). Hence, conscience performs the function of disclosing and understanding the reality of *Da-sein's* being or "somehow speaks of 'guilt'" (p. 258). As Buber (2002) cautioned, the concept of "guilt" (in German language *schuld*) refers to "indebtedness." It is not about feeling guilty about some wrong decisions or doings but about owing something to somebody.

"The they" owes the self-being to *Da-sein,* so conscience calls forth *Da-sein* to bring it back from its "lostness in the they" (Heidegger, 1996, p. 264). Heidegger (1996) noted the following:

> *Conscience reveals itself as the call of care*: the caller is Da-sein, anxious in throwness (in its already-being-in …) about its potentiality-of-being. The one summoned is also Da-sein, called forth to its own-most potentiality-of-being (its being-ahead-of-itself …). And what is called forth by the summons is Da-sein, out of falling prey to the they (already-being-together-with-the-world-taken-care-of …). The call of conscience, that is, conscience itself, has its ontological possibility in the fact that Da-sein is care in the ground of its being. (p. 256)

To put it simply, a person does not live or exist for the self, so conscience, the care of existence, calls forth a person to bring back the self from unreality of being for others to the reality of being for one's own. In this case, to follow one's conscience is to change the mode of caring, to change care of others into care of self. In other words, the only way to come back to the self being is to break away from being levelled down by averageness or publicness and being lost in the inauthenticity of everydayness. Acknowledging that language is the house for human existence, Heidegger (1968) did not trust the function of the word in conversation but appreciated experiencing the primal and vital being of the self by means of something like writing a poem from imagination and inspiration. This kind of in-depth communication with the self in a poetic and artistic way is to live out the uniqueness of being for the self.

Heidegger was right to admit that indebtedness actually will go back to the real primal guilt of being, but he failed to see that the wholeness of human life is essentially related to another self (Buber, 2002). Buber (2002) pointed out the following:

> Human life possesses absolute meaning through transcending in practice its own conditioned nature, that is through man's [sic] seeing that which he confronts, and with which he can enter into a real relation of being to being, as not less than himself, and through taking it not less seriously than himself. Human life touches on absoluteness in virtue of its dialogical character, for in spite of his uniqueness man can never find, when he plunges to the depth of his life a being that is whole in itself and as such touches on the absolute. Man can become whole not in virtue of a relation to himself but only in virtue to another self. This other self may be just as limited and conditioned as he is; in being together the unlimited and the unconditioned is experienced. (p. 199)

Thus, "the original guilt consists in remaining with oneself." The "cry of conscience" should be "where were you?"; "the saying of Thou by the I is the origin of all individual becoming" (pp. 249–250).

Heidegger was fully aware that a person stands in the world of relations, and the objects of understanding are the things and others, without which cognition and knowledge are impossible; however, being with others for him was psychical but not ontical (Buber, 2002). This is because for Heidegger, the relation with others out of carefulness and solicitude is incidental and of assistance but not essential; what is essential for him was the ultimate existence to reach the self-being. Therefore, Buber objected to Heidegger's notion of the self-being. He insisted that in an essential relation with others, the barriers of an individual being can be breached by the real mutuality: "one life opens to another"; both "the depth of one's substance" and "the mystery of the other" can be experienced (Buber, 2002, pp. 201–202). As he argued, Heidegger failed to recognize Feuerbach's point: "the individual does not have the essence of man [sic] in himself, that man's essence is contained in the unity of man with man" (Feuerbach in Buber, 2002, p. 203). Heidegger's search for an intimate communication with the self-being was merely an absurd mono-logical situation. His resolution of the communication dilemma of idle talk is still set in a closed system without openness to others. In this closed system, there is no desire to breach the barriers of the self: "there is no such Thou, no true Thou spoken from being to being, spoken with one's own being" (Buber, 2002, p. 204).

Under such circumstances, if human solitude regressed to such a degree that human beings could "no longer stretch out their hands to meet a divine form," which urged the death of God, then when the freedom of the self comes in the end, human beings will be unable to stretch out their hands to meet their fellow species and become impotent to love (Buber, 2002, p. 198). This may symbolize the real death of human beings. Therefore, the only way to pierce through the dullness and mediocrity of everydayness and to liberate the self from anonymous generality and being levelled off to averageness is the direct encounter or meeting with the difference or uniqueness of others through the openness of dialogue between I and Thou.

## The I–Thou Relation: The Foundation of the Dialogical Principle

According to Buber (2002), the earliest expressions of the consciousness of the I–Thou relation could be traced back to the end of the 18th century. He undertook a literature review of the dialogical principle using three different branches. The first branch is the discovery that the Thou is necessary to the consciousness of the I. From Jacob's "Pamphlets" he found such expressions: "The source of all certainty: you are and I am!" and "The I is impossible without the Thou" (Jacob in Buber, 2002, p. 250). A similar statement can be found in Fichte's work: "The consciousness of the individual is necessarily accompanied by that of another, that of a Thou, and only under this condition possible" (Fichte in Buber, 2002, p. 250). Buber values highly Feuerbach's idea—"the consciousness of the world is mediated for the I through the consciousness of the Thou"; and "man for himself is man, man with man—the unity of I and Thou is God" (Feuerbach in Buber, 2002, p. 250). The discovery of the Thou is necessary to the consciousness of the I.

The second branch is represented in Rosenzweig's theological understanding of Thou. For Rosenzweig, in order to direct Adam, there comes "the essential spokenness of the Thou"; God is "the originator and opener of the whole dialogue" between Adam and his soul (Buber, 2002, p. 253). Thus, Thou, as a spoken one, touched the core of the creation of human beings.

The third branch is reflected in Ebner's experience of "the solitude of the I" and the difficulty and disappointment in finding "the Thou in man" to have a dialogue. According to Buber (2002), Ebner postulated that a person should love not only God but also humans. However, one can only have a genuine dialogue with God instead of human beings: "where it is a question of the authenticity of existence, every other Thou disappears before that of God" (Ebner in Buber, 2002, p. 254). Hence, Ebner's experience reveals the following phenomenon: "the self-relating individuals who look at the world but are in the last instance acosmic, who love men [sic] but are in the last instance aanthropic" [sic] (Buber, 2002, p. 254).

As a matter of fact, Ebner's experience captures the core of the communication dilemma among human beings. He merely voiced Kierkegaard's claim, "God wants the Single Ones," but in a different way (Buber, 2002, p. 254). In other words, the precondition to have a dialogue with God is to be a single one. Although other human beings are obviously driven out of the dialogue between

I and God, human communication does not suffer too much because one still has God to talk to. However, once God is declared dead, and Heidegger's resolution of the communication crisis is mono-logical in a closed system, the belief that others could be the hell to the self makes human existence more isolated and miserable. Under such circumstances, an alternative to the deteriorating situation of the antagonism between the self and others seems urgent and imperative.

Influenced by Feuerbach's insight, Buber (2002) stressed that direct dialogical meetings with another self respond to the ontological call of human existence from the noumenon. "On the far side of the subjective, on this side of the objective, on the narrow ridge, where *I* and *Thou* meet, there is the real of '*between*'" (Buber, 2002, p. 243). For Buber, a human being, irreplaceable, is a creature of living in the "between"; of the happening between this person and that person that "cannot be reduced to a sum of two individuals or to a merely psychological reality within the minds of each" (Friedman, 2002, p. xviii). In other words, "man [sic] can attain to existence only if his whole relation to his situation becomes existence, that is, if every kind of living relation becomes essential" (Buber, 2002, p. 214). Therefore, what matters for the self is an essential relation with another self.

Genuine human relations produce genuine persons. Buber (2002) argued as follows:

> A great relation exists only between real persons. It can be strong as death, because it is stronger than solitude, because it breaches the barriers of a lofty solitude, subdues its strict laws, and throws a bridge from self-being to self-being across the abyss of the universe. (p. 207)

Buber (2002) did not downplay the role of the self in human relations. For him, the self, a real person, is a decisive fact and condition of the readiness and ability to have a full relation of one's life with the other self. The reason of becoming the self is "for the perfect realization of the Thou" (p. 207). In other words, the I finds its fulfillment in the Thou. Without Thou, I is useless because there is nobody for I to talk to. "The person who is the object of my mere solicitude is not a *Thou* but a *He* and a *She* .... But as there is a *Thou* so there is a *We*" (p. 208). For Buber, the faceless, nameless, and impersonal crowd or mass in which the I is entangled is not a We but "the they." Therefore, a person capable of truly saying Thou can make sense of *We* and know what it means to say *We*. *We* is the pronoun for *the I–Thou relation*, the genuine and embracing *I and Thou* rather than the sum of the two awkward and autistic selves.

Accordingly, the significance of dialogue is not in dialogue itself but in what sort of relationship is carried out. There are two possible relations in dialogue: one is the I–Thou relation while the other the I–It relation (Buber, 1959). The

I–Thou relationship is "a relationship of openness, directness, mutuality and presence" (Friedman, 2002, p. xii). It is a subject–subject relationship, which contains no thingness:

> When Thou is spoken, there is nothing. Thou has no bounds.
>
> When Thou is spoken, the speaker has no thing; he has indeed nothing. But he takes stand in relation ...
>
> The relation to the thou is direct. No system of ideas, no foreknowledge, and no fancy intervene between I and Thou. (Buber, 1959, pp. 4, 11)

By contrast, the I–It relation is indirect, not mutual but possessive. It is "the typical subject–object relationship in which one knows and uses other persons or things without allowing them to exist for one self in their uniqueness" (Friedman, 2002, p. xii).

The two relationships are not fixed but alter with each other. The I–Thou relationship cannot be preserved; it could only emerge in the process of a direct meeting with Thou. Only in this meeting can the indirectness of the world be presented to I and Thou. If the Thou is unresponsive, the emergence of the *It* will bring inauthentic personal and social life to human existence and make it unhealthy.

If meeting the Thou makes a conversation "speechifying," then what matters is to learn how to listen to others; however, as Buber contended, the mark of contemporary man and woman is that they do not really listen (Friedman, 2002, pp. xiii–xiv). It is also a mark of the lack of love or attention. As Friedman (2002, p. xv) commented, what underpins Buber's I–Thou relationship is love, which means "precisely the recognition of the other's freedom, the fullness of a dialogue in which I turn to my beloved in his otherness, independence, and self-reality with all the power of intention of my own heart." Therefore, Buber does not take dialogue, communication, and the I–Thou relationship "as a *dimension* of the self but as the existential and ontological reality in which the self comes into being and through which it fulfils and authenticates itself" (Friedman, 2002, p. xv). For example, when a mother hears her little boy learning to say "1, 2, 3, 4," she will say "good counting" to praise and encourage him. Here "1, 2, 3, 4" and "good counting" could be a piece of idle talk for passers-by, but for the mother and the child, it is not. This is because behind thought-language, there is always a human relation, and behind a human relation there are always human emotions and feelings. Thus, Buber (2002) remarked as follows:

> Only he [sic] who himself turns to the other human being and opens himself to him receives the world in him. Only the being whose otherness, accepted by my being,

lives and faces me in the whole compression of existence, brings the radiance of eternity to me. (p. 35)

This remark reveals the true essence of the I–Thou dialogical relation.

## Conscience Welcomes the Other

According to Levinas (1969), Buber has made "an essential contribution to contemporary thought"; however, "the I–Thou relation in Buber retains a formal character" and "does not determine any concrete structure" (p. 68). Specifically, who can be the Thou and where the Thou is and how to meet this Thou still remains a problem. Levinas (1969, p. 69) said that he has no "ridiculous pretension of 'correcting' Buber," but he merely tries "in a different perspective." According to him, the epiphany or irreducible relation of face-to-face encounters with any other makes a concrete Thou; the "other" is actually in a primordial reciprocal relation of "the thou-saying" (p. 68).

Levinas (1969) starts with the idea of the infinite. According to him, Western philosophy is dominated by the discourse of totality, which simply seeks for power and control and strives for domestication through order and system. In this discourse of totality, the meaning of life is defined by the ultimate meaning: "the last act changes beings into themselves" (p. 22). Accordingly, ethics built on the concept of totality is the war ethics of striving for being a master to be served by others. In this kind of the master mind, it is hard to find either the Thou or the other but only an I in the domain of self, which is marching toward a designed future in the mind. "The unicity of each present is incessantly sacrificed to a future appealed to bring forth its objective meaning"; people are "what they will appear to be in the already plastic forms of epic" (p. 22).

By contrast, the idea of infinity is based on "the metaphysical desire," which "tends toward something else entirely, toward the absolutely other" (Levinas, 1969, p. 33). This metaphysical desire does not need any actual satisfaction but "understands the remoteness, the alterity, and the exteriority of the other" and opens up "the very dimension of height" or "the Most-High" (Levinas, 1969, p. 34). The height here refers to Plato's idea that "knowledge only which is of being and of the unseen can make the soul look upwards" (Levinas, 1969, p. 34). For Levinas (1969), metaphysics is "to die for the invisible" (p. 35). In the same way, the idea of infinity "moves consciousness" and "sustains activity itself"; it is "not a representation of infinity" but "the common source of activity and theory" (Levinas, 1969, p. 27).

According to Wild (1969), Levinas's idea of infinity seeks for a higher quality of life, freedom, and creative advance. The systematic thinking and the holistic or panoramic view have their due places, but infinitizers are fighting against their constitutive violence, their tyranny of power systems, and their oppression of categorizing and manipulating people as objects to fit into the system. Thus, the infinitizers who believe in the idea of infinity look for not only what is said but also who and why that person is speaking in a living dialogue. As Wild commented, a concrete task Levinas set for himself was to resolve the antagonism between the self and the other in the dominance of the culture of totality.

For Levinas (1969), love runs the risk of sacrificing the self; only dialogue or language does not negate the I while this I speaks to her or him without letting me lose my own integrity; and it can also allow the other to perform the role of revealing herself or himself in her or his alterity. The coexistence of "we" is thus achieved. From this departure point, Levinas (1969) placed the idea of infinity on his phenomenological study of the other. According to him, the infinite does not present itself to a descendent thought or meaningful activity but in the other. The metaphysical movement to the other, to a simple presence of self to self, constructs transcendence. To meet the other is to have the idea of infinity:

> It is only in approaching the other that I attend to myself ... the Face I welcome makes me pass from phenomenon to being in another sense: in discourse I expose myself to the questioning of the Other, and this urgency of the response—acuteness of the present—engenders me for responsibility; as responsible I am brought to my final reality. This extreme attention does not actualize what was in potency, for it is not conceivable without the other. Being attentive signifies a surplus of consciousness, and presupposes the call of the other. To be attentive is to recognize the mastery of the other, to receive his command, or more exactly, to receive from him the command to command. When I seek my final reality, I find that my existence as a "thing-in-itself" begins with the presence in me of the idea of the Infinity. But this relation already consists in serving the Other. (Levinas, 1969, pp. 178–179)

Levinas (1969) captured the birth of human language through his phenomenological study of human face-to-face and eye-to-eye encounters. As he noted, when "the Other faces me and puts me in question and obliges me by his essence qua infinity," "that something we call signification arises in being with language because the essence of language is the relation with the Other" (p. 207). Hence, the direct face-to-face meeting with the other will initiate and necessitate communication between two real persons. "The language of eyes" that breaks through the mask is "impossible to dissemble": "the alternative of truth and lying, of sincerity and dissimulation, is the prerogative of him [sic] who abides in the relation of absolute frankness," "which cannot hide itself"; rather, "the eye does not shine, it speaks" (p. 66). Teaching also starts when people speak. Thus, "meaning is the face of the other, and all recourse to words takes place already within the primordial face to face of language" (p. 206).

From this face-to-face meeting and eye-to-eye communication, "the third party," the ethical nature of dialogue or language, comes into being. As Levinas (1969) argued, "language as the presence of the face" is justice because "the third party looks at me in the eyes of the Other"; "it is not that first would be the face, and then the being it manifests or expresses would concern himself with justice; the epiphany of the face qua face opens humanity" (p. 213).

Levinas (1969) revealed the phenomenology of the human face as follows:

> The presence of the face, the infinity of the other, is a destituteness, a presence of the third party (that is, of the whole of humanity which looks at us), and a command that commands commanding. This is why the relation with the Other, discourse, is not only the putting in question of my freedom, the appeal coming from the other to call me to responsibility, is not only the speech by which I divert myself of the possession that encircles me by setting forth an objective and common world, but is also sermon, exhortation, the prophetic word. By essence the prophetic word responds to the epiphany of the face, doubles all discourse not as a discourse about moral themes, but as an irreducible movement of a discourse which by essence is aroused by the epiphany of the face inasmuch as it attests the presence of the third party, the whole of humanity, in the eyes that look at me. (p. 213)

Accordingly, people's responsibility for the other is not a derivative feature of their subjectivity; instead, it gives them a meaningful direction and orientation to their subjective being in the world and being with the world. If one's surpassing of the phenomenal and inward existence is to offer one's being by expressing oneself, already in the service of the other, then this third party, the sense of humanity, appears in the process of any intimate communication. Nobody wants to hurt the other in genuine dialogue. Harm and damage often come after the failure of communication. Therefore, Levinas (1969, p. 89) argued, "the ground of expression is goodness." This ethical foundation is safeguarded by conscience.

Conscience, closely connected with humanity, encounters the other in a revelatory manner (Levinas, 1969). This has a transcendent purpose: "I am not alone ... in conscience I have an experience that is not commensurate with any a priori framework—a conceptless experience" (Levinas, 1969, p. 101). Further, conscience cannot assume and moral judgment is borne upon everyone; in the I–Thou relationship, my conscience welcomes the other; every other is You ("The interlocutor is not a Thou, he is a You ... pas un Toi, i lest un Vous"; Levinas, 1969, p. 101). Thus, the absolute other is you, who I am meeting face-to-face and eye-to-eye. Your face and eyes are my destituteness. You are the sunshine that enlightens and also enlarges my world. This you and I are not finite but infinite; it happens between every human being. The meeting between you and I accordingly makes conscience perform a transcendent function: to encourage one's ego to accept the fallibility of assuming things by other people, to resist one's selfish powers, and to call into question the naive sense of freedom to use such powers arbitrarily or violently. Morality thus develops.

## Dialogical Effect

Dialogue does not happen in a fixed, static, finite, and controlled manner; it brings "a new kind of mind" to its participants, as David Bohm (1985, 1994, 2004) claimed. This "new kind of mind" is an embracing effect of positioning human relationship among the participants above any topic one would like to bring to discussion tables with any preestablished purpose. Participants of dialogue "engage in a new dynamic relationship in which no speaker is excluded, and in which no particular content is excluded" (Bohm, 1985, p. 175). Bohm (1985) illustrated this dialogical effect by his phenomenological hermeneutic description of a weekend experience:

> The weekend began with the expectation that there would be a series of lectures and informative discussions with emphasis on content. It gradually emerged that something more important was actually involved—the awakening of the process of dialogue itself as a free flow of meaning among all the participants. In the beginning, people were expressing fixed positions, which they were tending to defend, but later it became clear that to maintain the feeling of friendship in the group was much more important than to hold any position. Such friendship has an important quality in the sense that its establishment does not depend on a close personal relationship between participants. A new kind of mind thus begins to come into being which is based on the development of a common meaning that is constantly transforming in the process of dialogue. (p. 175)

Accordingly, dialogue opens a new mental horizon, which comes in the service of people's being together and doing something together and above all, living together friendly. It is this harmonious togetherness maintained by dialogue that eventually protects not only a self but also a community.

However, in reality, the present culture is highly incoherent; it lacks the communal trust so that it hinders people from having genuine dialogue (Bohm, 2004). As Paul Klee showed by his painting, "Two Men Meet, Each Believing the Other To Be in a Higher Position," to increase one's own value in an alienated culture and society dominated by the discourse of totality is badly overdone sometimes (Klee in Blackburn, 2001, p. 2). It is not a rare phenomenon that some snobbish and arrogant elitists would preserve their social status without looking at the other. Meanwhile, some oppressed people would protect their dignity by keeping silent because speaking will expose their poor socioeconomic status. This sociocultural climate suppresses people's aspirations to see the wonder opened by dialogue on the basis of humility. Therefore, it is imperative to create a coherent culture for humankind to enter the arena of meaningful dialogue.

Freire is a key figure who has translated the dialogical principle into pedagogical theory and practice. He claimed that dialogue is an existential necessity for learning to live. To reiterate him, genuine dialogue cannot occur without the following requirements: love for the world and for human beings; humility "to learn more than they know now"; an intense faith in mankind, in human "power to make and remake, to create and recreate and becoming more fully human"; a strong hope for a better world because "hopeless is a form of silence, of denying the world and fleeing from it"; and critical thinking that urges further action while naïve thinkers simply look for how to accommodate themselves to "normalized today" (Freire, 1972a, p. 64). If to speak the true word will change the world, then the true word is not only available from the-culture-in-the-making through teaching and learning but also from an open and creative mind based on good conscience. If restoring humanity is an ontological and historical vocation, it must start with the cultural work of how to restore people's power and ability to speak and to listen, an essential prerequisite for dialogue.

## A Demonstration of the Transcendent Role of Love and Dialogue

Ontologically, love and dialogue are always bound up together as an enduring marriage in human relations and realities: Love will motivate dialogue while dialogue is at the service of love. In terms of transcendence, literature has its strength in demonstrating how transcendence occurs in concrete and particular situations. In this section, two novels, Dostoevsky's (1866) *Crime and Punishment* and Hesse's (2008) *Siddhartha*, are drawn on to elaborate how love and dialogue work in a transcendent way. The former highlights salvation through love based on Christian faith, the latter enlightenment through dialogue based on meaning seeking.

### Crime and Punishment

As Carr (1931) noted, through *Crime and Punishment,* Dostoevsky (1866) probed the deeper levels of moral feeling that pierce "the hollowness of the attempt to base ethics on egoism or on rational altruism" (p. 198).

The story of *Crime and Punishment* is plotted in a revolutionary background. It starts with Dostoevsky's main character, Raskolnikov, a university student of law, who lives up to his revolutionary principle of worshiping power and freedom and takes Napoleon as his living example. This is a true portrait of the cultural movement in the 19th century in Europe, in which every young university student wanted to prefer a person to a boot sole or a rag in the fierce battle of life (Carr, 1931). By the same token, Raskolnikov is "one of the innumerable 'innocent faces' which grimaced in the imitation of Byron and Bonaparte," since everyone at that time was believed to have an inviolable right to be a decent person (Carr, 1931, p. 192). Raskolnikov is a law student who lives in this historical and cultural context. He knows clearly that murder is a crime, but he is determined to discover the new "good" or another truth that is beyond the boundaries of ordinarily conceived good and evil. Raskolnikov's revolution of conventional morals starts from killing his landlady or money lender as a matter of principle. Inadvertently, when Raskolnikov kills the old woman with the axe, the woman's younger sister comes on the scene. He has no choice but to kill the poor girl as well. After the murder, he hides the money and jewelry and thereby no evidence can be found to connect him with the crime. Nonetheless, his deranged nerves and strange behavior have provoked a detective's suspicion. Coincidently, the suspicion of this detective in charge of the case is diverted by another man's false confession of committing the crime. Before his confession, Raskolnikov has experienced an unbearable psychological torture.

Raskolnikov's psychological torture, however, is not from the sting of his conscience but from the mental conflict between his revolutionary principles and the essential nature of human beings. Carr (1931) pointed out the following:

> The sequel reveals to us not the pangs of a stricken conscience (which a less subtle writer would have given us), but the tragic and the fruitless struggle of a powerful intellect to maintain a conviction which is incompatible with the essential nature of man. The tragedy for Raskolnikov is the collapse of the principle on which he has acted. (p. 195)

A dialogue between Raskolnikov and his sister makes this point clear. Raskolnikov tells his sister that he killed his landlady. His sister cries out in despair: "Brother, brother, what are you saying, you shed blood!" (Dostoevsky, 1866, p. 518). Raskolnikov defends himself by saying that he murdered a worthless, vile, and loathsome being, "who sucked the life-sap from the poor," so his murder is a virtue, "worth forty sins forgiven" (Dostoevsky, 1866, p. 518). Shedding blood is not a problem for his revolutionary principle:

> "Which everyone sheds," he picked up, almost in a frenzy, "which is and always has been shed in torrents in this world, which men spill like champagne, and for which they're crowned on the Capitoline and afterwards called benefactors of humankind.

But just look closer and try to see! I wished people well and would have done hundreds, thousands of good deeds, instead of this one stupidity—or not even stupidity, but simply clumsiness, because the whole idea was by no means as stupid as it seems now that it failed (everything that fails seems stupid!). By this stupidity, I merely wanted to put myself in an independent position, to take the first step, to acquire means, and later everything would be made up by the—comparatively—immeasurable usefulness .... But I, I could not endure even the first step, because I'm a scoundrel! That's the whole point!" (Dostoevsky, 1866, p. 518)

Raskolnikov does not regret his crime but hates his failure. He says, "I merely wanted to put myself in an independent position, to take the first step, to acquire means." Here the first step refers to the murder he committed. He has achieved that necessary revolutionary means: to kill "in an independent position." However, the problem is that Raskolnikov could not even endure this first step: He could kill but he is psychologically weak and fails to keep peace in his mind about the murder case. For him, a true revolutionary hero should feel indifferent to blood-shedding during and after killing with a heart of stone and iron. In fact, he is feeling unsettled, disturbed, and troubled. This is his failure, which makes him feel stupid and extremely disappointed. What is more, the root cause of Raskolnikov's failure is his weakness, which stops him from leading a revolution and turns his first revolutionary step into a murder case. In effect, he concedes he is not strong enough to become a Napoleon. This is why he hates himself and looks down upon himself as a scoundrel. According to Carr (1931), here Dostoevsky poses a fundamental ethical question: Does Raskolnikov fail merely because he is weak or fainthearted? Then what makes his heart weak or feeble?

It is clear that Raskolnikov's revolutionary principle cannot overcome and conquer his submoral consciousness of the guilt of murdering. It is the essential nature of human beings. To kill a person in any circumstance is against human conscience and thus offends human nature or humanity. If this is true, it is hard to explain the common phenomenon that occurs throughout human history: by means of shedding blood "in torrents" or like "champagne," "those who crowned on the Capitoline and afterwards called benefactors of humankind" as Raskolnikov cries out. Here Dostoevsky challenges the means of revolution through blood-shedding violence. He does not believe a better society can be built on the loss of humanity on a social scale. Thus, he highlights the role of love, which is exemplified and embodied in Sonya, an important heroine in the novel.

Sonya is a prostitute who supports her family by betraying herself. If Raskolnikov represents the extreme of self-assertion, Sonya lives out the extreme of self-sacrifice. If Raskolnikov kills others, Sonya, in Raskolnikov's words, murders herself for nothing. As Carr (1931, p. 198) commented, Dostoevsky does not give

Sonya's self-negation a smooth or glorious path; "no halo surrounds Sonya save the halo of suffering." However, suffering does not destroy purity, tenderness, and kindness of Sonya's heart. In front of her suffering and troubled mind and weeping face, Raskolnikov "bent all the way down, leaned towards the floor, and kissed her foot," telling Sonya, "I was not bowing to you, I was bowing to all human suffering" (Dostoevsky, 1866, pp. 321–322). While suffering may change a good person into a cold-blooded animal, it becomes the testimony and the purgatory of Sonya's Christian faith in love. It backs up Sonya not only to endure her sufferings of being in and with the world but also to be able to love the world and people.

From confession of his guilt to use of suffering for self-forgiveness, Raskolnikov displays a process of how conscience works in the ambience of Sonya's faith in love. Touched by Sonya's suffering, Raskolnikov tells Sonya about his murder case to let out his own insufferable mental anxiety. Sonya bids him to go to the crossroads to bow to people, to bow down and kiss the earth, which he defiled. With Sonya's help, Raskolnikov confesses his crime to the court and is sentenced to eight years in Siberia. However, Raskolnikov's confession is not the awakening of his conscience but the mere release from his nerve-racking mental struggle. Raskolnikov goes to Siberia repenting not of his crime but still of his failure to "hold out."

In any case, Sonya's strong Christian faith in love makes her feel determined about the salvation of Raskolnikov's suffering soul. She accompanies him to serve his sentence thither in Siberia. In particular, when Raskolnikov is very ill and stays in his prison hospital bed, his physical weakness makes his mind chaotic. Sonya talks to him and looks after him. Raskolnikov has been stuck in his solitary mental war to hold up his revolutionary principle for a long time. While this obstinate grip of his mind starts to become loose and blurred, the consciousness of life comes back to him. The moment Raskolnikov feels his love for Sonya and Sonya's love for him, his conscience and humanity come back to him.

As Dostoevsky (1866) accounted, "they were resurrected by love; the heart of each held infinite sources of life for the heart of the other …. Instead of dialectics, there was life, and something completely different had to work itself out in his consciousness" (pp. 549–550). Hence, for Dostoevsky, love, rather than violence based on hatred, is not only the most enduring way to resist human evils through the purgatory of sufferings but also the best way to salvation.

## Siddhartha

Hesse (2008) wrote *Siddhartha* to describe how Siddhartha in the time of the Buddha took a spiritual journey to look for the meaning of life or Om and the path to enlightenment by following his conscience. Om in *Siddhartha* signifies "God,

Creation, the oneness of all creation" (p. 120). For the Hindus and Buddhists, it is "the primordial sound, the first breath of creation, the vibration that ensures existence" (p. 120). Siddhartha's relentless search has enabled him to understand Om and thus to discover a transcendent inner space, where one can find a selfless universal spiritual self. By means of which, all things, both the inner spiritual world and the outer material world, can be unified and simply understood. At the end of the novel, Siddhartha takes up a selfless work of ferrying people by a river. "Ferrying" is a metaphor that suggests transcending people from the bank of the material world here to the bank of the spiritual world there.

The novel contains two parts. In the first part, Siddhartha rejects the material world. The Brahmins, Samanas, and Buddhists all maintain that the material world is an illusion that distracts a seeker from the spiritual truth. Adopting this belief, Siddhartha completely denies his body and, instead, focuses his efforts on refining his mind and memorizing the knowledge his teachers pass along to him. "I can think, I can wait, I can fast" is a vivid picture of his life for this period (Hesse, 2008, p. 51). In the second part, Siddhartha decides to embark on a material life with bodily pleasures. In a city, he stays with Kamala, a beautiful courtesan, who teaches him how to make love, and he learns the trade with Kamaswami, a merchant, who teaches him how to make money. Yet, an affluent life and physical pleasure cannot touch his spirit in any lasting way. The more he gains, the less he feels satisfied. In order to fill up the emptiness of his heart, he starts to gamble, drink, and dance, but he finds himself stuck in a downhill cycle of unhappiness. The relentless pursuit of carnal desires can simply greet him with "waited disillusionment and nausea" rather than any wisdom (Hesse, 2008, p. 61).

Siddhartha comes to realize that the material world is gradually killing him: "slowly, like moisture entering the dying tree trunk, slowly filling and rotting it, so did the world and inertia creep into Siddhartha's soul; it slowly filled his soul, made it heavy, made it tired, sent it to sleep" (Hesse, 2008, p. 60). When he stands near the river contemplating drowning himself, he hears Om again, the concept of perfection embodied in the unity of all things or the harmonious relationship with the world that he first encountered as a Brahmin boy. He comes to understand that life is not a continuous search for a philosophy that could only be accessed on an intellectual basis, and it cannot be split up into specific compartments to fit different paths in different times. In short, life is always an organic whole. Therefore, the essence of the world is life. The meaning of life is just life itself. Beings all around him essentially belong to Om. The Om of life itself is indestructible but in succession. Siddhartha realizes that he must try to merge himself with all beings in the world and learn to just "be." This is because enlightenment does not lie elsewhere but only comes from fully embracing the energy of Om. Then

Siddhartha wishes to learn how to keep inner peace from a ferryman, Vasudeva. Vasudeva, a wonderful listener, teaches him how to listen to the river nearby and have dialogues with it. Eventually, "They both listened silently to the water, which to them was not just water, but the voice of life, the voice of Being, of perpetual Becoming" (Hesse, 2008, pp. 84–85).

However, one day, on her pilgrimage to visit Gotama, Kamala approaches the ferry with her son. Before they manage to cross the river, a snake bites Kamala. Siddhartha and Vasudeva tend to Kamala, but the bite is killing her. Before she dies, she tells Siddhartha that he is the father of her 11-year-old son. Siddhartha falls deeply in love with his son. Yet Siddhartha's son dislikes the life with the two ferrymen and wishes to return to his familiar city and wealth. Being spoiled, cynical, and rebellious, his son treats Siddhartha badly. At the end, the boy steals all of his and Vasudeva's money and runs away. Siddhartha chases after the boy, but as he reaches the city, he realizes that the chase is futile. Vasudeva follows Siddhartha and brings him back to their home by the river, instructing him to soothe the pain of losing his son by listening to the river. The more Siddhartha listens to the river, the more aware he becomes of the complexity and entirety of Om. The meaning of the river that flows in front of Siddhartha and Vasudeva is just the water coming together and moving on. If the river bed that unites the opposing banks gives the form to a river to exist in flowing, the common ground between the material and spiritual world will embrace human experience. When Siddhartha comprehends that all possibilities are real and valid, and time itself does not exist, he finally achieves enlightenment or transcendence. As Freedman (1979, p. 235) commented, *Siddhartha* voices Hesse's interior dialectic: "All of the contrasting poles of his life were sharply etched: the restless departures and the search for stillness at home; the diversity of experience and the harmony of a unifying spirit; the security of religious dogma and the anxiety of freedom."

A central concern of studying Siddhartha in this book is what makes Siddhartha connect himself with Om and the universal self, that is, how he achieves enlightenment. First and foremost, the totality of all experiences, or the sum of conscious life events, plays a very important role in his journey to enlightenment. Without which, Siddhartha cannot approach understanding of reality let alone attain enlightenment. As a Chinese proverb says, one cannot know the full meaning of parents' mercy and love until she or he becomes a parent; one cannot know how hard it is to run a family until it is her or his turn to do it. Thus, human experience, an ontological foundation of life, should forever be highlighted. To live is to experience life.

However, experience by itself cannot lead a person to approaching Om. It is reflection or meditation upon experience that leads people to Om. It is crucial to identify what sensitizes and motivates Siddhartha to think deeply about the meaning of life and finally to make connections between himself and the universal self. Weil's (2002b) notion of suffering is helpful here. According to her, "suffering: superiority of man [sic] over God" contains the function of "teaching and transformation"; it is the most immediate source of seeking the knowledge of life without losing the soul (pp. 80–83). This is true. Deep thinking often originates from suffering. If *Siddhartha* is read closely, Om approaches Siddhartha's heart at the two key moments of his experience of suffering. One is the most disillusioned time, in which he could not see any hopes of achieving his life goal or spiritual enlightenment. The other is his son's rebellion and escape, which made him feel the pain in love, a deep affliction in his bones. Both occurrences of suffering drive Siddhartha to the river, the metaphor of reflection, to listen to his conscience. The former moment of disillusionment and despair makes him become reconciled with the world and accept life. The latter moment of the pain in love leads him to find the universal self or his moral self. Specifically, the river is like a mirror, in which Siddhartha finds the resemblance of his face with his father's. He starts remembering how once, as a youth, he left his father and never returned. "Had not his father also suffered the same pain that he was now suffering for his son? Had not his father died long ago, alone, without having seen his son again? Did he not expect the same fate?" (Hesse, 2008, p. 102). From this reflection of the same pain, Siddhartha sees his natural bonds with his father, his son, and anybody he knows. Through these natural bonds he finds the sameness or oneness: Everybody is longing and desiring in loneliness and suffering. This marks the awakening of his moral self in the universal self. From that moment on, he becomes accepting, embracing, and understanding. All that is false and true, good and evil, joyful and sorrowful, living and dead, to be more exact, all these polarities are "interwoven and interlocked, entwined in a thousand ways," but they are coexisting at the same time (Hesse, 2008, p. 105). Therefore, all possibilities, voices, goals, and yearnings are united in the spirit of the universe: "all them together was the world, the stream of events, the music of life" (Hesse, 2008, p. 05). At this critical moment, "his Self merged into unity" (Hesse, 2008, p. 105), Siddhartha has understood Om and achieved enlightenment. He has completed the most important project in his life: to become reconciled with himself. At the end, he takes over the ferrying job from Vasudeva and becomes a selfless ferryman like Vasudeva used to be. This indicates not only that he liberates himself from the smallness, narrowness, and darkness of the cave of a bigoted egoistic self but also that he starts the work of ferrying others. The essence of transcendence is no more than this.

Accordingly, the core of transcendence is to find out one's moral self. As Zhu Xi (1983), an ancient Confucian philosopher, remarked, "when one finds out about one's moral self one will naturally know the reasons for everything, so that one could suddenly be enlightened about everything" (pp. 35–36). According to Hamilton (2008), this moral self will gain metaphysical empathy, the awareness or the identification of one's own self through sharing the universal subtle essence in the universal self. This universal self, "emerging from the noumenon," finds its most immediate expression or "the innermost voice" in conscience, which is not only universal but also personal (p. 147). Owing to this universal self, religious people communicate with God; secular people judge their inner self and maintain their natural bond with others; and those few "great cosmopolitan spirits" could transcend social conventions and embrace "the whole human race in their benevolence" (Rousseau in Hamilton, 2008, p. 159).

Given that human beings are social by nature, deep reflection upon experience motivated by suffering cannot happen without the intervention of the two ontological means of human existence: love and dialogue, the two main recurring motifs that permeate the whole text of the novel. For example, while Siddhartha considers drowning himself but instead falls asleep on the riverbank, Govinda happens to pass by. Not recognizing who he is, being afraid that he might be bitten by a snake, Govinda watches over the sleeping Siddhartha and protects him until he wakes up. If Govinda walked away from a stranger as many people do, then Siddhartha could have died of snake bites in his sleep. This is only a small episode in the novel, but it makes Govinda's merciful heart of love and benevolence shine. Vasudeva, the ferryman, a sage, is a master of dialogue. He has acquired a high skill of listening to his interlocutors and even to the river. He also knows how to conduct his dialogue with Siddhartha in less necessary words but more attentive care.

Further, dialogue and love do not work in an isolated and separated way. A dialogue between Siddhartha and Govinda is a good illustration of how love and dialogue can function dialectically and interactively in the process of transcendence:

Siddhartha: Love is the most important thing in the world … it is only important to love the world, not to despise it, not to hate each other, but to be able to regard the world and ourselves and all beings with love, admiration and respect.

Govinda: I understand that, but that is just what the Illustrious One [Buddha] called illusion. He preached benevolence, forbearance, sympathy, patience—but not love. He forbade us to bind ourselves to earthly love.

Siddhartha: How, indeed, could he not know love, he who has recognized all humanity's vanity and transitoriness, yet loves humanity so much that he devoted a long life solely to help and teach people? … also with this great teacher …. Not in speech or thought do I regard him as a great man, but in his deeds and life. (Hesse, 2008, pp. 113–114)

After this heartfelt and insightful dialogue, Siddhartha kindly invites Govinda to kiss his forehead. When Govinda bends near to Siddhartha and kisses him on the forehead, enlightenment is unfolding itself in Govinda's mental horizon:

> Govinda saw that this mask-like smile, this smile of unity over the flowing forms, this smile of simultaneousness over the thousands of births and deaths—this smile of Siddhartha—was exactly the same as the calm, delicate, impenetrable, perhaps gracious, perhaps mocking, wise, thousand-fold smile of Gotama, the Buddha, as he perceived it with awe a hundred times. It was in such a manner, Govinda knew, that the Perfect One smiled. (Hesse, 2008, p. 116)

The tremendous interactive work of love and dialogue eventually enables Govinda to find a universal self—a new larger spiritual world. This episode epitomizes how the love/dialogue nexus makes transcendence happen. Once love releases people's spiritual energy, dialogue will simultaneously pull out the wonders and miracles of being in the world and being with the world, or vice versa.

When people love, they understand and try to communicate; when people communicate, they promote their love and understanding. Therefore, the love/dialogue nexus is conducive not only to opening people's minds but also to opening people's hearts. As De Mello (1990, p. 160) remarked, "If the mind is unobstructed, the result is wisdom .... If the heart is unobstructed, the result is love." If people are sensitive to or become aware of the real world and pay attention to what is happening around them, wisdom and love can go dialectically to tell them how to listen and how to observe the mystery and meaning of life. In fact, any form of human civilization and of gifts given by nature are all there to reveal and talk to people in multiple unique ways about the *mauri* of things in the universe. (*Mauri* is a Maori word. It means that everything in the world has a life and a spirit, the vital life force. It has a strong sense of love of and respect for life.) This principle can be demonstrated, for instance, in a poem, some prose, a film, a TV show, a piece of music, a painting, a sculpture, a photograph, a scientific invention, a style of architecture, a flight of a bird, a song of a stream, a shape of a big rock, a dropping flower in the rain, the roaring sea, and the movement of grass in the breeze. If the scope and the content of love and dialogue are thereby enriched and enlarged, people will not only achieve self-dependence but also find themselves living in communion with people, nature, and the universe.

CHAPTER SIX

# The Integration of the Cultivation of Conscience Into Conscientization

This chapter seeks a guideline for integrating the cultivation of conscience into conscientization, determines the distinctive and irreplaceable functions and roles that both the cultivation of critical consciousness and the cultivation of conscience assume, and identifies the new features conscientization gains after the integration.

## Freire's Dialectical Meetings With Marx and Christ: A Guideline

There are two main reasons for the integration of the cultivation of conscience into conscientization. One is that conscience may bend in front of armed injustices or system problems no matter how important it is to morality. The other is that the practice of cultivating conscience must carry on in a dialogical approach on a social scale to transform self-conscience of inner harmony into social conscience of justice. Thus, once the cultivation of conscience is integrated, it is important to ensure that conscientization must still proceed on Freire's unyielding revolutionary, critical, dialogical, and praxical track. Freire's dialectical "meetings" with Marx and Christ are instructive for completing this project.

As mentioned in the first chapter, Walker (1980) called into question Freire's treatment of existentialist Christianity and Marxist liberation. He argued that they are contradictory. However, Freire himself did not consider this a problem:

> My meetings with Marx never suggested to me to stop "meeting" Christ. I never said to Marx: "Look, Marx, really Christ was a baby. Christ was naïve." And also I never said to Christ, "Look, Marx was a materialistic and terrible man." I always spoke to both of them in a very loving way. You see, I feel comfortable in this position. Sometimes people say to me that I am contradictory. My answer is that I have the right to be contradictory, and secondly, I don't consider myself contradictory in this. (Horton & Freire, 1990, p. 246)

Accordingly, only those who with closed minds or are uncritical in thought, only those who read Marx mechanically without asking serious questions, would think that there are irreconcilable contradictions between Marx and Christ (Horton & Freire, 1990).

In an interview, Freire (2012, video file) said, "I stayed with Marx in the worldliness ... looking for Christ in the transcendentality." This explains why Freire did not find himself in a contradictory position. It also pinpoints the respective unique roles of both the cultivation of critical consciousness and the cultivation of conscience. However, it needs further elaboration of how Freire stayed with Marx in the worldliness and how he looked for Christ in the transcendence.

## Legacies From Marx

According to Freire, Marx's theory of social explanation offers him a powerful sociological instrument to understand critically what happens in the world. He said that the more he read Marx the more he became convinced that "we really should have to change the structures of reality, that we should become absolutely committed to a global process of transformation" (Horton & Freire, 1990, p. 246). It is necessary to identify which legacies Freire inherited from Marx should be retained for the cultivation of critical consciousness.

For revolutionary social change, Marx's materialist concept of history provides a solid foundation. According to Marx (1977, p. 157), "the human essence is no abstraction inherent in each single individual. In its actuality it is the ensemble of social relations." As Balibar (1995) noted, Marx chose the French word "ensemble" to indicate that social relations are more of a fluid network than the merely static totality or the whole in the German philosophical tradition.

Therefore, according to Marx (1977), social relations or productive relations are not stationary and fixed forever but will change as long as productive forces develop. When productive relations become fetters to the development of productive forces, the production of life materials will become a problem. However, a ruling class, people with productive means and materials, do not give up the power and the privilege they have obtained to improve productive relations. They would maintain their economic base by means of state apparatus such as law making and armed forces to legalize and keep the order for what they have and what they want to have. The only solution to remove these fetters for bettering productive relations is to have a revolution. Thus, human history by itself moves on by the ongoing development of productive forces, driven by the development of technology and continuous revolutions to ameliorate and harmonize productive relations. Both revolutions and the development of technology will go hand in hand toward a humanist historical vision: human emancipation, the maximization of human powers.

Marx (1977) offered a liberating definition of the subject. According to him, human beings are not passive sensible beings; they are the subject of their "'revolutionary,' 'practical-critical' activity" (p. 156). At the same time, he claimed that "the philosophers have only interpreted the world, in various ways; the point is to change it" (p. 158). That is, the transformative character of human subjectivity embodies itself in concrete practices—the expression of definite ways of life. As Osborne (2005, p. 31) pointed out, Marx used the word "interpret" to suggest that those philosophers do not really understand the world, because to change the world "is both the point (telos, end) of human activity and the appropriate perspective from which to understand it." Therefore, "the subject is practice ... the subject is nothing other than practice which has always already begun and continues indefinitely" (Balibar, 1995, p. 25). Thus, the subject is always the subject in praxis.

As Marx (1977) claimed, philosophers cannot stay away from the real world but must make philosophy the *head* of human emancipation to give *spiritual weaponry* for the proletariat, the *heart* of human emancipation. That is, philosophers should not close people's thinking with absolute truth and abstract knowledge about the world. They must try to find a way to overcome the gap between the universality of philosophy and the particularity of the social world. This is to take philosophy as worldly philosophy, to be more exact, as "journalistic criticism" based on concrete social contexts (Osborne, 2005, p. 66). It is true that the weapon of criticism cannot supplant "the criticism of weapon," however, the theory or truth it contains "will become material force as soon as it seizes the masses" (Marx, 1977, p. 69). As Marx (1977, p. 65) argued, "Criticism ... no longer pretends to be an end in itself but only a means. The essential feeling that animates it is indignation, [and] its essential task is denunciation." Freire's concepts of "indignation" and "denunciation" have a genealogical source here.

In the same way, Marx's economics, a type of historical anthropology, also offers a way to critique (Osborne, 2005). As a historical realist, Marx acknowledged amorality and violence of history. He condemned the hypocrisy of the political economy that presented capitalism in essentially moral terms. Thus, he employed economics as a powerful instrument to disclose the true nature of capitalism. According to Marx (1964, 1976), there are two basic inner contradictions in the capitalist mode of production. One is the contradiction between social production of life materials and private possession of the means of production and the wealth produced. The other is the contradiction between private production with a plan and social production without a plan. Consequently, uncontrolled material production increasingly expands; by marked contrast, most people's ability to purchase these manufactured products becomes more and more limited. Under such circumstances, economic crisis and recession become an inevitable and necessary readjustment of uncontrolled social production. Moreover, endless fierce competition fueled by the capitalist mode of production produces fewer winners and more losers. Therefore, the ferocity of capitalism lies in the fact that "the increasing wealth of the few and rapid increase of poverty and misery for the vast majority of humanity" and the "nature of capitalism" are "intrinsically evil" (Freire, 1998a, p. 114).

Marx (1964, 1976) strongly believed that the mode of production or the way of labor in a certain society creates and determines the certain mode of being for men and women. Whatever form of labor people take in their work, they produce not only life materials including cultural objects but also themselves. Their identities are simultaneously shaped by certain productive relations. By this logic, in the capitalist mode of production, the relationships of capital make individuals subordinate to others through their access to and ownership of capital. Alienation of labor occurs accordingly. Capitalists' incessant pursuit of surplus value reduces all human beings, including themselves, to slaves of money and tools of capital. Workers are estranged from their products, their life activities, and their generic being. They also lose fellowship with other people. However, the same universal suffering has been experienced differently by two different classes:

> The propertied class and the class of the proletariat represent the same human self-alienation. But the former feels comfortable and confirmed in this self-alienation, knowing that this alienation is its own power and possessing in it the semblance of a human existence. The latter feels itself ruined in this alienation and sees in it its impotence and the actuality of an inhuman existence. (Marx, 1977, p. 134)

Accordingly, Marx (1964) showed deep and acute moral concerns for the working-class people in his time. He vividly portrayed the living conditions of those workers in factories as the cogs in the machine, with their bodies mortifying and their minds ruining.

Marx's critical and revolutionary spirit is vitally important. More than 2,000 years ago, Confucius said that a corrupt government is more ferocious than tigers when he and his students were taking the route to pass the Taishan Mount in China. Bette Bao Lord (1990) wrote this into a Chinese tale, as follows:

> Once a sage passed by a cemetery where a white-haired woman was wailing. "What tragedy has befallen you?" the sage asked.
>
> "In these parts," she replied, "there lived a man-eating tiger. Two months ago, it devoured my eldest. A month ago, my second son. This week, my youngest."
>
> "Why did you flee from these ills?"
>
> "Because more ferocious than man-eating tigers is a corrupt government." (p. 230)

In the same light, Aristotle (1981) remarked succinctly, as follows:

> Injustice armed is hardest to deal with; and though man is born with weapons which he can use in the service of practical wisdom and virtue, it is all too easy for him to use them for the opposite purposes. (p. 61)

Therefore, among all these dehumanizing problems, a problematic social system is one of the biggest. No matter how strong an individual's morality, it is not strong enough to resist the destructive nature of a problematic system. As Marx and Engels (1972) argued, if class oppression, social injustice, and inequality prevail in a social system, talk of conscience and compassion undoubtedly adds insult to the injury of the poor oppressed people and turns out to be a spiritual way of oppressing them. If conscientization can be understood as "learning to perceive social, political, and economic contradictions, and to take action against the oppressive elements of reality" (Freire, 1972a, p. 15), then its critical, praxical, and revolutionary spirit based on social justice is clearly what Freire inherited from Marx's philosophical standpoint and economic analysis.

## A New Concept of Revolution

As mentioned earlier, Freire is "looking for Christ in the transcendentality." If looking for Christ is understood as looking for the way to love, then "looking for Christ in the transcendentality" is actually to love in the transcendence. This notion of love in the transcendence enables Freire to offer a new concept of the revolution.

As a historical fact, Marx's theory of communism had ignited the worldwide communist movement. In particular, the victory of Lenin's revolution in Russia gave hope to the proletariat revolution all over the world. However, the means of the revolution still repeated the old stereotype of a blood-shedding struggle for power. In many countries, the criticism of weapons evolved into many cruel head-on civil wars, which cost millions of human lives. Consequently, the end of total redemption of humanity was fulfilled by a dehumanizing means of revolution. The means of revolution is separated from its end.

For many revolutionaries, the end of building up a socialist system will justify the means of the revolution through violence. For example, I still remember Mao's remark that I learned at school: "Communism is not love. Communism is a hammer, which we use to crush the enemy." The logic here is that if there is oppression, there will be anti-oppression. However, the dilemma arises: Violence in a war subverts the whole foundation of community life, shatters the whole fabric of human solidarity, and eventually erases humanity away. It is highly questionable that human beings can build an ideal and fair society on the foundation of blood-shedding battlefields, the loss of humanity on a social scale.

Being antisectarian and antifanatic for all his life, Freire (1972a) offered an alternative to this means problem. He did not take a reactionary position of anti-revolution and treat unnecessary human suffering as the will of God. Rather, he cherished the revolutionary aim of creating a better world through social change, a fundamental way for "the overcoming of alienation" and "the affirmation of men [sic] as persons" (p. 21). However, his concept of the revolution was obviously different from those revolutionaries in the Maoist tradition. For him, the end of restoring humanity must be achieved through a humanizing process because the means itself is an integral part of the end. Rather, the means of the revolution does not necessarily exclude or oppose its end of restoring humanity. To fight for social justice and equality does not necessarily mean the loss of humanity. As Freire (1972a) argued, "I am more and more convinced that true revolutionaries must perceive the revolution, because of its creative and liberating nature, as an act of love" (p. 62). He elaborated the attributes of love as follows:

> Because love is an act of courage, not of fear, love is commitment to other men [sic]. No matter where the oppressed are found, the act of love is commitment to their cause—cause of liberation. And this commitment, because it is loving, is dialogical. As an act of bravery, love cannot be sentimental; as an act of freedom, it must not serve as a pretext for manipulation. It must generate other acts of freedom; otherwise, it is not love. (p. 62)

If the revolution is defined as an act of love, the connotation of love should not be confined to the comradeship based on the working-class people construed by the social class perspective. It must extend to enemies. Love extending to enemies is the only way to avoid "a pretext for manipulation." This requires the pedagogy of both indignation and tolerance. Accordingly, Freire (2004) wrote about the pedagogy of indignation because it is a psychological precondition for denouncing injustices. He never concealed his anger with moral integrity in the face of those who were shameless and corrupted to abuse government power for serving their own interest. At the same time, he stressed tolerance because it creates necessary conditions for transcendence of not only the oppressed but also the oppressors. Therefore, Freire did not take "love your enemies" dogmatically and mechanically but critically and creatively. His way of treating "enemies" is to admonish their "evils" with indignation but count them as human beings with tolerance.

There could be at least two reasons for doing this. The first reason is that enemies are a social product of social and ideological conflicts. For example, those who are "shameless" (a word Freire often used to admonish the corrupted officials in his country) are people's enemies because they betray people's interest. People are the enemies for those who are shameless because people are obstacles to their further betrayal. Therefore, these social and ideological conflicts are merely living witnesses of these inner social, political, and economic contradictions in a given society. The aim of social change is to reconcile these conflicts or to address these contradictions. However, there is no social system without social contradictions because there is no society in which people think and feel unanimously all the time. As the French revolution shows, when old enemies were eliminated, conflicts between revolutionaries generated new enemies. This is also what happened in the Soviet Union and China when the socialist system was established. The social conflicts (taking the form of class struggles) between "comrades" often produced new "enemies." Eventually, finding ways to crush enemies made revolutionaries deviate from their original goal of the revolution: the total redemption of humanity. In such a case, if enemies are not treated as human beings but as devils for revolutionaries to destroy, the destruction of enemies, in fact, human beings, is endless.

The second reason is that power works in power relationships. Freire (2007) strongly believed that people are always the primary source of power. If people, the majority of the weak, stand up together, those few who hold power in office in a dominant position automatically become weak. The communist movement worldwide has borne out this truth. However, if the image of oppressors occupies people's minds, a victory of a military revolution only turns out to be a victory of the number of the majority, which lacks a fundamental change. This may turn all revolutionaries into the victims of change, as Freire (1998a) cautioned.

Therefore, Freire focused on system problems and consciousness problems rather than on people or individuals. This requires more of the dialectical and interactive work of indignation and tolerance based on dialogue, but dialogue needs an ethical foundation. Then what can serve such an ethical foundation? It is to treat both the oppressed and the oppressors as human beings. This requires love. Accordingly, Freire cited Guevara: "Let me say, with the risk of appearing ridiculous, that the true revolutionary is guided by strong feelings of love. It is impossible to think of an authentic revolutionary without this quality" (Guevara in Freire, 1972a, p. 62). Certainly, the power of love is "the most crucial characteristic of dialogue and constitutive force animating all pedagogies of liberation" (McLaren, 2000a, p. 171). Here, McLaren's (2000a) comment is thought provoking:

> Only when the other is encountered behind the door can the self find its authentic eyes, ears, and voice in the act of dialogue, reciprocal understanding. Love both embodies struggle and pushes it beyond its source. In Freirean terms, revolutionary love is always pointed in the direction of commitment and fidelity to a global project of emancipation. In this respect, Freire's concept of love coincides with that of Che [Guevara]. The commitment of revolutionary love is sustained by preventing nihilism and despair from imposing their own life-denying inevitability in times of social strife and cultural turmoil. Anchored in narratives of transgression and dissent, love becomes the foundation of hope. In this way, love can never be reduced to personal declaration or pronouncements but exists always in asymmetrical relations of anxiety and resolve, interdependence and singularity. Love, in this Freirean sense, becomes the oxygen of revolution, nourishing the blood of historical memory. It is through reciprocal dialogue that love is able to serve as a form of testimony to those who have struggled and suffered before us, and whose spirit of struggle has survived efforts to extinguish it and remove it from the archives of human achievement .... Freire understood that while we often abandon hope, we are never abandoned by hope. This is because hope is forever engraved in the human heart and inspires us to reach beyond the carnal limits of our species being. (pp. 171–172)

Freire said he spoke to both Marx and Christ "in a very loving way" (Horton & Freire, 1990, p. 246). Certainly, this "very loving way" enabled him to embrace both a historical vision of emancipation and a theological view of salvation. It allowed Freire to stand on a spiritual summit, on which he was able to have contemplative dialogues with both Marx and Christ.

However, it is crucial to note that Freire did not make any compromise between Marx and Christ. For him, Marx's critical social explanation formed "an objective basis to continue to be Christ's comrade" (Freire, 2012, video file). It bears the similarity with Confucius's bottom-up way of learning: to seek the fundamental truth of Heaven by starting with philosophizing on feet the worldliness of human affairs (Yang, 1980). It is not only a holistic philosophical and theological approach but also a manifestation of conscience and of how Freire, like Confucius, cared about, was concerned for, and loved humanity profoundly and dearly. This accounts for why Freire devoted his whole life to "a more human, fraternal, and solidarity-based vision for the world" in the company of other "great masters of humanity" (Andreaola in Freire, 2004, p. xliii). It also accounts for necessity of the cultivation of conscience through love, which begins its formation in the push and pull of the human heart. McLaren (2000a) remarked as follows: "The day that the *corazon* of humanity becomes filled with the collective love of its people, the abyss [of human suffering] will disappear, and the bridge across it will no longer be necessary" (p. 176).

Although Freire did not write systematically about how to integrate the cultivation of conscience into conscientization, his dialectical meetings with Marx and Christ provided a fundamental approach to humanization. They also offered a guideline for identifying and specifying the main functions and roles of both the cultivation of critical consciousness and the cultivation of conscience.

## The Cultivation of Critical Consciousness: Functions and Roles

To integrate the cultivation of conscience into conscientization is not to undermine the functions and roles of the cultivation of critical consciousness. Rather, it reinforces them. With its political and revolutionary spirit, the cultivation of critical consciousness awakens the oppressed people's critical consciousness of a just existential place in society and the subject position in making history.

### Awakening the Consciousness of a Just Social Place

To reiterate Gramsci's (1971) view, the dominant class depends more on cultural hegemony than on overt forces to win the consent of subordinate groups and thus maintain their obtained interests and existing social order. To win this consent could be organized in various ways, but education is a main site for *the war of position*. Bourdieu, an influential French sociologist, made Gramsci's insights more concrete by investigating these concepts such as social capital, cultural capital, habitus, and symbolic violence. His sociological study of education revealed that in the practice of education, curriculum and pedagogical processes are employed to serve the interest of the dominant class by keeping the status quo.

Influenced by Marx, Bourdieu (1984, 1990) investigated how capital works. He based his ideas on Marx's (1973) belief that capital is a "dialectical process of development" (p. 99) rather than a simple relation. Because capital moves, according to Marx, it interacts dynamically in multiple forms and various ways in people's economic, social, and cultural life. Therefore, Bourdieu divided capital into at least three forms: economic capital, social capital, and cultural capital.

For Bourdieu (1990), economic capital refers to people's command over economic resources such as cash and assets. Social capital is basically about social resources based on group membership, relationships, and networks of influence and support. It is "the sum of the resources, actual or virtual, that accrue to an individual or a group by virtue of possessing a durable network of more or less institutionalized relationships of mutual acquaintance and recognition" (Bourdieu & Wacquant, 1992, p. 119). Cultural capital refers to intellectual and educational resources, such as knowledge and expertise, competencies and skills, and educational advantages (Bourdieu, 1990). Top-class university qualifications play an important part in educational advantages because they may give their possessors a higher status in society.

Different forms of capital are dialectically interwoven together. Bourdieu's (1984) focus is to distinguish cultural capital from economic capital and social capital. For him, there are three subtypes of cultural capital, which may be obtained in three different ways. The first is embodied cultural capital. It refers to *properties* not only acquired consciously but also *inherited* passively. What can be inherited is not in the genetic sense but in the sense of acquisition over time. Hence, embodied cultural capital is not transmissible instantaneously as a gift or bequest given by someone. Rather, it is received over time by means of *habitus*, shaped by socialization based on people's family background and their parents' social networks.

The second subtype is objectified cultural capital. It is physical cultural goods such as scientific instruments or works of art. This kind of cultural capital is acquired through one's access, use, and consumption of their facility.

Institutionalized cultural capital is the third subtype Bourdieu identified. It consists of institutional recognition most often in the form of academic credentials or qualifications. The institutional recognition process plays its most prominent role in the labor market. It is in this process that credentials or qualifications allow a wide array of cultural capital to be expressed in a single qualitative and quantitative measurement. Eventually, with the help of their parents' social contacts, middle-class graduates can easily get good positions with good pay in the labor market.

Bourdieu unmasked a key fact: middle-class parents' economic capital is transformed into their children's cultural capital, their university qualifications; then after university graduation, their parents' social capital again secures their children to find a high status job in the labor market; finally these children's cultural capital will be transformed into economic capital in turn. As Bourdieu (1990) argued, by every single kind of capital, middle-class students will maintain a similar social position as their parents. By marked contrast, working-class children will be marginalized. When they finish schooling and enter into the labor market, it is very hard for them to find a fair *place* in society.

In this context, a key question arises: What underlies the interactive movement of these three subtypes of cultural capital for the middle class to preserve their social privileges from one generation to the next? Or, what fundamentally maintains educational success for middle-class students? According to Bourdieu (1990), *habitus* is a key to understanding this social phenomenon. *Habitus* refers to people's disposition or character handed down intergenerationally. It is about lasting ways of perception, thought, and action that people may have acquired in their sociocultural surroundings, primarily, family background. For example, language, in particular, accent, grammar, spelling, and style, can be a showcase of how people may present themselves to others through their way of communication learned from their surrounding culture. By the same logic, the food one chooses to eat, the clothes one chooses to wear, the friends one chooses to make, and so forth, play an important role in forming one's *habitus*. Taste is a good representative of a person's *habitus*.

In the same way, educational success, according to Bourdieu, entails a whole range of cultural behaviors, such as the way to hold a pen or a book, gait, dress, and accent. However, these are not taken as nonacademic features. Children from intellectual family backgrounds have already learned this kind of behavior as required, as have their teachers. They fit the pattern of their teachers' expectations easily and feel as comfortable within their schooling environment as fish in water. Thereby, they are also thought to be docile and get more care and attention. By contrast, children of unprivileged backgrounds have not developed these behaviors and habits. They are found to have difficulties at school. Seemingly, the ease the privileged children experience is out of their natural ability; but as Bourdieu (1990) investigated, this *ease or natural ability* depends largely on the part of *habitus*, nurtured by their parents.

Bourdieu (1984) used symbolic capital to account for how these disadvantaged working-class children respond to their school failure and their middle-class peers' success. According to him, together with cultural capital, there is symbolic capital. It is a kind of capital that goes unnoticed, such as prestige, honor, and attention, but it forms a crucial source of power. That is, symbolic capital will produce symbolic power. When the holder of symbolic capital uses her or his symbolic power against an agent who holds less prestige and honor and seeks to alter this agent's actions, symbolic violence is being exercised. Symbolic violence fundamentally tends to perpetuate the dominant structures and impose categories of thought and perception upon those dominated social agents without their consciousness. As a result, the dominated will take the social order legitimated by the dominant class to be "*just*" and their own miserable position to be "*right.*" Accordingly, working-class children often come to view the educational success of their middle-class peers as always legitimate, seeing what is often class-based inequality as the result of hard work or even natural ability. Thus, to some extent, symbolic violence is much more powerful than physical violence. When the dominant class uses symbolic violence to impose the specter of the legitimacy of social order, this kind of specter will penetrate deep into the very modes of actions and structures of individuals' cognition. This is why working-class students often internalize their feelings about their educational failures at school.

Sociologically, each individual should occupy a just position in a multidimensional social space (Bourdieu & Wacquant, 1992). However, those working-class people are marginalized and are forced to have an unjust place in society by not only overt forces but also symbolic violence. For this reason, sociology should be employed as a combative means to counter symbolic violence (Bourdieu & Wacquant, 1992).

Bourdieu and Wacquant's (1992) investigation showed that although the bourgeoisie class, as Marx theorized, has become stratified in some ways, the actuality of domination remains intact. As mentioned early, the middle class, known itself by knowledge and expertise, not only dominates social classes and cultural reproduction but also forms the main trunk of the government body and other public sectors. Hence, class consciousness does not disappear but takes deep root in all walks of life. Accordingly, discrimination has taken on subtle and sophisticated forms, self-alienation often produces its excruciatingly corrosive effect on human existence, and oppression has become not only inter-multilayered but also internalized. In this sociocultural climate, it is imperative to use sociological analysis to expose the unthought structures beneath social agents' physical (somatic) and thought practices, laying bare the unseen areas where one should have been free (Bourdieu & Wacquant, 1992).

If what happens in the educational field practice is the cultural reproduction of social classes and inequality rather than the production or construction of knowledge and culture, as Bourdieu showed, education in this postindustrial society, portrayed by some progressive educationalists as based on autonomy, equal opportunity, and high social mobility, is merely a myth. This speaks significantly and powerfully of Freire's criticism of banking education or domestication.

As mentioned in the first chapter, Walker criticized Freire, noting that Freire's dialogue is a misapplication of Marx's notion of class struggle and it will undermine workers' powerful agent role in the revolution. However, Walker failed to see that the formation of the working class has already changed in this consumption age. He ignored that it is the practice of education that produces who will stay in the middle class and who will stay in the working class. Accordingly, class struggle turns out to be the *war of position*, as Gramsci argued. It would seem that Walker's reading of Marx is mechanical and uncritical.

Roberts (2005) remarked as follows:

> Freire makes it clear, however, that there are multiple ways of participating in the process of social transformation, and sometimes the most effective approaches, *in the long term*, are the quiet, unnoticed forms of gentle intellectual 'subversion' practiced by educationalists and others as they go about their daily work. (p. 453)

The cultivation of critical consciousness as cultural action or "subversion" does offer an effective sociological tool to wake the political consciousness of the oppressed. It can make those individuals sensitive to what is happening in the real world and help them engage in transgressing symbolic violence.

## Strengthening the Subject Position in Making History

To be conscious of one's social positioning is imperative for social change and combating symbolic violence. However, it is insufficient. According to Freire (2007, 2004, 1997, 1998a, 1996, 1994b), if people's view of history is fatalistic, deterministic, and static, they will take the status quo for granted and see what is happening to them as their unchangeable destiny. This will eventually draw the oppressed back to the social order designed and arranged by the dominant class. Therefore, to take revolutionary acts necessitates a clear historical vision, which is brought about by the awakening of people's historical awareness.

Freire (1998a) saw making history as to live out opportunity, hope, and possibility. This enabled him to associate the historical vision with human existence in concrete social discourses. He stated the following: "I am not angry with people who think pessimistically. I am sad because for me they have lost their place in history" (p. 26). This poignancy strongly suggests that to lose one's place in history means to lose one's existence in society not only today but also tomorrow. To accept this loss constitutes a deep level of resignation, passivity, and hopelessness. Given that history is society-in-movement, to make history is therefore to restructure people's social positioning based on their historical vision. It is responsiveness to human beings' unfinishedness in time. In other words, if human beings are ontologically historical and praxical, to make history is to make sense of human life, to fulfill and honor human finite being with dignity. It is fundamental not only for revolution but also for being in and with the world.

However, because of cultural hegemony, history is conventionally believed as the outgrowth of those great heroes and the record of their stories maintained by the dominant power/knowledge regimes. For the oppressed, they can make their own history but not under circumstances of their own choosing. Their capacity to respond historically to the finiteness of their being is controlled by oppressors. They are compelled to accept so-called personal destiny. In most cases, they are deprived of their human right to make history. *The True Story of Ah Q*, a Chinese novel written by Lu Xun (1972), illustrates this point well.

Lu Xun (1972) claimed ironically in the first chapter that he could not recall nor verify Ah Q's correct name. *Ah* in Chinese is a diminutive prefix for names, and Q is an English letter; its pronunciation is closer to *Quei* in Chinese. The name symbolizes a name for the nameless. Ah Q is a rural peasant with little education and no definite occupation. He often lives in a deserted memorial temple for worshipping the God of Land and Crops. The story of him traces all his tragic "adventures." The following are only some of his tragedies.

Ah Q's parents died early, so Ah Q cannot remember his family name. Owing to the Chinese tradition of guilt or honor by association, Ah Q claims that his family name is also Zhao. This is because Zhao is the family name of an honored landlord in Ah Q's village. At first, some villagers suspect Ah Q may have no true association with the landlord Zhao. Instead of questioning the matter closely, most villagers give Ah Q more respect for a time. However, when Zhao's son passes an important examination for entry to a high status school, Ah Q thinks, if he shares the same family name with the landlord, it means long ago his and the landlord's ancestors could have lived in the same family. On this special occasion, it is appropriate for him to go to Zhao's house to say "congratulations" to him. When he turns up, the landlord swears at Ah Q, saying that Ah Q is not qualified to be named after Zhao because he is so poor and uneducated. The landlord makes his point very clear: He does not want Ah Q to have Zhao as his family name. He warns Ah Q that every time he hears Ah Q saying that his family name is Zhao, he will ask his people to thrash him without any consideration. Then he sends his servants to beat Ah Q away.

Ah Q is a bullying object for most of the people in his village, to let out their feelings of discontent. Having been oppressed continually, Ah Q also has acquired an instinct to oppress others. He dares not bully those strong ones, but he attempts to bully those who are weaker than him. For example, in order to make himself feel better and to blame his problems on the weaker ones, he harasses a young nun unscrupulously by pinching her on the cheek. The nun throws the worst curse in Chinese culture at Ah Q: "You will have no male heir!" This curse makes Ah Q feel miserable and he starts his adventure of love. When he works as a part-time coolie for the landlord Zhao, he takes a chance and kneels down in front of Wu Ma, a housemaid, awkwardly begging her to sleep with him. Being terribly horrified, Wu Ma runs away and cannot stop crying. In order to comfort Wu Ma, the landlord Zhao asks his servants to catch hold of Ah Q and teach him a good lesson. Ah Q's love story thus ends up tragically with the humiliation of being whipped.

When a revolution in his county breaks out, Ah Q does not know the meaning of the revolution but mechanically imitates those revolutionaries in the town and shouts "revolution, revolution." During the period of the revolution, Mr. Qian, a county official, is afraid of revolutionaries so much that he asks the landlord Zhao to hide some of his treasure in Zhao's house and then runs away to escape the revolution. However, revolutionaries rob Zhao of nearly all his treasure, including Qian's. When the revolutionaries get the power, both landlord families, the Zhaos and the Qians, pretend to espouse the revolution. As a result of this pretense, they reestablish their power and acquire more property in the new regime. Mr. Qian thereafter requests that Zhao pay him back his treasure. Zhao tells Mr. Qian that his treasure was robbed by revolutionaries. Mr. Qian orders Zhao to get his treasure back from the revolutionaries. Wanting to shake off Qian, Zhao comes up with a malicious plan to bribe a new police officer in the new local government and asks him to arrest Ah Q, who thereafter becomes Zhao's scapegoat.

Ah Q wants to call himself a revolutionary and join the revolution so that he can rob the rich of their wealth. Yet, "a false foreign devil," as Ah Q often calls him, does not permit him to participate in the revolution. When the revolution ("revolutionaries" looted Mr. Zhao of his treasure and split it among themselves) took place, Ah Q happened to be sleeping in the temple. He therefore had nothing to do with the looting. Despite his innocence, he was nonetheless arrested by the bribed police officer, who saw the situation as a golden opportunity to ease the ongoing tension between the Qians and the Zhaos.

During the court hearing, when Ah Q is asked if he participated in the looting, he tells the judges that "they did not wake me up." Ah Q speaks his mind. He believes that someone would have woken him if the revolution had ignited, but in fact, he was sleeping at the time. He is still disappointed that he did not take part in the looting. To the court, this explanation simply confirms his guilt by intent: He wanted to be an accomplice but just missed the opportunity. He did not join the looting this time because he was asleep, but he did other times. Oddly, however, looting is part of the revolution for the "revolutionaries" and can be condoned by the judges, but for Ah Q, it becomes a serious crime because nobody recognizes him as a "revolutionary." Ultimately, Ah Q is sentenced to death for this crime.

To show that his sentence is legal on behalf of "justice" and "the reverence to the law," the judges get Ah Q to sign his name on the court verdict. When Ah Q tells them he has no name and does not know how to write either, they ask him to draw a circle as his signature instead. Ah Q tries his best to do so, but with a trembling hand, his circle ends up with a tail. His circle and tail look more like the English letter Q than a circle. Ah Q's name is formally justified by this drawing at last, but ironically, he has signed his own death warrant without knowing what he is actually doing.

Although this narrative only covers certain aspects of Ah Q's life, it nonetheless aptly illustrates his oppressive life circumstance. He is not allowed to choose a name for himself, let alone make history. Given this situation, Ah Q's participation in the revolution turns on one political precondition being met: Ah Q must be allowed to participate in the revolution of fighting for a better world. However, there can be two options under this political precondition. One is to train Ah Q to become a good soldier. The other is pedagogical politics to convert him into a true revolutionary.

The former option may enable Ah Q to obtain a "master" status in a new society, but it does not necessarily lead him to the subject position of making history. If Ah Q does not understand that the aim of the revolution is to change the social and political system that maintains Zhao's and Mr. Qian's oppression and exploitation, nothing really will have changed except the actors on the stage. Instead, Ah Q will still regard the purpose of revolution as to loot the wealth from the rich, to get what he wants, and to kill anyone he hates (because the word "revolution" in Chinese translation means to kill one's life). Ah Q will continue to become another Mr. Qian or Zhao; the people whom he is now going to oppress will become new Ah Qs, like he used to be. A master of a new society is no more than another oppressor with an advantage obtained by means of looting. As Freire warned, the image of oppressors still occupies the minds of the oppressed. Therefore, through *The True Story of Ah Q*, Lu Xun shows that the victory of the revolution led by Kuomintang in the early 1900s is only a substitution of one set of masters for another. Oppression still exists or remains intact; nothing is changed fundamentally.

The latter option is desirable. In fact, in *The True Story of Ah Q*, Lu Xun attacks two main characteristics symptomatic of the Chinese persona. One is Ah Q's "spiritual victories," the way Ah Q tried to persuade himself mentally that he is spiritually "superior" to his oppressors when he runs into extreme defeat or humiliation. For example, when bullied or beaten, he would repeat his pet phrase, murmuring, "What is the world coming to nowadays, with sons beating their parents!" He managed to escape the bitterness of day-to-day hardships by muting or dulling his consciousness of suffering in this way. Hence, "spiritual victories" is Lu Xun's euphemism for the criticism against the typical Chinese tendency toward verbalism or self-talk and self-deception—a behavior that thus reinforced the status quo heralding tyranny and suppression.

A second feature of Chinese society that Lu Xun was reacting to in his novel was the "mob mentality" or "onlookers' apathy." Here, the oppressed do not display empathy for the oppressed in the face of injustice but assume the mindset of an oppressor instead. They gloat over the misfortune of the oppressed. For example, when Ah Q harasses the nun, instead of protesting and intervening to stop Ah Q's bullying, the crowd nearby laughs, amused at both the nun's insult and Ah Q's misbehavior. The message that Lu Xun wants to give is that the oppressed need to wake up from their slumber, to recognize how their indifference toward human suffering is indicative of their immature state of consciousness. This is also where the significance of Freire's pedagogical politics lies—to awaken the oppressed from their anesthetized consciousness and numb nerves due to oppression, to encourage them to face social reality directly and unyieldingly, and to act together with them heroically. Awakening or a psychological revolution initiated by cultural revolution is certainly the first step.

Part of the problem of this awakening is undoubtedly the pain that arises when people realize their own social reality (Hooks, 1994). Roberts (2000) remarked as follows:

> It could be argued against Freire that those who come to view their situation critically might remain as powerless as ever to effect change, given the overwhelming dominance of certain groups, but be more frustrated, more unhappy, more resentful, and more bitter than ever before. (p. 134)

This is why Ah Q uses "spiritual victories" to cope with the pain of realizing his reality, not that this line of argument should stop anyone from becoming conscientized. It only brings to prominence the question of how to transform the pain into self and social empowerment in exercising conscientization.

Westrheim's (2009) research offers a compelling answer to this problem. By looking into the PKK (Kurdistan Workers Party) education under Freire's pedagogical theoretical framework, Westrheim maintained that there is a connection between the armed guerrillas and education. One of her informants said the following:

> When we look at the progress we made, we realise that everything is somehow related to education. I am thinking of education in the sense of having a personality,

developing a culture, and developing moral values and critical thinking. In that sense, we are an education movement. (p. 21)

According to Westrheim (2009), education empowers the oppressed if it is anchored in their daily life. Moreover, the key to a successful revolution is the extent to which a person can be changed. True revolution starts with the self and the person. Citing an informant, this change is captured:

Yesterday I was nothing, I was obliterated and ignorant. Today this emptiness is filled with the PKK. I have gained a community perspective on all my doings and have a love for all human beings. I have put my individual freedom in the PKK. I am now more conscious of who I am and of my surroundings. (p. 21)

Here human dignity and confidence shine when they are inscribed in revolutionary praxis. Westrheim's (2009) research shows clearly how self and social empowerment go hand in hand with self and social transformation through education. PKK's mountain-top education speaks profoundly for the need of Freirean pedagogical politics—without which, nothing can generate resulting change of social habits and a new mode of thinking.

In just the same way, Ah Q's revolution must start with education. It starts with helping Ah Q choose a name for himself and teaching him how to read and write it. In Chinese culture, to help a person choose a name is common. Taking Ah Q's oppressive condition into account, it is not common for him. It is a sign of social recognition for his autonomous existence and the beginning of his revolution. As Freire and Macedo (1987) claimed: "Anyone who takes history into his or her own hands can easily take up the alphabet" (p. 106); dialectically, when the oppressed take up the alphabet, they also start their journey of history-making. With the progress of reading a word, together with reading the real world through dialogical or democratic education, Ah Q will experience self and social empowerment. With the growth of his critical consciousness will also come a transcendence of his reliance on "the image of the oppressors," "spiritual victories," and "the mob psychology." Without shunning and escaping cynically and pessimistically from reality, Ah Q will come to know the true meaning of the revolution.

Nevertheless, any educational commitment and effort require an essential prerequisite: to love people and live with people as Freire (1985) stressed. Without the presence of love, nothing educational will "most deeply and intimately begin" (Hooks, 1994, p. 13). What matters is to love Ah Q as a human being and to see him as a subject rather than a nameless feature of the landscape. In dignifying every human being, the climate is thus created for those like Ah Q to grow, not only conscious of but also accountable for what he is doing to himself and to others.

He will know the importance of loving others and treating others as subjects. Fashioned as a subject, when the revolution comes to its most mature phase, Ah Q will not oppress Zhao and Mr. Qian as enemies in vengeance but will treat them equally as human beings in the same way as he is treated. This is a fundamental way of uprooting oppression and resorting humanity. It begets a true revolution.

Freire's pedagogical politics of conversion is to transform the climate of indifference that we have created historically and accepted as "normal"—in which people are mere objects of history—into a climate where people see themselves as active subjects of history based on the "unique fusion of social theory, moral outrage and political praxis" (West, 1993, p. xiii). That is, Freire's linking of social theory of countering oppression and domestication to narratives of human freedom and justice allows him to put a premium on democratic dialogue, which "is attuned to the concrete operations of power (in and out of classroom) and grounded in the *painful* yet *empowering* process of conscientization" (West, 1993, p. xiii, emphasis added). As the previous narrative illustrates so well, in the process of making history, the cultivation of critical consciousness reinforces the subject position of the oppressed people in their transformative praxis.

## The Cultivation of Conscience: Functions and Roles

In contrast with the functions and roles of the cultivation of critical consciousness, the cultivation of conscience plays a foundational role in building moral character and an instrumental role in maintaining Freire's claim of a universal human ethic.

### A Cornerstone to Build Moral Character

The work of conscience eventually embodies itself in conscientious decisions and acts. However, conscientious decisions and acts can be seen either frequently in most occasions or temporarily in a few occasions. The cultivation of conscience looks for the constancy and consistency of conscientious decisions and acts inscribed in a person's personality. It aims at building up moral character. This necessitates a brief look at Aristotle's characterological approach first.

According to Aristotle (1976, p. 337), character improvement or virtue training can provide a remedy for many human ills because good character "through education in goodness" can enable a person to resist the pressure of bad situations. This is known as a characterological approach. It makes heavy use of a set of robust and enduring traits that are expressed in specific patterns of action in all the varying situations in which people find themselves. However, variations on it are common in modern sociology, psychology, and political philosophy. Opposite to characterologists, situationists doubt the characterological approach and the lack of virtue at an individual level as the primary cause of human problems or "evils." For them, the focus on character is inadequate to explain inhuman events such as genocide by reference to the bad characters of the perpetrators.

Zimbardo (2007) is a key figure who lays stress on situations. He draws on many experiments and human disasters to show how situations can create roles, de-individuate people, and make their own character traits, values, and ideals become dysfunctional. Even "heroic imagination," for Zimbardo, is also born out of concrete situations. According to him, under the right or wrong situational circumstances, to do something good or bad is possible for everybody. Nothing that some humans do is foreign to others. Being brought up in the ways of virtue, as Aristotle suggested, people will not be sufficient to protect them from doing something bad. To raise children to be virtuous cannot be the solution to the problem of crime. Circumstances are much more powerful determinants of behavior than are individual factors such as character. They have the power to override character. Accordingly, it is a mistake to attribute the actions of people to their individual characters without considering the situations they go through. To say that the Nazi Holocaust occurred because the Nazis were evil men is actually to deny the truth that all humans could be capable of doing terrible things, in situations like those that prevailed in the Third Reich.

There is nothing wrong with stressing the situational or discursive forces over merely focusing on characterological approach. However, to rely on situational explanation dogmatically and deterministically is a pretext for inaction, which is due to the lack of conscience. In the face of a dehumanizing situation or living in an unjust society dominated by a problematic political and economic system, the real issue is this: Should the being of human beings always succumb to that social system like a tree leaf drifted by wind to mire? Should human beings allow their conscience to go on holiday in a bad situation? If the answer is yes, then there will be nobody like Gandhi, Mandela, Dalai Lama, Mother Teresa, or other great heroes and heroines of humanity. People respect and admire them just because their great characters are all built up by living out their conscience.

In an educational discourse, there are fewer things more central and important than moral character or personality building. Here, Buber's (2002) view on education of moral character is relevant and compelling. According to him, it is character that coheres with the active life and represents the unity of being in different situations. As he argued, every living situation calls for "a reaction which cannot be prepared beforehand" (p. 135). Any situation functions as a touchstone to test out a person's moral character. "A great character" is thus the "one who by his actions and attitudes satisfies the claim of situations out of deep readiness to respond with his whole life, and in such a way that the sum of his actions and attitudes expresses at the same time the unity of his being in its willingness to accept responsibility" (p. 137). Hence, the worse a situation is, the greater the responsibility demanded. In short, adversity is the test of moral character.

In the same light, Mencius (2003) pointed out the following:

> That is why Heaven, when it is about to place a great burden on a man [sic], always first tests his resolution, exhausts his frame and makes him suffer starvation and hardship, frustrates his efforts so as to shake him from his mental lassitude, toughen his nature and make good his deficiencies. (p. 143)

Therefore, moral character is not formed in the calm repose of a luxurious life situation but in hardships and longsuffering. It is tempered in this kind of conscious resistance of the pressure of a bad situation. "Only then do we learn the lesson that we survive in adversity and perish in ease and comfort" (Mencius, 2003, p. 143). In this context, "survive in adversity and perish in ease and comfort" is about one's moral life. When a person shoulders a greater ethical responsibility to live out these high principles such as benevolence and righteousness, she or he is morally alive. Otherwise, she or he can be morally dead.

Nevertheless, it is these high principles that substantiate a person's moral life. They give life to people's morality. Moral character is in fact living out these high principles. However, there is some distance between these high principles and concrete situations. If these high principles cannot be associated with these situations, they will become redundant. Thus, there needs to be a bridge to connect these high principles with these daily realities. As previously discussed in Chapter 4, serving as the basis of morality, conscience can fulfill this role of bridge and meet this crucial need. With its affective and sentimental power, conscience knows concrete demands called by concrete life situations and thereby generates corresponding ethical responsibility. With its function of practical reason, it makes timely connections between these high principles and specific realities so that these high principles can serve as a conscious resistance to pressure in hard-life situations.

As Weil (2002a) argued, when social and ethical obligations, viewed as fundamentally having a transcendent origin and a beneficent impact on human character, are fulfilled, and when spiritual life in the conscience of most citizens is awakened, a society to become more just and protective of liberty will come true. High moral principles only make sense when they are lived out as one's personal intrinsic spiritual need and social obligations to community. Hence, the ultimate goal of the cultivation of conscience is to help people see true vision of a good life maintained by these high moral principles. Only when a person can follow and will live out these high moral principles freely, constantly, and consistently in different life situations with unshakeable moral responsibility, comes the maturity of moral character.

## An Effective Means to Maintain a Universal Human Ethic

Any high principle enables people to cope with specific hardships in their specific sociohistorical and cultural conditions. This is also true of Freire's (1998a, p. 23) "universal human ethic." It can provide people with a powerful spiritual support to overcome alienation and commercialization of humanity at this globalization age.

As Freire (1998a, p. 23) stated, humanity "is betrayed and neglected by the hypocritical perversion of an elitist purity" and "affronted by social, sexual and class discrimination," so he claimed "a universal human ethic" in the same way as he claimed "humanization" in his *Pedagogy of the Oppressed* (1972a). In this context, the fundamental principle of "a universal human ethic" is that under no condition and circumstance can market ethics be placed above human ethics. It is no more than to treat human beings as human beings, rather than commodities.

For Freire (1998a), a person's being in and with the world is not just about being but more about *presence*. A presence will distinguish "I" from "not I" and thereby forms the basis of self-recognition. This presence is able to reflect upon itself and also to know itself as presence. Because human presence expresses itself through speaking, thinking, and dreaming, it exists in such areas as decision, evaluation, elimination, freedom, and option; therefore, "the ethical necessity imposes itself" (Freire, 1998a, p. 26). In other words, human beings are conditioned genetically, socially, and culturally, but they are not pure products of genetic, cultural, and class determination. They must take their ethical responsibility for their actions.

Freire's (1998a) universal human ethic is speaking of "something absolutely indispensable for human living and human social intercourse" (pp. 24–25). If Freire's work and life are studied closely and holistically, this "something absolutely indispensable for human living and human social intercourse" can be his central concern of love, a common thread that brings together all these essential human qualities and virtues. As he told Myles Horton, "I did not have any other door but to love the people" (Horton & Freire, 1990, p. 245); it is loving people that pushed him "to meet with workers and peasants in Recife's slums, to teach them and to learn from them" (Horton & Freire, 1990, p. 247). Even when he was dying, the notion of love was still lingering in his heart and mind: "I could never think of education without love and that is why I think I am an educator, first of all because I feel love" (Mayo, 1999, p. 17).

The scope of Freire's concept of love is broad. It includes love of the self, of people, of nature, and of the world. What it all boils down to is love of life. Freire's notion of love of life extends from "cities" to all the forms of life in the whole ecological world, such as trees on mountains and fish in rivers. Therefore, he strongly criticizes the deplorable practice "that pollutes the air, the waters, the fields, and devastates forests, destroys the trees and threatens the animals" (Freire, 2004, p. 120). If there is a key principle in Freire's universal human ethics, it must be love of life.

In all difficult situations, high principles are powerful weapons to help people resist the pressure and darkness in bad situations and endure hardship caused by regression of humanity. So is love of life. Two examples are used to illustrate how this high principle impacts human life significantly. One is a story of face washing. I was told this story by a friend when I was in China 10 years ago. It is about an episode in a Jew's life in a German concentration camp during the second World War. Feeling hopeless, meaningless, and disappointed in a dehumanizing condition, the Jew did not want to wash his face in the morning. One of his cellmates asked him the following:

> Why don't you wash your face in the morning? I know we are not sure how long we will live. Maybe we are going to be killed this afternoon or tomorrow. Yet if we are still alive now, we must live as human beings. They do not treat us as human beings, but we must treat ourselves as human beings and live with dignity and decency. We must respect life. Go and wash your face together with me. We wash our faces to start a day for ourselves.

Face washing is not a huge task, but in this unbearable dehumanizing situation, it became an extraordinary thing: conscience of one's existence and dignity. It is the application of the high principle of love of life—however hard a situation is, one must treat oneself as a human being and know how to cherish and respect life. Just because of this strong faith in life, the Jew finally managed to escape from the concentration camp and survived.

The other example is from Tolstoy's (1993) novel *War and Peace*. Pierre, one of the important heroes in the novel, comes to the following understanding after his deep reflection upon his hard life situation in captivity:

> Life is everything, life is God. Everything changes and moves and that movement is God. And while there is life there is joy in consciousness of the divine. To love life is to love God. Harder and more blessed than all else is to love this life in one's sufferings, in innocent sufferings. (Tolstoy, 1993, p. 838)

In other words, to love life is the most difficult but also the most essential thing, particularly when one is suffering.

If love of life as a high principle can pull out people's courage, strength, and perseverance to counter disappointment and despair at extremely difficult times, it will make humanity shine in various ways on normal occasions. The cultivation of conscience certainly helps create a new culture, in which love and dialogue will become the mainstream. It will serve as a practical means to maintain Freire's "universal human ethic."

## Conscientization in a New Light

As this chapter shows, once the cultivation of conscience is incorporated, it does not abandon and contradict the cultivation of critical consciousness. Rather, it adds new elements to conscientization.

While the cultivation of critical consciousness seeks social change with strong political and revolutionary spirit, the cultivation of conscience attempts to build moral character to maintain a universal human ethic. While the former aims at decoding the limit-situations, the latter focuses on the transcendence of consciousness problems such as egoism, greed, lust, and ambition. While the former looks at human emancipation from a historical perspective, the latter looks for human salvation from a spiritual angle. Therefore, their distinctive functions and roles are irreplaceable.

Nonetheless, the cultivation of critical consciousness and the cultivation of conscience are dialectically related and interdependent. They interpenetrate, interact, and complement with each other in the process of conscientization. On the one hand, the cultivation of conscience, with its sentimental power, stimulates and motivates critical consciousness to work; with its practical reason, it gives a strong ethical foundation and direction for the cultivation of critical consciousness. Thereby, it draws the practice of conscientization much closer to humanization and makes this ethical ideal more specific, tangible, and practical than it used to. On the other hand, as revealed in the third chapter, conscience works at the site of consciousness. The development of critical consciousness by itself is the development of conscience. The passivity, hibernation, and death of consciousness bring the same consequences to conscience. Therefore, any social critique and cultural criticism are powerful manifestations of both the self and social conscience.

CHAPTER SEVEN

# Conscientization: Educational Necessity and Cultural Significance

Conscientization is a praxical need in current educational and cultural contexts. It offers an alternative to counter the antihumanist character of globalization and neo-liberalism. At the same time, it also fits in with the progressive trend of postmodernism and thus plays a significant role in promoting a more free and democratic culture across the globe.

## The Educational Necessity of Conscientization

It is widely believed that the end of the Cold War (the collapse of the Berlin wall and the Soviet Union) and the advanced development of information technology have brought capitalism to its latest version: globalization, an economic form underpinned by the ideology of neo-liberalism. The most basic philosophical assumption of neo-liberalism is that human beings are *homo economicus*. As Hayek (2001) claimed, it is to fulfill "the 'End of Economic Man'" (p. 208). Thus, by taking the notion of individual freedom as a political underpinning, neo-liberalists stress the free play of competition and the free market system as an economic arena. In such a discourse, the notion of equality and state intervention becomes a social obstacle to entrepreneurship, but inequality is hailed as a good thing, a stimulus to drive a person to be strong, competitive, and successful. As Sen (1987) contended, Hayek's notion of free economic beings merely makes human beings isolated from society and turns them into a self-interested, rational, and utility maximizer.

In response to this kind of philosophical impact, globalization, a shared global market, has come into being. As Murphy (2004) argued, globalization is the integration of a "circuit board of contemporary capitalism" (p. 130). While capital is still positioned in key strongholds, at first every walk of life, in particular, labor, is segmented; then the specific business areas that have advantages and potentialities are exploited for producing more profit or making more money. The more the globe is divided into distinct spatial segments, "the better to organize and squeeze profits from the flows between them of objects, people, data, and money" (p. 130). Consequently, inequalities and injustice caused by the free market system have produced serious self-alienation and moral decadence. Although the Third Way politics attempted to reconcile the increasingly intense social contradictions, neo-liberal political practice and the deep-rooted ideology of neo-liberalism still stay firmly intact across the globe. Most people today are living in both a market economy and a market society.

There is a great deal of literature criticizing neo-liberal ideology and its political practice. The discussion here focuses on how the antihumanist character of neo-liberalism, as Freire (1998a) argued, has detrimentally affected current educational practice and why conscientization is praxically needed. Four aspects are explored: robotic vocationalism maintained by "busnocratic" rationality, money idolatry caused by commercialization and marketization, indifference to the loss of humanity and unnecessary human suffering, and the reiteration of Freire's claim of the absolute necessity of conscientization.

## Robotic Vocationalism

As Freire often stressed, education is forever ideological and political. Education dominated by neo-liberal politics is an example of this assertion. Based on the basic assumption of "the efficiency of the market as a superior allocative mechanism for the distribution of scarce public resources" (Peters & Ghiraldelli, 1999, para. 13), education, reduced to a subsector of economy (McLaren, 2000a), is treated as a commodity that generates an individual good rather than a social one. Thus, everybody should pay for their own education, and education can thereby be marketized for essential competition. Consequently, nearly every country on the planet has attempted to create a quasifree market of education. Considering the sale of educational products, almost every type of education has been channeled as a pathway to the labor market. This has increasingly reduced the role of education to merely vocation training, providing students with the skills required by the workplace. Under these circumstances, as Marshall (1997) argued, a new vocationalism has emerged.

There are at least two main features with regard to this new vocationalism. The first feature is that knowledge and understanding give way to information and skill-training. Influenced by information technology, the information economy has started to reconstitute people's subjectivity or identity and the established notions of rights, power, and authority, and to restructure not only social and cultural relations but also curriculum (Marshall, 1997). However, information on its own is not knowledge. Drawing on Peters (1966), Marshall (1997) argued that whatever form information takes, it requires knowledge and general theoretical understanding to make sense or critical assessment of it; otherwise, it is worthless. The problem of the new vocationalism is that the user of the new technology misses and goes without knowledge and understanding, this first crucial step of using information (Marshall, 1997). That is, general knowledge and understanding as required are presupposed within certain programs, are already located in software and hardware, and thus cannot be open to criticism and evaluation for the user of the new technology.

The second feature is that "these 'busnocratic' values, particularly, the notion of the autonomous choosers, are characteristic of the new vocationalism" (Marshall, 1997, p. 318). Here, the core is "busnocratic rationality":

> Central to this notion are concepts and stances taken in promoting skills, as opposed to knowledge; and the view that it is the consumers, especially industry, who define and determine quality, as opposed to the providers. There is a view of human nature in these agendas in which people are 'constituted,' produced and reproduced as autonomous choosers. (Marshall, 1997, p. 318)

In this way, the notion of "busnocratic rationality" marks off the new vocationalism. Given that "the autonomous chooser is a unit in an enterprise and consumer-driven market totality," all educational provisions and choices are totally determined, controlled by, and imbued with business values (Marshall, 1997, p. 320). If human beings are treated as autonomous choosers who only hold consumer values with the aid of the new technology, to place information above knowledge will automatically pave an easy and convenient way to translate any knowledge into a business package. In fact, the educational policy making in almost every country has shifted from the liberal arts curriculum, essential for human development, to a vocation-oriented curriculum. In order to handle the information economy and its concomitant electronic communication, identifying, analyzing, synthesizing, evaluating, locating, organizing, gathering, retrieving, processing, and using different types of information are thus set as a basic educational goal.

Accordingly, what dominates the educational field is basically skill-training rather than cultural and knowledge production. Knowledge is no longer viewed either as social and cultural achievement or as a liberating humanizing tool that is conducive to free and critical thinking but is downplayed as a set of exchangeable "credits" or a "currency" of skills. Qualifications no longer "qualify" the attributes and capabilities of students but come to be commoditized as "credentials." In this educational milieu, teachers are no longer supposed as an integral part of curriculum making but as merely a tool to implement market-oriented curriculum made by educational administration offices. In the same way, parents are thought to exercise their right of consumer sovereignty. They are forced to make calculations between investment for schooling and economic return in the job market. As a result, students are cast in the ongoing learning and re-skilling processes of dealing with information and thereby become slaves and robots of the intelligence of others in this new vocationalism.

## Money Idolatry: The Core of Marketization

In the international educational market, the First World has increasingly enhanced its educational export for further marketing in the Third World. Any subject or course that seems to guarantee the investment for a qualification that paves the way to a future highly paid job has already been cherry-picked to put on an international sale. In the end, money idolatry has driven those international multinational corporations to such a point that they even forget masking the ugliness and shamelessness of the animal spirit driven out of the corporate greed. This is well illustrated by an article, "The Future of Education Under the WTO" (Frase & O'Sullivan, 2005), bidding for education to be included as a commodity to trade under the umbrella of the World Trade Organization (WTO).

The article begins with its authors' self-complacence about their corporate dream:

> With their hands in the pockets of the various multinational corporations, they [international corporate CEO] have succeeded in establishing a New World Government based on profit. This is a government of and for the corporation—an extremely undemocratic, authoritarian institution. What better way to institutionalize corporate rule, than to create a mild, corporate-run education system to reproduce standardized people. All hail ... WTO. (Frase & O'Sullivan, 2005, p. 1)

Education evokes them to "salivate" over money:

> What entrepreneur wouldn't salivate over, what corporate CEO could resist ... a trillion dollar industry? How is it possible then, that such a market has yet to be fully explored and exploited? How is it possible that many of us are completely unaware that this market exists at all? Normally, we don't think of students, teachers, faculty, and staff as profit-making resources. Normally, we don't view the institution of

education as a market. But then, most of us are not trade representatives or corporate CEOs. (Frase & O'Sullivan, 2005, p. 1)

Accordingly, they want education to adapt to a mono-culture of business: "Now all you have to do is to learn English!"; "As education standardization is institutionalized through international equivalency, the uniqueness of each educational institution will vanish"; "the most powerful corporations and countries will control the educational agendas of the world" (Frase & O'Sullivan, 2005, p. 3). For them, "if educational systems cannot compete, they will be taken over and assimilated," and "smaller universities, liberal arts universities, and poor universities will be forced to expand, or perish" (Frase & O'Sullivan, 2005, pp. 4–5). They believe that the way of the future is the business, corporatization, and commercialization without the inference of government.

As Frase and O'Sullivan (2005) claimed, "no longer will truth be sought, but rather, whatever suits the interests of multinationals" (p. 2); "any idea that education should build democratic culture or work towards the betterment of humanity is rejected, in favour of moulding education into the training division of the transnational corporations" (p. 4). This is morally reprehensible! The antihumanity notion of education as such will reduce students to merely money-making machines and turns them into spiritually dead *homo economicus*.

## Indifference to the Loss of Humanity and Unnecessary Human Suffering

As Freire (1998a) warned more than a decade ago, if people are unaware of the injurious impact of neo-liberalism upon people, they will feel anesthetized to the loss of humanity and human suffering caused by inequality and injustice. Neo-liberalism still dominates people's minds in theses developed countries. It has also spread to some developing countries with the introduction of the market economic system. Its basic assumptions are therefore taken by some people as fundamental principles that account for and justify various inhumane social realities in these countries. The "Ma Jia-jue Accident" and some relevant comments along with it on the Internet can be used as an example to show how people are still anesthetized in neo-liberal ideology ("The Ma Jia-jue Incident," 2009).

The "Ma Jia-jue Accident" is a murder case. In February, 2004, Ma Jia-jue killed his four roommates with a big stone hammer in his dormitory at Yun-nan University in Yun-nan Province, the People's Republic of China. This murder case shocked the whole country. Before his execution, he wrote a confession letter from prison, telling the world of his life story and why he murdered his roommates.

According to Ma ("The Ma Jia-jue Incident," 2009), he was born in a very poor peasant family in a village in Bing-yang County in Gang-xi Province. His parents toiled hard in the farm field. In order to make some money, his mother did ironing for others and got paid 5 Jiao RMB (nearly 8 U.S. cents) per item. As an outstanding student with excellent academic performance, Ma was presented with high status awards such as the "Second Prize in the Chinese Physics Olympic Contest" and "Good Student in Moral, Intellectual and Physical Education of Gang-xi Province." In 2000, in the national matriculation for university entrance, he scored 50 marks over the enrollment benchmark for top universities. However, considering his family's socioeconomic status and his parents' ability to pay, instead of choosing the universities he dreamed of, he went to Yun-nan University, which is not too far away from his hometown. The tuition fee of 5,000 RMB Yuan was all borrowed. During his nearly four-year university life, in order to lessen the financial burden on his parents, he kept doing part-time coolie jobs and did not go home during university holidays. In order to comfort his parents and to make them happy, he lied to them, telling them that his life was good and that sometimes he was invited to have dinner in his teachers' homes. In fact, his life was very hard. He tried to save every cent he could. As he wrote, one time he had no shoes to put on and, feeling ashamed, he did not enter the classroom until he got a student hardship grant to buy a pair of cheap slippers. In order to save money, he did not take warm showers in winter but endured the chill to take cold showers. He often bought one meal from his university canteen but made it last for two meals. He used to have two steamed buns for a whole day though he still did hard physical work. According to him, in those desperate conditions of hunger and poverty, he never thought of stealing and robbing. He kept telling himself to work hard so that after his university graduation, he could take good care of his parents and pay back their love and toil for him.

However, Ma's life in poverty aroused the contempt of most of his classmates. They often hurt him, sometimes deliberately, but other times not. One of his roommates urinated on his quilt. Not liking the cold water in winter, his roommates gave him one or two RMB Yuan and asked him to wash their clothes. Needing the money, Ma did the washing for them. Nearly all his fellow students had girlfriends. Encouraged by one of his classmates, Ma wrote a love letter to a girl he fell in love with. When he handed the letter to the girl, she took it as an insult and tore the letter into pieces publicly. Ma said he did not care too much because he knew his limitations; for instance, his family background did not match up to hers.

Ma used to work during university holidays to support his life and study. In the last winter holiday of Ma's university life, his classmates returned early to search for jobs. In order to kill time, Ma's three classmates asked Ma to play cards with them. Because of his high intelligence, Ma often won while the other three often lost. They suspected that Ma was cheating. Ma insisted that he did not cheat. An argument ensued and they started attacking Ma's character with disdain by reminding him of all the unhappy things that had happened to him, including the girl who tore apart his love letter. As Ma wrote, these who he played cards with were all his "friends" who had not treated him badly before. Now he found out that they actually looked down upon him because of his poverty and hard life situation. Ma wrote that he could endure the others' poor treatment, but he could not endure the insults from those whom he took to be his "friends." It seemed to Ma that they had pretended to treat him equally when things were going well but started to humiliate him aggressively when the dispute arose. When their hypocrisy was uncovered, Ma felt his heart was bleeding and he decided to teach them a lesson. As Ma explained further, he was a strong person, not beaten down by the hardships of life, but he could not bear his dignity and character being denigrated by those who enjoyed some economic advantage over him. That is why he committed the murders.

When he put on the prison uniform, he told the prison policemen that it was the best he had ever worn in his life. According to the webpage ("The Ma Jia-jue Incident," 2009), after hearing this, the policemen were moved to tears. At the end of the confession letter, Ma said he felt regretful that he would not have a chance to reward one of his classmates who had not insulted him but had instead bought him a meal. This had made him realize how valuable true human love was in a world where people can often be very cruel.

Ma's confession letter may not be an entirely factual account because it was written while he was in an abnormal mental state. Nonetheless, one fact is certain: Ma had gone through a situation where he had felt belittled and depressed. From his letter, it is not hard to see that these experiences of degrading treatment had wounded Ma in the heart and had hurt him psychologically. The attacks on his character that aroused his desire for revenge brought him to an extreme point and served as the trigger that set him off to club his classmates to death. This is not to say he was psychologically sound and healthy. It may be that Ma had an inferiority complex and an anger problem from his longtime poor living conditions. The way he sought to regain his sense of dignity was, however, devastating and out of proportion to what he had endured. In killing his four classmates, he lost his own humanity and brought great suffering to the families, relatives, and friends of the murdered ones, in addition to his own parents.

According to the webpage ("The Ma Jia-jue Incident," 2009), many in the public believe that the unjust social circumstances of Ma's life are to blame. They think that such issues as Ma's poverty and the degrading treatment he endured are causally significant. However, in the face of such a tragedy, what is even more shocking is that some intellectuals showed no social conscience and reacted callously to the human suffering evident in this case. Portraying herself as rational, Li Mei-jin, a professor of psychology, offered a report based on a questionnaire survey she designed for the murderer. According to Li, if Ma hated those who scorned him, he should have killed the rich students who used to oppress him, but he did not. His victims were all poor like him. Therefore, the professor concluded that society is not to blame, that this is a character problem, not a social problem. For her, it was the criminal's own distorted, depressed, and defective character that caused him to commit the murder, in particular, egocentrism: Ma's philosophy of life.

An anonymous editor disagreed with Li's analysis ("The Ma Jia-jue Incident," 2009). According to this editor, egocentrism is not a character defect. Rather, it reflects a natural human trait—selfishness. For this editor, selfishness agrees with *homo economicus's* rationality: to maximize self-interest. The editor contended that selfishness is not only a human instinct but also the basis of modern society. Therefore, egocentrism is not to blame. The editor used an idea of the classical economics of Adam Smith to defend selfishness or egocentrism; that is, people provide the goods and service for others to enjoy not because they are selflessly generous but because they can profit from them. Even though altruism is truly desired by some people, it is hard to be altruistic because people have different values. Thus, for individuals, they know what is good or bad for them. From this standing point, the editor maintained that egocentrism is good because it can support people in making their own decisions and pursuing their own lives. Hence, the editor argued that Ma's problem was not because of his egocentrism but because of his indifference to life.

It is clear that both Li's asocial view and the editor's *homo economicus* rationality are deeply rooted in the neo-liberal ideology. Li failed to see that social injustice and inequality break down human solidarity. That is, when social justice and equality do not pertain, some negative and corrosive feelings such as hopelessness, indifference to life, discontentment, and anomie build to a point of hatred where they become the psychological triggers for a backlash against the society that lacks love and warmth. As a matter of fact, in a problematic social climate, nothing will guarantee that people's personality and character can always remain in good order. This by no means suggests that Ma's murderous response to his tough social situation was right. Rather, as Marx and Engels (1972) argued, when criticizing this kind of hypocritical moralism in *The German Ideology*, the root causes of these crimes cannot be determined dogmatically and/or assigned simplistically to individual character and personality without taking into account a wider picture of society. Injustice and inequality must not be ignored. In addition, it is not hard to understand why Ma did not kill the rich students who bullied him. Ma admitted that he got used to the oppression from the rich, but it was hard for him to endure the insults from his classmates who were his socioeconomic equals and usually treated him fairly. Lu Xun (1972) described this psychology clearly and vividly in *The True Story of Ah Q*.

The editor ("The Ma Jia-jue Incident," 2009) used Ma's indifference to life to account for his committing the murder. This is seemingly true. However, the editor failed to see the antihumanist character of neo-liberalism; that is, the root cause of indifference to life lies precisely in *homo economicus's* rationality. As mentioned earlier, *homo economicus's* rationality places the ethics of the market above all other ethical concerns. In particular, it embraces and celebrates inequality. If inequality is justified, discrimination is automatically legitimated. By this logic, *homo economicus's* rationality in fact justifies the principle that those who have money will get more respect and those who do not have money will be looked down upon. Therefore, *homo economicus's* rationality values capital more than human beings and makes people subordinate to money. If Ma had lived in a just and equal society, he would not have thought of killing others. That is, if he is rich, he will work hard to protect his property and money; if he is poor, he will use every means to earn money. However, when the justification and practice of inequality corrode social conscience of justice, meritocracy is paid lip service but without substantive reality.

Equality of opportunity needs to be built into the very fabric of society or the social system rather than something people try to get for themselves. In an unequal social climate, although Ma was an academically excellent student, he did not have equal opportunity to find a good job and earn good money, compared with the students from the privileged family background. Neither do students like him today. Moreover, when inequality and injustice prevail in a society, the acts of what is morally good do not count and the acts of what is morally bad do not matter. According to Wilkinson and Pickett (2010), there is a close correlation between inequality and crime. They used statistics to show that "more people are imprisoned in more unequal countries" (p. 148). If Ma's character was warped, then it is at least partly because of the social discourse shaped by *homo economicus's* rationality. As Freire (1998a) argued, neo-liberalism shows no moral concern. It is plausible to say that *homo economicus's* rationality lacks respect for life at its core. If Ma had not been scorned over a long period of time because of his poor family background, he would not have become so vengeful and gone to the extreme of committing a murder. In this sense, Ma and the classmates he killed are all the full victims of the neo-liberalist ideology, the chief criminal. Further, to suggest that egocentrism based on *homo economicus's* rationality will lead people to a respect for life and a love of life is a self-deception. It is to take the whiff of poison as if it is spiritually soothing.

Therefore, the danger is that many people, particularly in the developing countries with the introduction of the market system, are still anesthetized in the neo-liberal way of philosophizing the nature of reality. If the antihumanist character of neo-liberalism criticized by Freire is not unveiled, the social contradictions that caused Ma's murder will remain unattended. The same tragedy will repeat. This gives good reason to pay due attention to Freire's claim of the absolute necessity of conscientization.

## The Absolute Necessity of Conscientization

Freire identifies two main dehumanizing problems of neo-liberalism. One is its transgression of human ethics with an antihumanist character (Freire, 1998a). The other is its fatalistic and deterministic way of philosophizing the world and history (Freire, 1996, 1997, 1998a, 2004, 2007).

For Freire (1998a), neo-liberalist ethics of the market have made all fundamental human values, interests, and ideals submit solely to the law of profit. In particular, freedom of commerce is no more than issuing the license to put profit above everything else. It aims at creating favorable conditions for those few with privilege to increase their own political and economic power but shows no moral concern on the suffering of the dispossessed, disadvantaged, and oppressed. As Marshall (1996) used Foucault's vivid parable, the practice of neo-liberal freedom is those few free foxes among many free chickens. Economic globalization turns out to serve the interest of those few with power to control the world for meeting their insatiable corporate greed. While the power minority uses scientific and technological advances to "squander the fruits of the earth" and become richer, the majority of humanity are marginalized and become poorer (Freire, 1998a, p. 93). As a result, opulence goes side by side with mass hunger and unemployment. A lot of people are even hard-pressed to survive in misery and suffering. For example, sometimes those who suffer in famine and poverty are driven to search among the rubbish for something to eat and wear in the public rubbish dump in some polluted areas. One woman went so far as to make her family's Sunday dinner with pieces of an amputated female breast she dug out of the rubbish dump (Freire (1997, 1998a), further indicating that sometimes dehumanizing conditions can be heart-rending.

In order to make people accept the dehumanizing practice of globalization and the new world order as natural and inevitable, neo-liberalism tends to immobilize the world and justify the status quo by "the death of history theory" (Freire, 1998a, p. 102). That is, history is not to be lived as possibility but as determinism. The historical past is not problematized for critical understanding; tomorrow is simply the perpetuation of today, and things happen today because they have to (Freire, 1998a). Events are merely *faits accomplis* and facts are too omnipotent for human beings to redirect and alter; then there is no room left for decision making, choice, and change (Freire, 1998a). By the same logic, globalization and the dominance of capital are inalterable. Accordingly, Freire (2004) noted the following: Neo-liberalism "speaks about the death of dreams and utopia and deproblematizes the future" (p. 110). For example, one of the speakers at an international meeting of nongovernmental organizations reported "hearing an opinion, frequently bandied about in the First World, that the Third World children suffering from acute diarrhoea ought not be saved because we would only prolong lives destined for misery and suffering" (Freire, 1998a, p. 23). Without any human compassion, this kind of cynical fatalism tries to justify the degradation and dehumanization of human beings. It calls upon the wretched of the earth to accept their wretchedness as their unchangeable fate. It sings "a hymn of praise to resignation" (Freire, 1998a, pp. 73–74) to deny a defining human capacity, to think and to imagine the world differently and to negate the right to do so. This is the core of the death of history theory.

As Freire (1998a) remarked, once time stops to be a matter for people to reflect upon so as to interfere in it, actually the negation of human existence is solemnly pronounced. Therefore, to think dead of time and history is the negation of a defining human feature of existence: making history. It anesthetizes people's consciousness and domesticates their capacity to dream; thereby, their vigor of action for change can be brutally sapped. It is clear that the neo-liberal fatalist way of philosophizing the world and history attempts to improve the oppressed people's capacity to adapt themselves to that inevitable negation of their essential humanity. Thus, Freire stated with indignation, "the capitalist system reaches, in its globalizing neo-liberal crusade, the maximum efficacy of its intrinsically evil nature" (p. 114). Specifically, globalization just means the globalization of misery, sin, and destruction of natural resources worldwide (McLaren, 2000a).

Under such circumstances, it is immoral to adapt oneself to human suffering and misery such as hunger, disease, and the lack of hygiene and to allow them to persist. Freire (1998a) declared his position:

> I cannot, therefore, fold my arms fatalistically in the face of misery, thus, evading my responsibility, hiding behind lukewarm, cynical shibboleths that justify my inaction because "there is nothing that can be done." The exhortation to be more a spectator; the invitation to (even exaltation of) silence, which in fact immobilizes those who are silenced; the hymn in praise of adaptability to fate or destiny; all these forms of discourse are negations of that humanization process for which we have an unshirkable responsibility. (p. 72)

He continued: "We have an unshirkable responsibility" because humans have an ethical nature and capacity to "spiritualize the world," to make the world either beautiful or ugly (p. 53). He strongly believed that in human existence, there is always "a radical and profound tension between good and evil, between dignity and indignity, between decency and indecency, between the beauty and the ugliness of the world" (p. 53). From this ethical standpoint, Freire called for "the universal ethics of the human person" to act against "the perverse era of neoliberal philosophy" and "the instruments of change and transformation" to make "a world worthy of human habitation" for "real people" (p. 115).

Freire (2007, 2004) maintained that hope, this ontological need, can only be born out of the indeterminateness of history and the openness of future. Accordingly, to change the world or make the history is to change oneself and one's fate; people can make future but future cannot make people. Thus, Freire (2007, 2004, 1998a) strongly opposed a deterministic way of understanding history, emphasized that humans are conditioned but not determined, and urged us to dare to dream and imagine what is different from the status quo. For him, such dreaming engages in people's hope and anticipation in their own becoming. It opens up more living spaces for anybody, both public and private, and unfolds more possibilities. This unfolding allows people to see the truth of the strong conviction that change is hard but possible.

If the banking mode of technical training is the educational representative of the neo-liberalist ideology for domestication currently, then to practice conscientization is to take a radical, critical, and revolutionary means to humanize and beautify the world. Freire (1998a) made this point clear, as follows:

> In the 1960s, when I reflected on these obstacles I called for "conscientization," not as a panacea but as an attempt at critical awareness of these obstacles and their raison d'être. In the face of pragmatic, reactionary, and fatalistic neoliberal philosophizing, I still insist, without falling into the trap of "idealism," on the absolute necessity of conscientization. In truth, conscientization is a requirement of our human condition. It is one of the roads we have to follow if we are to deepen our awareness of our world, of facts, of events, of the demands of human consciousness to develop our capacity for epistemological curiosity. Far from being alien to our human condition, conscientization is natural to "unfinished" humanity that is aware of its unfinishedness. It is natural because unfinishedness is integral to the phenomenon of life, which besides women and men includes the cheery trees in my garden and the birds that sing in their branches. (p. 55)

Considering hard situations of those poor people in the present economic recession and depression across the globe, thinking of those disappointed and miserable expressions on the faces of so many dying children and parents in Somali due to the famine in 2011, taking into account the fact that political illiteracy, nihilism, and disillusionment prevail among the younger generation worldwide, it is not hard to see that education did not perform its role of giving directions to people. On the contrary, domestication makes nearly everybody deeply ensnared as slaves in information technology and electronic communication. In this context, Freire's claim of "the absolute necessity of conscientization" is still relevant, valid, and compelling today.

## The Cultural Significance of Conscientization

Freire's critical pedagogy for human emancipation and freedom has taken deep root in the modernist discourse of humanism, so his work and theory are challenged by critics such as Ellsworth, Weiler, Hill, Andreotti, and others arguing from a postmodernist perspective. This requires reconsideration of whether Freire's critical pedagogy is adequate for addressing the specifics of oppression complicated by different discourses. For this purpose, a number of key concepts of Foucault's and Lyotard's cultural criticism of oppression and domination are employed to examine Freire's work and theory—in particular, the aspects of Freire's conscientized subject in his humanism, his claim of a universal human ethic, his certainty of the socialist orientation, and above all, whether his critical pedagogy will produce another new form of oppression and hegemony. This examination not only illuminates Freire's attitude toward postmodernism but also draws out the cultural significance of practicing conscientization.

### Freire's Conscientized Subject in His Humanism

To become a subject is central to Freire's notion of humanization and conscientization. However, the critique of universal thought and the demise of subject-centered reason in the postmodern discourse seem to mount a serious challenge to Freire's subject. As Roberts (2000) noted, while Freire has capitalized his notion of the knowing, praxical, and dialogical subject, postmodernists try to decenter this notion of subject and reject "the ideal of a self-directing, self-knowing, individual agent" (p. 147). In this context, it is imperative to determine a number of main features of Freire's conscientized subject in the light of Foucault's notion of care of the self.

According to Foucault (2002), human beings are caged in the structure of rationality and segmented by human sciences such as biology, philology, and economics. If Nietzsche tends to knock down Christianity and metaphysics, Foucault attempts to dismantle the cultural structure of rationality and human sciences.

As Marshall (1996) commented, if to be autonomous means to act morally and to act morally means to act rationally, these particular "new, unthought things, experiences and pleasures" can never be perceived, conceptualized and legitimated; by contrast, they can "enter the arena of thought concerned with caring for oneself through an appropriate exercise of liberty" (pp. 174–175). Therefore, while Marx discovers self-alienation in labor, Foucault discovers self-alienation in culture (Marshall, 1996).

In the rationalist episteme, abstraction and generalization often exercise reductionist violence on human life experience in specific discourses. Because self is always in a specific situation and a concrete discourse, the most fundamental way to defend human freedom must start with care of the self. Accordingly, Foucault (2000) advocated for the ethics of care for the self as a practice of freedom and building a different epistemology that favors the local and ethnocentric. However, it is equally important to note that Foucault's care for the self is not in an antagonistic position against care for others. Foucault (2000) declared clearly that care for the self essentially includes care for others. In this context, care for the self requires an in-depth concern for the being of both self and others.

Freire's (1998a) humanism grew out of the modernist discourse. However, his humanism was not caged in a rational structure of humanism or segmented by the modernist episteme; he merely cherished the modernist goal of human emancipation, liberty, and social justice. In a strict sense, his notion of the subject is a dialectical synthesis of an existential self and a historical being.

On the one hand, as an existential self, Freire's subject is not an abstract notion of a universal human being, normalized or prescribed by certain essential attributes. His humanist self is deeply influenced by existentialism. Freire (1972a) pointed out the following:

> A naively conceived humanism often overlooks the concrete, existential, present situation of real men. Authentic humanism, in Pierre Furter's words, "consists in permitting the emergence of the awareness of our full humanity, as a condition and as an obligation, as a situation and as a project." (p. 66)

Therefore, Freire (1972a) claimed the following: "Reflection upon situationality is reflection about the very condition of existence" (pp. 80–81). In fact, Freire's deep, sensitive, and attentive care of human existence in a local, specific, and present situation extends to some daily trivial things, normally ignored by other people.

In *Letters to Cristina*, Freire (1996) mentioned an elderly janitor. A group of scholars sat around a table discussing some theories. They kept asking the janitor to bring a coffee or to buy something from the nearby shop. The janitor rushed for different items in several runs. In the end, the elderly man became upset and asked why these people could not give him a list so that he could serve them once rather than several times. The janitor complained that these scholars were so occupied with their own thinking and talking that they had no time to say "thank you" to him. In this context, to say "thank you" is neither idle talk nor a matter of shallow politeness in a diplomatic way, but a means of showing sincere respect for this janitor's work, time, and above all, his being as a person. Freire often stresses the importance of humility. This small incidence of saying "thank you" to the elderly janitor illustrates that humility is in truth a manifestation of profound love of people and the world. It bears out the unique authenticity of Freire's ethics of care: care of the self starts with caring of others.

On the other hand, as a historical being, Freire's subject deviates from existentialist individualism but takes deep root in human praxis based on the metaphysical hope of making history. To be more precise, Freire conceptualizes the subject as a praxical and dialogical agent, conditioned but not limited by concrete sociocultural discourses. Accordingly, Freire's conscientized subjects are *on the move*, to shape social reality and to be shaped by social reality with the flexibility to resist different oppressive structures (Roberts, 1996). As Roberts (2000, p. 152) remarked, owing to its dialogical nature, "concerned with expanding the range of discourses within which people might actively and reflectively participate," Freire's language of conscientization is compatible with the language of discourse analysis.

Moreover, Freire fought against oppression in the front line together with those oppressed people. Because the oppressive and dominant system turned people into objects, to be a subject is to fight for the right of human existence. In this context, to be a subject is the deepest concern for those oppressed selves. This accounts for why Freire's conscientized subject stresses the consciousness of consciousness or the common sense beyond common sense. In particular, there is nothing wrong with emphasizing the notion of subject in educational discourse because an object can never learn. Hence, Freire's conscientized subject cannot be equated simplistically with a self-contained, self-constituting, abstracted, and stable subject.

Freire's epistemology is also different from the modernist episteme, the segmentation or alienation of human natural being as Foucault (2002) criticized. Freire rejects reducing a human being to "a thing," or merely a rational agent at the service of reason or labor by exercising the violence of metaphysics. He gives significance to the being of an entire human person. As Roberts (2010) commented, "Freire's philosophy became, in Pierre Hadot's (1995) terms, *a way of life*, rather than mere intellectualizing" (p. 34). Even knowing for Freire (1997) is a holistic whole: "I know with my entire body, with feelings, with passions, and also with reason" (p. 30). This is a manifestation of "functional moments," Foucault's (2002) comment on "the Classic episteme" (p. 338). Therefore, human affective, intellectual, and spiritual power are harmonized and unified in a conscious, concentrative, active, and curious process of knowing in teaching and learning (Freire & Shor, 1987). Emphasis should be placed equally on both feeling and understanding.

As mentioned in the first chapter, considering the changing nature of oppression in her practical dealings with students in a real concrete pedagogical situation, Ellsworth (1989) noted that "if these assumptions, goals, implicit power dynamics, and issues of who produces valid knowledge remain un-theorised and untouched, critical pedagogies will continue to perpetuate relations of domination in their classrooms" (p. 297). However, as Freire (1993a) claimed, "oppression must always be understood in its multiple and contradictory instances, just as liberation must be grounds in the particularity of suffering and struggle in concrete, historical experiences, without resorting to transcendental guarantees" (p. x).

Ellsworth (1989) was insightful to see that "there are no social positions exempt from becoming oppressive to others ... any group—any position—can move into the oppressor role" (p. 322). This reflection is a good departure point of conscientization. However, unfortunately, Ellsworth stopped there. Thus, it is essential to clarify that the whole point, the ultimate aim and the soul of conscientization, is that a teacher as a cultural worker can work out a humanizing teaching and learning program so that every student is cared for and loved as a real person in a healthy, dialogical, and humane atmosphere and thus real learning can occur. In other words, conscientization prompts a teacher to conduct deep, critical, and intimate research into the internal relation between students and teachers, between human beings and the social reality, and between specific sociocultural conditions and the irreducible meaning of life. If anything drawn from any thinker's theory including Freire's stops the realization of this ultimate aim, it should be abandoned immediately. Therefore, the assumption of all assumptions, the goal of all goals, and the principle of all principles in Freire's liberating education is humanization: to make humanity alive in educational settings, either the formal learning in a classroom or the informal learning outside a classroom.

## Freire's Universal Human Ethic

Freire (1998a) claimed "a universal human ethic" (p. 23). This makes people associate Freire's claim with the concept of metanarratives. In order to clarify whether Freire's universal human ethic is a metanarrative, a study of Lyotard's conceptualization of metanarratives is imperative.

A metanarrative is a term Lyotard (1984) used to identify the postmodern condition of knowledge. According to Lyotard, a metanarrative is a metadiscourse that contains universal rules and principles. These rules and principles are appealed to resolve a dispute that arises between the "small discourses" or "language games" (*petits recits*), in which different people are engaged. For him, the history of Western philosophy is replete with metadiscourses such as the absolute Spirit, the hermeneutics of meaning, the emancipation of the working and rational subject, the creation of national wealth, and so forth. In any case, the appeal to a metadiscourse is an attempt to legitimate one's own discourse. However, this legitimation, characteristic of modernity or the modernist practice, fails eventually. In the postmodern condition of knowledge, it is no longer possible to call for universal rules and principles that can apply across all discourses. That is, there are no universal rules and principles but merely language games or small discourses instead, defined themselves by their own set of rules.

In the discourse marked off by the absence of metadiscourses, there must be conflict between two language games or small discourses. Nonetheless, when this conflict occurs, each game or small discourse should try to dominate others by totalizing its own field with its own internal rules and principles. In this case, there could be two consequences: either the conflict remains unresolved or one discourse is dissolved into a totality dominated by the other discourse.

Any conflict between at least two parties cannot be equitably resolved. This is due to the lack of a rule of judgment applicable to both or all arguments. Lyotard (1988) defined this phenomenon as a *differend*, the effect of the death of metanarratives. The core of a differend is to respect differences and to put every *wrong* into phrases. Within a totalizing discourse, the wrong arises in the first place by virtue of the fact that the rules of discourse of the wrong are not legitimated and recognized as valid. That is, the wrong does not necessarily mean it is wrong in truth but only that the victim loses legitimatization and recognition. According to Lyotard (1988), there is a multiplicity of small discourses; to import a question from one discourse to or impose that question upon any other small discourse amounts to oppression. Oppression is an ethical problem. To respect differences avoids oppression, but it needs justifying differends. The justification requires waging a war against totality. Failing to do so gives rise to injustice and perpetuates wrongs such as the wrong suffered by the Jewish people under Nazism or the wrong suffered by the oppressed people everywhere. In this case, a matter of life and death for stopping this unnecessary human suffering and these tragedies, such as what happened to Jews, is to respect and justify differends.

The way Lyotard (1988) offered for anti-oppression or to respect differences was to present the unpresentable or to make the unpresentable visible. Since something legitimated as wrong does not necessarily mean it has no right to exist, it is injustice to forbid that wrong to have the chance for game playing. The binding force of the normativity or the rule of just game playing always lies in game playing itself. Hence, Lyotard (1988) argued, the first crucial step to fight against totalization is to awaken and sharpen the consciousness and sensitivity of presenting the unpresentable. This requires reflecting on what is not there in familiar discourses or some small discourses legitimated as wrong. Since the unpresentable is not there and cannot be put into phrases, it is decisive to develop a feeling for it. This feeling is Kant's reflective judgment, which can be generated from reflecting upon thinking (Lyotard, 1994).

Like Lyotard, Freire (1993a, 1998a) also stressed the need to respect differences. His education for conscientization in essence is an effective weapon to counter the domestication of any forms of metanarratives and to represent the unpresentable of the oppressed by means of cultivating critical consciousness. In this context, "a universal human ethic" should not be understood as a metanarrative uncritically and simplistically.

As Roberts (2005) remarked, "we must take some things as given if we are to ask a thoughtful question or develop a coherent line of critique or pose a well-conceived problem" (p. 452). These "some things as given" are important because they give criteria or standards when people make judgments and evaluations in the process of their criticism. By the same logic, Freire's universal human ethic serves as a moral code to uphold the inviolability of human dignity with moral certainty. Its fundamental claims are as follows: All human beings are human people; they are entitled to fulfill human potential and become more human. Therefore, under no condition and by no means can human beings be alienated and made into units of production or into commodities. The word *universal* used by Freire is not to deny the facts of historical and cultural specificity and obscure the dignity of being an individual human person. Rather, it indicates a shared ethical standpoint as well as a shared understanding of humanity underlying these specific facts. From this shared ethical standpoint and understanding of humanity, these dehumanizing issues such as inequalities and injustices can be well examined and identified.

Freire (1998a) stated clearly that a universal human ethic is employed to battle against these humiliating and degrading living and working conditions that mortify the human body and stultify the human mind at this globalization age. In short, it is the antihumanist character of the market ethics that drove Freire to claim a universal human ethic. As he explained, a universal human ethic speaks of an ethic that dares to condemn dehumanizing exercises such as "the ideological discourse" of market ethics; "the exploitation of labour and the manipulation that makes a rumour into truth and truth into a mere rumour"; "the fabrication of illusions, in which the unprepared become hopelessly trapped and the weak and the defenceless are destroyed"; "making promises when one has no intention of keeping one's word, which causes lying to become an almost necessary way of life"; "the calumny of character assassination simply for the joy of it"; and "the fragmentation of the utopia of human solidarity" (p. 23).

Therefore, Freire's claim of a universal human ethic is not a metanarrative imposed top-down by the dominant power groups to justify their own interests and hegemony. It is a practice of conscientization, a resistance to the metanarratives of market ethics, a respect for the differences of the wretched of the earth, and an advocacy for making their unpresentable suffering and misery presentable.

## Freire's Certainty of His Socialist Orientation

Andreotti (2009) criticized Freire's certainty of his socialist orientation from her pluralist postcolonial epistemological perspective. She argued that future possibilities are better left open to negotiation.

The defence of Freire's political certainty helps to illuminate Freire's viewpoints on the limitations of postmodernism. Freire had a high opinion of power relations and respecting difference espoused by those postmodernist thinkers. However, he cautioned against "sacrificing some of modernity's most laudable goals" because "excursions into the discourse of postmodern social theory are often purchased at the price of sacrificing narratives of freedom underwritten by an ethical imagination" (Freire, 1993a, p. x). In the same light, McLaren and Leonard (1993) pointed out that the postmodernist thought in its "most conservative form" lacks "a political will," and the proliferation of new, complex, difficult language that expresses postmodernist ideas obfuscates these ideas and makes them meaningless and ineffective to ordinary people (p. 6). To put it simply, difficult language without a political will and altruistic concern have made many people, in particular, the younger generation, politically illiterate. In this cultural milieu of political apathy and disempowerment, who can participate in the negotiation about future possibilities and speak for people's will is highly questionable. Thus, Freire (1993a) argued as follows: "Current epistemological and ontological shifts taking place in social theory must be firmly grounded in human narratives of emancipation and social justice" (p. x). His certainty of socialist orientation is no more than a manifestation of his political will.

Indeed, epistemological pluralists are deeply concerned about the dehumanizing disasters brought about by metanarratives. However, while they may offer some useful ideas for creating a space in which difference is recognized and allowed to speak, pluralist negotiation without certainty of social change courts political passivity and encourages a culture of silence. These are features that sustain the hegemony of the dominant system. Effectively, pluralist thinkers have found a theoretical home, but the problem of oppression remains (see further, Clothier, 2000).

In the age of globalization, the market ethics espoused by neo-liberalism is perhaps the largest meta-narrative that exists. To divert the attention of the oppressed to negotiate for fear that in the future, another form of oppression and domination will be produced, is a gross misunderstanding of how power works. It is to throw away the apple because of the core. As Freire (1997) warned, while the Right is becoming stronger in solidarity, "we tend to divide forces fighting among and against ourselves, instead of fighting the common enemy" (p. 86).

More importantly, sometimes social contradictions are hard to reconcile through any negotiation. Therefore, in a revolutionary social change discourse, it is praxis rather than negotiation that ultimately determines future possibilities. If actions are ignored, negotiation will not add up to anything meaningful and constructive. The best way to counter oppression and domination can only be found in the practice of struggling against oppression and domination. An ancient Chinese fable used by Mao (2009) is a powerful illustration of this point:

> There is an ancient Chinese fable called "The Foolish Old Man Who Removed the Mountains." It tells of an old man who lived in northern China long, long ago and was known as the Foolish Old Man of North Mountain. His house faced south and beyond his doorway stood the two great peaks, Taihang and Wangwu, obstructing the way. He called his sons, and hoe in hand they began to dig up these mountains with great determination. Another greybeard, known as the Wise Old Man, saw them and said derisively, "How silly of you to do this! It is quite impossible for you few to dig up those two huge mountains." The Foolish Old Man replied, "When I die, my sons will carry on; when they die, there will be my grandsons, and then their sons and grandsons, and so on to infinity. High as they are, the mountains cannot grow any higher and with every bit we dig, they will be that much lower. Why can't we clear them away?" Having refuted the Wise Old Man's wrong view, he went on digging every day, unshaken in his conviction. God was moved by this, and he sent down two angels, who carried the mountains away on their backs. Today, two big mountains lie like a dead weight on the Chinese people. One is imperialism; the other is feudalism. The Chinese Communist Party has long made up its mind to dig them up. We must persevere and work unceasingly, and we, too, will touch God's heart. Our God is none other than the masses of the Chinese people. If they stand up and dig together with us, why can't these two mountains be cleared away? (para. 3)

In this technological age, the problems people face are more complex, specific, and subtle than Mao's time. However, these problems will not undermine the praxical spirit expressed in this passage: The fount of power and change is praxis. Keeping the status quo yields no hope, and to rely too much on negotiation often ends up with the Wise Old Man's fatalist verbalism. Even in the course of negotiation, what is available for negotiating about what to do tomorrow is often what is happening now and what people are doing today.

It must be noted that a certain social orientation is an essential prerequisite for human revolutionary praxis. Talk of social change cannot go without knowing what sort of society is going to be built. Without a social orientation, people's actions will be directionless. This will not only narrow down the scope of living history as possibility but also lurk the risk of killing people's sociohistorical responsibility. Therefore, Freire's certainty of the socialist orientation is a showcase of his sociological and historical imagination.

Nevertheless, in terms of the socialist orientation, two key points must be made clear. First, it is not the certainty of the future that oppresses people. Rather, it is the domestication of thinking about the future that oppresses people. This is why Freire (2007) advocated for daring to dream. Second, no social orientation is flawless. Any social orientation must be subject to praxis and dialogue. Likewise, Freire's socialist orientation should not be treated as the unchangeable absolute truth, permanently right and good. It should be open to critical reflection and the test of practice.

Freire feels certain about socialism, but he was fully aware of certain historical lessons from previous socialist practice. Hence, in his later years, Freire (1996, 1997) proposed to build capitalist democracy on the basis of socialism. It would seem that Freire attempted to draw on the advantages of both socialist and capitalist systems—that is, to introduce the superstructure of capitalist democracy on the top of a socialist economic base. However, Freire did not develop his political theory of socialism in theoretical thoroughness, and he did not work out how to put it into practice.

There are at least two preconditions for realizing true socialism by means of introducing capitalist democracy as a superstructure. One is to ensure that state planning based on common ownership can serve as an effective engine to uphold high levels of cooperation and coordination, while productivity is enhanced without undermining individual welfare. The other is to form a stronghold with the majority of intellectuals who can function as the social conscience to maintain genuine liberty and democracy in a socialist system. It is hard to deny that one of the mainstays of capitalist democracy is its "organic intellectuals." Therefore, to build capitalist democracy as a superstructure based on socialism ultimately necessitates the support of the "organic intellectuals" of socialism, as claimed by Gramsci. Otherwise, the capitalist democratic system is hard to incorporate into a socialist economic system. In this case, the foremost task is a long-term cultural revolution and also evolution to subvert the ideological hegemony of private property based on individualism, deeply rooted in nearly everybody's mind. This again speaks loudly for the necessity of practicing conscientization.

## Freire's Critical Pedagogy: Another New Form of Oppression and Hegemony?

Hill (2001) contended that, compared with Foucault's antiparadigmatic approach, Freire's paradigmatic approach may lead to another new form of hegemonic ideology to maintain another new dominant world order and social structure. This challenge, out of a profound concern for genuine freedom and democracy, draws out the cultural significance of conscientization.

Hill (2001) argued that within the discourse of care of self, Freire can be criticized on the grounds that he combats the limiting ideas of others but only at the cost of advancing his own socialist and Catholic variations. However, this does not necessarily mean that Freire's critical pedagogy theory, influenced by socialism and the theology of liberation, will produce another new form of oppression and hegemony. If Foucault's (1980) concept of power is taken into account, it is the nature of the power/knowledge regime, to which Freire's theory is applied, that determines whether his theory will fall into another form of oppression and hegemony. For example, in a dictatorship power/knowledge regime, if every word Freire says is taken as universal and absolute truth while all other thinkers' theories are denied, his theory, either with or without paradigms, will inescapably yield another new form of oppression and hegemony. However, if in a liberating and democratic power/knowledge regime, everybody's theories, including Freire's, are subject to critical judgment and examination, Freire's theory cannot find a channel to generate another new form of oppression and hegemony. This accounts for why Freire attempted to introduce Western capitalist democracy into socialism to counter the system problem of dictatorship. Therefore, what really matters is what sort of power/knowledge regime people find themselves in.

In this context, three insightful points in Foucault's (1982) analysis of power deserve attention. One is that power is exercised through action, over or upon action, by means of power relationships. Thus, he argued, "a society without power relations can only be an abstraction" (Foucault, 1982, p. 791). If power works in a relationship, then if one party is stronger while the other is weaker, the stronger party is likely to be in a position of domination. It is crucial to realize that where there is domination, there is the danger of oppression. This is because domination often ruins the equilibrium of a power relationship. Furthermore, power relations permeate all walks of life. Among them, two power relationships are most likely to produce unbearable domination. One is the relationship between an individual and the social system. An individual is always on the weak side and thus is easier to oppress. The other is the relationship between the ruling class and the ruled class in a class society. The ruling class, controlling the government and instruments of power, is often in a position of domination. However, for Foucault, there are always ruptures, tensions, and contradictions in any power relationship, and these ruptures, tensions, and contradictions bring about change time after time. As Freire (1985) remarked, where there is domination and oppression, there will also be anti-domination and anti-oppression. Therefore, the dominant power is not permanent and invincible, and those who hold power in office are not determined and predestined.

The second point is that any power relationship takes deep root in the social nexus (Foucault, 1982). In this case, power is in fact multifaceted and power relationships vary from one discourse to another. For example, a male worker may be oppressed by his boss, but he can be an oppressor to his wife and children (Weiler, 1991).

The third point is the most important: Every piece of knowledge is inscribed in power (Foucault, 1980). This inseparable nexus of power and knowledge forms the being of human beings and makes them the subjects of power. It is known as the power/knowledge nexus: power as constitutive of identity and knowledge as constitutive of power.

Combining Foucault's analysis of power relationships and the power/knowledge nexus gives a new analyzing tool for understanding the dialectical relation between historical events and power/knowledge notions. Since all disciplines, including political, economic, cultural, and educational forces, are inscribed in the power/knowledge nexus, it would seem that conventional ways of viewing history are burdened by unfolding causal forces. That is, historical events and facts cannot be understood as inevitable historical processes, as Hegel and Marx claimed. Rather, because historical events can shape and be shaped by the power/knowledge nexus, historical processes are no more than organization and reorganization of these power and knowledge relations. At the same time, individual and social identities are also shaped by relations of knowledge and power. If history is examined in this way, these power/knowledge regimes, either at present or in the past, should not be seen as inevitable end results of historical movements. They must be seen as possible end results of human invention in specific historical contexts, passing themselves off as historically necessary. As human invention, they change in accordance with the change of their social and discursive conditions. In this sense, to take contingent happenings as necessity and natural laws of history is only to play the language game of metanarratives. Therefore, Foucault contributes an alternative narrative of human history and a revolutionary way to understand it.

His power/knowledge nexus not only reveals the deepest reality of history but also shows a fundamental way to human freedom.

Nonetheless, in order to dismantle a dominant and oppressive system, it is necessary to establish another form of oppression and coercion. At the same time, the new hegemonic cultural discourse must be created simultaneously to destroy the previous oppressive discourses or hegemonic culture. In this way, old power/knowledge relations must be replaced by new power/knowledge relations. This is why, as human lived experience witnesses, once a new power/knowledge regime is established, there is the danger that it will come to exercise domination and oppression again. Furthermore, political judgments, conclusions, choices, and decisions in any power/truth regime inevitably yield ethical consequences. Because human beings have not found a perfect social system, and problems of human consciousness such as egoism, lust, greed, and ambition perennially exist, nothing and nobody guarantee that people in a new dominant power/knowledge regime will draw right conclusions and make flawless judgments, decisions, and choices all the time. Then what matters is how to make any human choices and judgment in a dominant power/knowledge regime subject to regular evaluation, criticism, and readjustment. Under such circumstances, it is imperative to forge a critical and emancipatory power/knowledge regime, whose discursive practice not only works as a conscious resistance to oppression and hegemony but also prevents itself from falling into a newer form of domination and hegemony (Giroux, 1992).

If Foucault shows where the seeds of social change for liberation are, then Freire illustrates how to make them grow. By examining the concept of history in a revolutionary discourse from both a materialist and existentialist perspective, Freire combines the praxis of making history with human existence in everyday lives with acute consciousness of incompleteness. With such sound and profound philosophical underpinnings, education for conscientization, as a practical and fundamental way for developing people's sociohistorical awareness of existence, serves as an effective revolutionary human intervention to fight against any forms of domestication of the fatalist way of philosophizing the world and history. While the cultivation of critical consciousness performs the function of social criticism and examination, the cultivation of conscience fulfills the role of self-criticism. Therefore, with its ethical commitment to humanization, with its political will of emancipation and social justice, and with its authenticity of being critical, praxical, and dialogical, conscientization promotes a cultural practice of genuine freedom and democracy. It is compatible with the progressive trend of postmodernism. It does play a significant educational role in not only creating a critical and liberating power/knowledge regime but also in upholding its ongoing humanizing performance.

# CHAPTER EIGHT

# The Pedagogical Possibilities of Conscientization

Conscientization, the cultivation of critical consciousness and conscience, as a main agency of cultural subversion, is pedagogically feasible. It has the potential to be realized in concrete daily pedagogical situations.

## Conscientization Maintains Humanizing Education

Conscientization can fundamentally uphold humanizing education. Its theoretical worthiness may reenvision education as a revolutionary intervention and a human act that fosters pedagogical love and simultaneously nurtures and protects epistemological curiosity. This reenvisioning also encourages the posing of new and different questions to better understand the notion of the individual in the formal educational settings.

### Conscientization Promotes Education as Revolutionary Intervention

To engage a humanizing education process fully, it would seem necessary to better understand, for instance, the nature of the individual person. Here, Bruner's (1990) cultural explanation of human beings is helpful. Bruner is a psychologist who stresses folk psychology and narrative explication but objects to explaining human beings biologically. For him, human biological inheritance is not the universal cause of human action and experience, so it cannot direct or shape human life but impose constraints on the human mind. He attempts to propose a view that will reverse the traditional relation of biology and culture with respect to individuation, and particularly, human nature. He remarked as follows:

> Cultures characteristically devise "prosthetic devices" that permit us to transcend "raw" biological limits ... it is culture that gives meaning to action by situating its underlying intentional states in an interpretive system. It does this by imposing the patterns inherent in the culture's symbolic systems—its language and discourse mode, the forms of logical and narrative explication, and the patterns of mutually dependent communal life. (p. 34)

Hence, an individual person cannot be an individual without culture in which socialization occurs. As Bruner quotes Polkinghorne, "Self, then, is not a static thing or a substance, but a configuring of personal events into a historical unity which includes not only what one has been but also anticipations of what one will be" (Polkinghorne in Bruner, 1990, p. 116). Therefore, socialization precedes individuation. An individual person is always a social product of individuation out of socialization. She or he, either young or old, cannot be abstracted from the metaphysical study of human beings.

In the study of the mental and social life of babies, Kaye (1982) determined that a socialization process naturally starts with the mutual accommodation between an infant and parents. Through a period of time of social interaction, a child's consciousness of rules, signs, and other people develops to a stage of her or his realization that she or he is actually a member in a particular system, which she or he shares with other individuals. This marks off the consciousness of self. As Kaye quotes Pliny, "Man [sic] is the only one that knows nothing, that can learn nothing without being taught. He can neither speak nor walk nor eat, and in short he can do nothing at the prompting of nature only, but weep" (Pliny in Kaye, 1982, p. 54). Without mentioning an infant or a child, whose individuation is interdependently born out of the attachment to parents for self-protection, even for an adult, running into a foreign environment, socialization starts again. If the being or life of human beings is always in a becoming process, socialization will never stop throughout life.

Indeed, when an individual is born into the world, she or he is definitely cast into certain social and cultural relations, which have already been given. Fitting in and becoming familiar with certain social and cultural customs and norms become a necessity for both individual and social survival. This defines one of the essential meanings of education. It makes Dewey's (1916) educational view relevant:

The primary ineluctable facts of the birth and death of each one of the constituent members in a social group determine the necessity of education. On one hand, there is the contrast between the immaturity of the new-born members of the group—its future sole representatives and customs of that group. On the other hand, there is the necessity that these immature members be not merely physically preserved in adequate numbers, but that they be initiated into the interests, purposes, information, skill and practices of mature members: otherwise, the group will cease its characteristic life. (p. 2)

Thus, Dewey believed that education through schooling plays a pivotal and unavoidable role of socialization. However, education as socialization is always carried out in concrete sociocultural and historical contexts. Given that education is forever political and ideological, Freire preferred the term *intervention* to *socialization* with regard to the role of education. The question for Freire, as Roberts (2000) pointed out, was not "How can one, as an educator, avoid intervening in the lives of others?" but "What *form* will this intervention take?" (p. 127).

According to Freire (1998a, 1972a), education as intervention takes two basic forms. One is domestication, trying to reinforce people's adaptability to the status quo. This type of education performs the function of making people conform to "a given and 'unchangeable' situation" (Freire, 1998a, p. 73). The other form is liberation, trying to empower people's capacity to take a radical, critical, and revolutionary position for nonconformity. This form of education requires not only denouncing the injustice in the existing system but also announcing the dream or a new utopia of a new society. Conscientization, targeting social justice and freedom, will make education act as a revolutionary human intervention, thus allowing teaching and learning to happen in an open, humane, free, democratic, and dialogical environment. It will play a positive, constructive, and helpful role in shaping every individual's being-formation and becoming more.

## Conscientization Turns Education Into a Human Act

Education as dialogical intervention is ethical at every moment. In short, teaching is a human act (Freire, 1998a). An episode from my supervision of a student teacher's teaching practice in China more than 10 years ago sheds light on this point.

Ningrong Hu, a student teacher, was giving her English lesson in a primary school. The pupils were about 7 or 8 years old. She told students that if any of them could answer her question, she or he would get an apple as a prize. The apple was actually prepared to teach students the English word "apple." Unexpectedly, two boys shouted the answer nearly simultaneously. Because of their young age, each of them ran to the student teacher in the platform and tried to grab the apple for his own. This kind of occurrence in classroom teaching is very hard to predict in any lesson preparation in advance. However, with a quick response to this new situation, Hu asked the whole class promptly, first in English and then in Chinese, "Can we destroy our friendship because of one apple?" The whole class answered "no" and the two boys stopped grabbing the apple immediately and stood timidly in the front of the classroom. Hu then asked the class how to deal with the matter. The whole class answered, "To halve the apple." Then Hu cut the apple into two parts and gave a half to each boy as a prize for the right answer.

If Hu did not care about the friendship among those pupils and only focused on subject transmission, there could have been two outcomes. One is that she could have abused her teacher's authority to scold the two students for their dispute so that her teaching could carry on. The other is that she could have neglected to control the two boys' argument, leaving her teaching disrupted. Both cases would turn a learning incentive into a painful experience.

This is merely a moment in Hu's teaching practice, but it suffices to show that teaching is a human act every moment rather than merely a transfer of knowledge and technical training. As a matter of fact, many teachers have caring personalities and desire to help their students achieve highly at school. Nel Noddings is a good example: "School had played a central role in Noddings' life as a student herself, and her early experiences with caring teachers contributed to a career-long interest in student–teacher relations" (Flinders, 2001, p. 210). However, the evaluation of both students' and teachers' performance is based on the workload prescribed by curriculum making controlled by the scaling system, in which those disadvantaged are often excluded by normalization of scaling test marks. This will shift teachers' authentic care and attention from students as human persons to knowledge transfer and at the same time reduce students' school performance to only academic reports. Conscientization will encourage teachers to shift from merely transmission of subject knowledge such as English language, mathematics, physics, and technical training to the care of the well-being of human development. It helps fight against the banking mode of education, including the scaling of students' performance in a discriminative and inhumane way.

Therefore, "it must do everything to ensure an atmosphere in the classroom where teaching, learning, and studying are serious acts, but also ones that generate happiness" (Freire, 1997, p. 90). Freire (1998a) listed a number of fundamental human qualities and virtues for carrying out an authentic progressive democratic education, such as "a generous loving heart, respect for others, tolerance, humility, a joyful disposition, love of life, openness to what is new, a disposition to welcome change, perseverance in the struggle, a refusal of determinism, a spirit of hope, openness to justice," eagerness to start a dialogue, and willingness to listen (p. 108).

In this case, conscientization will not play a troublemaker role to turn classroom teaching and learning into a political battlefield, full of unhappy and unsettled disputes, as some critics feared. It also will not pose some extraordinary hardships to teachers and students. It only aims to turn education into a human act.

## Conscientization Fosters Pedagogical Love

If education is intrinsically and forever ethical, it should become a project of love first. The importance and the unique meaning of love to education are well spelled out by Tolstoy's educational experience. In her book *Teacher*, Ashton-Warner (1963) described how Tolstoy taught and lived with his pupils. When the idea of opening a school to teach the peasant children for his county forcibly and clearly comes to Tolstoy as the most important thing of all, he realizes his dream. Tolstoy discards the standard and well-regulated school systems, all existing traditions and the methods already in use, and rejects all these punishments. He fathoms each peasant child's mind first and allows the students to teach himself the art of teaching. Tolstoy encourages his pupils to choose their own subjects freely and to work as much as they desire. He tries best to proffer assistance for each individual child in each case. Eventually mutual passionate affection develops between both the teacher and the pupils. Basil Borosov, one of Tolstoy's pupils, said the following 50 years later:

> Hours passed like minutes. If life were always as gay no one would ever notice it go by …. In our pleasures, in our gaiety, in our rapid progress, we soon became as thick as thieves with the Count. We were unhappy without the Count, and the Count was unhappy without us. We were inseparable, and only night drew us apart …. There was no end to our conversations. We told him a lot of things; about sorcerers, about forest devils …. (Borosov in Ashton-Warner, 1963, p. 30)

Here schooling or education becomes an act of displaying humanity and goodness. Tolstoy's pedagogical love transformed the schooling environment into a cozy home, in which those pupils were able to learn freely and grow happily. Conscientization is conducive to fostering pedagogical love. With cultivating conscience, it helps build a good rapport between teachers and students to maintain joyful teaching and learning.

## Conscientization Upholds Epistemological Curiosity

At the very beginning of his *The Metaphysics*, Aristotle (1933–1935) remarked that, by nature, all men and women are yearning for knowledge; it is an indication of the esteem for human senses. In the same light, Freire (1998a) argued that curiosity is the foundation for knowledge production:

> Among us women and men, we recognize our unfinishedness, and this awareness necessarily implies our insertion in a permanent process of search, motivated by a curiosity that surpasses the limits that are peculiar to the life phenomenon as such, becoming progressively the ground and the foundation for the production of knowledge, for that curiosity is already knowledge. (p. 55)

Thus, it is not education that makes human beings educable; rather, it is human historical awareness of being unfinished, finite, and mortal (Freire, 1998a). This awareness of unfinishedness or incompleteness motivates and activates human "epistemological curiosity," a term Freire (1998a, p. 55) employed to denote leaning and knowing curiosity. Epistemological curiosity is an ontological human condition for existence; even the domestication or the banking concept of education cannot extinguish it (Freire, 1998a). However, this does not mean that students' epistemological curiosity does not suffer in a domestication schooling system. Conscientization, aiming at removing social fetters and creating favorable schooling environment for real leaning and knowledge production, will play an important role in nurturing and protecting epistemological curiosity and promoting its development.

## Potentialities for Realizing Conscientization in Daily Pedagogical Situations

Education as human intervention can go both as the preservation of the status quo and as the service of social change. However, it is a fundamental error to take education as simply an instrument for the reproduction of the dominant ideology or as merely an instrument for unmasking and dismantling the hegemonic ideology (Freire, 1998a). The project of denouncing injustice and announcing a possible utopia of a new society cannot be perceived naively or simplistically as if it can be accomplished fundamentally and easily. In fact, any revolutionary educational intervention inevitably takes place in a domesticating educational atmosphere of the preservation of the status quo sponsored by the dominant political and economic system. This makes the work of unmasking or decoding the dominant ideology more complex and more difficult.

Nonetheless, the nature of education is dialectical (Freire, 1998a). The domestication maintained by the dominant power is hard to change, but this does not suggest that change is impossible. Under domination and domestication, there are always contradictions, tensions, and ruptures in the social sphere of schooling. This is because domestication cannot erase away all teachers' ethical responsibility for their students. In particular, any dominant power cannot stop these virtuous and compassionate teachers' spiritual willing and pursuit of the good for those disadvantaged students. Herein reside great potentialities for realizing conscientization in pedagogical practice. Mr. Mattingly's intervention helps to elaborate this point.

## Mr. Mattingly's Intervention

Mr. Mattingly's educational intervention, highlighted in this section, is abridged from Adam Howard's life story based on his article, "Lessons of Poverty: Towards a Literacy of Survival" (2005).

Adam was born into a small poor community in eastern Kentucky. He was the second child of his parents; he had an elder sister and a younger brother. His father began preaching at 13 and travelled from one small town to another across Kentucky and Tennessee and thus met his mother as a travelling evangelist.

Both of Adam's parents were jobless because of disabilities and poor health. His father had been sick since he was a child, but unable to afford proper health care, he was not exactly sure what was wrong with him. Adam only knew that his father had a stomach problem and when a spell came to him, it could nearly take his life. As Adam recalled, these spells hit his father frequently and made him bedridden, curled in a fetal position for days or weeks. They could not afford proper medical attention, and Adam's father was only medically attended to when these spells tortured him unbearably. Adam's mother had a psychological illness of inability to be around people. This illness was untreated and undiagnosed for all her life. She was also a diabetic and died of a heart condition in her early 40s.

Adam's family lived in a small house next to his father's parents until he was 4, using money from a government subsidy for his father's disability. Then the government money was cut off due to welfare reform. Adam's father had worked as a groundskeeper at a local cemetery right after high school, but one of his spells at work had made him lose that job. He had not held a job since. When the reform took place, his father's unchanged health condition did not allow him to find some backbreaking jobs, practically available in the area. Without the government subsidy, the only source of income, the family could not manage to pay their rent and bills. Having no place to go, they moved into the basement of the church where his father served as the preacher and stayed there for a year. They survived on food given generously by churchgoers. Desperate for money, Adam's father had unnecessary surgery that year. This was his 10th surgery. Most of those surgeries were not necessary and made his condition even worse. In the end, the surgery could only serve as evidence to prove his father's disability and made him eligible to again receive disability benefits from the federal government. With this income, they could afford to rent a house of their own.

From a very young age, Adam could see how much pain his father was in when the spells struck him. His mother was not one of those parents who hid the hardships of life from her children. Adam, his brother, and his sister saw the facts and details of living in poverty with their own eyes. They knew how difficult it was for their parents to make ends meet, to clothe and feed themselves and to deal with their own health problems. Adam's father had graduated from high school and his mother had completed 10 years of formal schooling, which was a higher level of literacy than most people in their local community. Owing to the pressure of survival, they did not read to Adam and his sister and brother; they also did not spend time with them rehearsing the alphabet and numbers. They simply taught the children different lessons about knowing what life in poverty was like and how to struggle for survival.

However, the formal schooling system did not take into account the specifics of these learning experiences in poverty. Without considering the fact that most adults in the community were illiterate, Adam's school placed unrealistic expectations on the students from those poor and illiterate families. According to Adam, even at the kindergarten level, children were expected to have some necessary preschool preparations and some preliterate behaviors or skills, for example, to be able to recite the alphabet, to do some basic counting, to write one's name, and to know the right way to hold books. This expectation of cultural habits was not a problem for the young children who were able to learn about reading and writing in a literate home environment. However, for students like Adam, the school environment was strange and unfamiliar and had little to do with their previous lived experiences at home and in their own community. Therefore, they felt uncomfortable.

Adam's painting lesson is a good example. According to him, painting took up a big part of his teacher's curriculum. All the other pupils in the class loved painting and considered it a special treat because they had no materials to paint at home. However, this was not the case for Adam. He worried about ruining his clothes. It had something to do with a barn painting experience he had gone through together with his grandfather and his brother the previous summer. Before painting the barn, his grandfather told the two brothers not to ruin their clothing by fooling around with the paint; otherwise, he would get scolded by their mother. Adam listened to his grandfather and did not get one speck of paint on his clothes. But his brother didn't listen and got paint all over him. When they arrived home, Adam's mother had an argument with his grandfather and punished his brother for not listening. In the painting class, Adam felt like his teacher was asking him to do something wrong that his brother had done, which was against his grandfather's warning and would lead him to his mother's punishment. Facing a white piece of paper, brushes, and small cups filled with paint provided by their teacher, most of the pupils set about drawing pictures such as a house, a tree, and a cat as assigned. But Adam refused to follow the teacher and left the paint untouched. His protest lasted until he received his mother's permission to paint, when she asked him to paint a picture for her birthday.

For needy children, clothes, shoes, and schoolbags might mean more than learning. Adam wrote the following:

> This is the first, but not the only, memory I have of the conflict between the lessons that I learned from my family about living in poverty—in this case, *don't ruin your clothes because we don't have money for new clothes*—and the lessons that I learned at school—in this assignment, *don't worry about getting paint on your clothes*. I did have to worry. At five, I knew Mom and Dad couldn't afford to buy me new clothes if I ruined what I had. I was well aware of how hard it was for my parents to not only make sure we had clothing on our backs, but also a roof over our heads. I learned that, in part, from my experiences living in poverty and the everyday reality my family faced in their struggle to make ends meet. Along with what I learned from my experiences, though, I was taught important lessons about living from my family; lessons that were often disregarded and misunderstood in formal schooling. (Howard, 2005, p. 80)

The living in poverty seen, experienced, and learned in Adam's family and community not only shaped his identity, his value of life, and his understanding of the world, but it also taught him particular habits of knowing, learning, and doing, and certain ways of feeling and thinking. However, the schooling community normalized by the system made knowledge, beliefs, actions, and habits of the children like Adam physically and culturally irrelevant and disconnected. Consequently, real learning hardly came to them. Adam's brother and several of his classmates graduated high school functionally illiterate.

In the same way, Adam experienced being singled out and excluded in his school at the very beginning. Because of speech problems and his lack of preliterate skills, Adam was diagnosed with a learning disability. He was regarded as the child from a poor family neither with intellectual abilities to learn nor with the necessary family support to help him learn. Finally, he was placed in a remedial class together with students with behavior disorders, housed together in the ground floor of his school. Adam could be excluded by the educational system if he did not meet Mr. Mattingly in class. As Adam said gratefully, it was Mr. Mattingly who established him a cultural bridge, a connection between the "literacy of survival" (as Adam called it) and the discursive practice of formal schooling.

Mr. Mattingly came to know Adam in his seventh-grade English class. Before long, he discovered the secret that Adam was actually illiterate. That is, his learning problems were caused by his illiteracy. As Adam wrote, before Mr. Mattingly, his poverty was misdiagnosed as a learning disability and was also mistaken as stupidity by his school officials and most of his teachers at school. His identity was equated with his poverty. According to Adam, his previous teachers maybe had noticed his status of being illiterate, but they had not known how to deal with it or refused to know the everyday realities he and his community faced. After Mr. Mattingly found out Adam was still illiterate, he asked Adam to stay after school and gave him extra lessons. Adam uttered something he had never spoken. Genuine dialogues started to go on between Mr. Mattingly and Adam. Adam's educational experiences changed after his seventh grade. From then to his high school graduation, for nearly seven years, Mr. Mattingly offered Adam additional instructions to help him reach a sufficient level of academic proficiency for college.

Mr. Mattingly's continuous effort changed Adam's life and fate. Through Mr. Mattingly's mentoring, Adam attended college and found his own way of walking out of poverty. According to Adam, many of his classmates or peers had dropped out of school and entered the workplace. Some abused or sold drugs, and some had already been put in prison. For them, failures at school were taken as normal, but successes at school were seen as a rare phenomenon, out of their anticipation. Adam's parents wanted him to be successful at school, but they did not know how to help him with his school work. It was Mr. Mattingly who gave Adam help and support, which was beyond his parents' reach. It was Mr. Mattingly's intervention that provided Adam with an alternative to a normalized life trajectory and made college attendance a reality for him.

## A Critical Reflection

Mr. Mattingly's intervention is only an outworking of the potentialities of implementing conscientization in a daily classroom. Adam did not mention whether Mr. Mattingly knew Freire's theory of conscientization. If those who are not happy with Adam's case and think it is out of date and fails to cope with the complexity in a contemporary classroom, particularly in these developed countries, they could refer to Darder's (2002) *Reinventing Paulo Freire: A Pedagogy of Love* for more insights. However, Mr. Mattingly's intervention is chosen because it can provide a much fuller picture of how conscientization is carried out in concrete pedagogical practice. In other words, it is instructive for the application of conscientization in real educational settings in various ways.

In the first place, education begins with teachers meeting with students. Teachers cannot avoid meeting students. In this process of meeting, a teacher comes across different kinds of students. Some are physically strong, while some are physically weak; some are economically rich, while some are economically poor; some are politically privileged, while some are politically unprivileged; some are intellectually clever, while some are intellectually limited. These relative and dialectical concepts and realities always exist, so the phenomenon of teachers meeting with those students who are in a disadvantaged position is inevitable. However, the stories of meeting different students cannot be reduced to one plot. This is because these meetings cannot be anticipated beforehand and may often vary from one situation to another. Even for the same student, life is different for her or him every day. Accordingly, the care that each student demands in a real educational setting is uneven. This makes the pedagogical ethics of care a practice of caring attunement. Conscientization calls for teachers to give attention and care to the weak and the disadvantaged during their meetings with students. It orients toward the needy. This essence is well displayed in Mr. Mattingly's meeting with Adam. Mr. Mattingly does not take the school's misdiagnosis of Adam's learning ability for granted but pays sensitive and conscientious attention to Adam's realities and goes to help him readily.

A practice of conscientization starts with reading the word together with reading the world. Knowledge learning is forever an organic part of human experience. As Adam narrates, Mr. Mattingly does not cut off his knowledge learning at school from his previous experience. Rather, he has built an effective bridge between the knowledge he gained from his family background and the knowledge required by the school's curriculum. Owing to this bridge, Adam not only feels connected and has a departure point from which to start his learning but also feels hopeful and has a solid foundation to envisage his future world. Therefore, making connections between what has been learned at school and what has been happening in the real world of students generates real learning and knowledge production.

Conscientization stresses a good rapport between teachers and students, which facilitates real teaching and learning. Mr. Mattingly has an empathetic understanding of the deepest realities of Adam's life situation so he is able to respond to them lovingly and sensitively. This response results in a new relationship between Mr. Mattingly, a teacher, and Adam, an ignored and excluded student. According to Adam, this relationship stimulates and inspires him to explore and discover a new world ahead of him, which is not defined and limited by poverty. From this relationship, Adam finds another kind of fatherly love that can compensate for the love he wanted from his father but his father was unable to give. Although Mr. Mattingly's fatherly love can never fully replace the love Adam needs from his own father, it has transformed Adam's schooling into a happy and successful part of his life experience.

Students' critical consciousness and conscience can only be authenticated by the authenticity of teachers' critical consciousness and conscience. The best way for teachers to cultivate these characteristics is to use what they do, feel, and think to show students what critical consciousness and conscience really are. In other words, teachers' ability to read students' realities and to react to them sensitively, lovingly, and responsibly, and above all, teachers' power and capacity to love and to learn, have a leavening transformative effect upon students. As Adam said, from Mr. Mattingly's fatherly love, he learned how to love another human being in a caring and respectful way. Hence, students' critical consciousness and conscience are often awakened, nurtured, and developed in their teachers' critical consciousness and conscience embodied in their work and dialogue with students.

Teachers are always the main agent and practitioners of conscientization in an educational arena. This is because teachers are on the front line. They have an intimate knowledge of not only the inner workings of the educational system and the subject knowledge they are going to teach but also the students they are going to meet. It is teachers who decide what content to teach and what method to choose. Hence, teachers are masters of culture-in-making. They shape the whole learning atmosphere, either teaching in class or mentoring after class. They bring students educational possibilities as well as hope for a better life. Moreover, in social spheres such as schools, conscientious teachers with moral integrity often exercise power as a positive force to create a different new culture of resistance. At present, unprivileged children are excluded by the dominant system that dictates what is "normal." Good teachers can help these unprivileged children break away from this situation. Hence, without teachers, anything educational will become an empty shell. It is teachers who make conscientization possible, not the other way around. Taking into account the complexity and specificity of discrimination and oppression in this postmodern age, the career of being a teacher is more demanding than it used to be. A teacher is supposed to become a caregiver in various ways, such as an intellectual mentor, a learning facilitator, a school activity organizer, a social worker, a cultural worker, a psychologist, and a healer.

Conscientization, as Freire portrays it, rejects constructing a clear-cut model or method for all teachers to follow. Nobody can offer an exact example of practicing conscientization for other teachers to follow. This is because any established model might destroy the uniqueness of particular pedagogical situations and thus limit the possibilities for a teacher to know, to learn, to act, and to create. Therefore, conscientization encourages teachers to become their own model creators out of their own realities shaped by their own sociocultural discourses. In the same way, the application of conscientization must be always set in the discourse of praxis. Multifarious realities are always beyond theories as landscapes lie beyond their maps. Through praxis, the practitioners of conscientization make close connections between theories and different specific situations. Thereby, human beings are able to approach and understand the deepest realities of human life experience in society. In the final analysis, praxis changes the world by giving people "self-determination," "cultural aspirations," "mediation of socio-economic impediments," and "a collective vision" (Smith, 1999, p. 38). Accordingly, the energetic life, illuminating power, and inexhaustible source of thousands of possibilities for exercising conscientization only express themselves in concrete pedagogical praxis.

Conscientization has originally been located by Freire in the humanizing vocation of history making through revolutionary social change and cultural creation with strong political will and sociological imagination. This is because, if the system of cultural reproduction of social classes cannot be changed, the life situation of students with family backgrounds like Adam's can never be changed. Adam could have been another victim of the system if Mr. Mattingly had walked away from him, as other teachers did. Hence, the political nature of education can never be downplayed. Mr. Mattingly's intervention indeed represents a number of key elements of conscientization. However, in order to ensure that conscientization proceeds down the track of Freire's critical pedagogy, a bigger social picture should be considered. That is, if Mr. Mattingly's intervention is carried out on a social and collective scale, every teacher can become alert to any form of discrimination and exclusion and act responsibly to support and help those who are weak, poor, disabled, and disadvantaged. Otherwise, Adam's success only serves as a foil to enhance the school successes of the middle-class elites.

If conscientization is applied to educational practice, all these principles of the cultivation of critical consciousness and the cultivation of conscience boils down to one fundamental principle: the pedagogy of love. The pedagogy of love must be embodied in a teacher's desiring and looking for the good of students. Sometimes, it is hard to keep a critical and attentive eye on realities and discover something such as a wrong diagnosis of Adam's educational ability. However, it was even harder to give Adam continuous extra help after school for nearly seven years. This intervention shows how important a teacher's commitment and determination can be when something good can be done for a disadvantaged student such as Adam who was living in poverty. Without a profound pedagogical love, this is impossible. As Adam noted in citing bell hooks (1994) at the end of his article, "to teach in a manner that respects and cares for the souls of our students is essential if we are to provide the necessary conditions where learning can most deeply and intimately begin" (bell hooks in Howard, 2005, p. 81). In truth, nothing cares and respects for "the souls of our students" and makes "conditions where learning can most deeply and intimately begin" except love. Only love transforms teachers' conscientious attention, sensitive care, and sincere respect for their students into responsible actions, heartfelt support, and practical assistance. This ultimately helps students change the concrete realities of their lives and thus builds them a pathway to a good, happy, and meaningful life.

# Conclusion

The internal logic of the topic of this book, cultivation of conscience and conscientization, is that the love and dialogue nexus performs a transcendent role in transforming people from the dark cave of self-indulgence into the moral sphere. This is the sphere in which the work of conscience will uphold social and cultural criticism against oppressive elements within a given political and economic system. In particular, love of the good and life and dialogue—meeting the other face-to-face, eye-to-eye, in the I–Thou relation through one's conscience of welcoming the other—make conscientization and any other genuine educational act possible, not vice versa.

Love and dialogue might seem fragile in the face of dehumanization such as armed injustice. However, this should not lead to an exaggeration of brutal force such as military weapons, falsely conceived as greatness in a tradition of totality, and end up with idolatry of the political power of the state apparatus. This is because any users of cannons and tanks are human beings. It is crucial to realize that love and dialogue not only create a spiritual home for human existence but also hold the greatest transforming and constructive power for building a humanizing community.

It must be noted that the well-being of love and dialogue might be affected by three regressive trends in contemporary sociocultural discourse. One is that the erosion of traditional forms of justification of morality brings about the worship of the self, nihilism, and spiritual exhaustion. Another trend is that a new form of domestication is sponsored by the hegemonic ideology of market ethics. Idolatry of money and its by-product—political corruption—make alienation deteriorate. The third trend is that the production of cultural objects is manipulated by consumerism. This, in turn, leads to the mass media—such as television stations, filmmakers, and Internet service providers—trying to please contemporary audiences in a mediocre and artificial way. Serious in-depth truth seeking and original minds become anathema to the mainstream culture. Shallowness and meanness in feeling and understanding tend to paralyze our noble impulses and magnanimous sentiments. In many people's minds, there are only legal laws but no moral laws. An ensuing lack of political and social responsibility from a decline in moral courage results in a corresponding lethargy in the pursuit of justice.

Nonetheless, this does not mean the current situation is eternally hopeless and incurable. It only calls for a greater moral responsibility to build a new and invigorating culture to overcome domestication and alienation. As a Chinese proverb says, "the tendency of human nature to good is like the tendency of water to flow downwards." Ontologically, the human soul is longing for something beautiful, bright, sublime, noble, benevolent, pure, and thought provoking. Conscientization, a revolutionary and empowering educational intervention, will offer *a* way but not *the* only way of such a cultural work to open our minds and hearts. It encourages the development of the ability to love and fosters engagement in praxical dialogue with other human beings.

To conclude, the ultimate aim of conscientization must forever be humanization—a historical vision of the ongoing emancipation of human energy and the development of human power and potential. To become more is our ontological need and the audacity of human hopefulness. The meaning, dignity, and worthiness of being in and with the world as human beings are all inscribed in endless cycles of transformative praxis generated by a loving, critical, and creative spirit.

# References

Alschuler, A. (1976). Foreword. In W. Smith, *The meaning of conscientization: The goal of Paulo Freire's pedagogy* (pp. v–viii). Amherst, MA: Centre for International Education.
Andreotti, V. (2009, July). Cognitive adaptation versus epistemological pluralism in discussions around the shifting conceptualizations of knowledge and learning in the 21st century. Paper presented at the research seminar at College of Education, University of Canterbury, New Zealand.
Apple, M. W., Gandin, L. A., & Hypolito, A. M. (2001). Paulo Freire. In J. Palmer (Ed.), *Fifty modern thinkers on education* (pp. 128–133). New York, NY: Routledge.
Arendt, H. (1972). *Crises of the republic*. New York, NY: Harcourt Brace Jovanovich.
Arendt, H. (1978). *The life of the mind*. New York, NY: Harcourt Brace Jovanovich.
Aristotle. (1933–1935). *The metaphysics* (H. Tredennick, Trans.). London, UK: Heinemann; Cambridge, MA: Harvard University Press.
Aristotle. (1976). *Ethics* (J. Barnes, Trans.). New York, NY: Penguin Books.
Aristotle. (1981). *The politics* (T. A. Sinclair, Trans.). New York, NY: Penguin Books.
Arnold, M. (1994). *Culture and anarchy*. New Haven, CT: Yale University Press.
Aronowitz, S. (1993). Paulo Freire's radical democratic humanism. In P. McLaren & P. Leonard (Eds.), *Paulo Freire: A critical encounter* (pp. 8–24). London, UK: Routledge.
Ashton-Warner, S. (1963). *Teacher*. London, UK: Secker & Warburg.
Balibar, E. (1995). *The philosophy of Marx*. New York, NY: Verso.
Bao Lord, B. (1990). *Legacies: A Chinese mosaic*. New York, NY: Alfred A. Knopf.
Bentham, J. (1996). *An introduction to the principles of morals and legislation*. Oxford, UK: Clarendon Press.

Berger, P. (1976). *Pyramids of sacrifice: Political ethics and social change.* London, UK: Allen Lane.
Blackburn, S. (2001). *Being good: A short introduction to ethics.* Oxford, UK: Oxford University Press.
Bloom, A. (1979). Introduction. In J. J. Rousseau, *Emile* (pp. 3–28). New York, NY: Basic Books.
Bohm, D. (1985). *Unfolding meaning.* London, UK: Routledge.
Bohm, D. (1994). *Thought as a system.* London, UK: Routledge.
Bohm, D. (2004). *On creativity.* New York, NY: Routledge Classics.
Bourdieu, P. (1984). *Distinction: A social critique of the judgment of taste* (R. Nice, Trans.) Cambridge, MA: Harvard University Press.
Bourdieu, P. (1990). *An introduction to the work of Pierre Bourdieu: The practice of theory* (R. Harker, C. Mahar, & C. Wilkes, Eds.). New York, NY: St. Martin's Press.
Bourdieu, P., & Wacquant, L. J. D. (1992). *An invitation to reflexive sociology.* Chicago, IL: University of Chicago Press.
Bowers, C. A. (1983). Linguistic roots of cultural invasion in Paulo Freire's pedagogy. *Teachers College Record, 84*(4), 935–953.
Bowers, C. A. (1986). Review of Freire, P. *The politics of education: Culture, power, and liberation. Educational Studies, 17*(1), 147–154.
Bowers, C. A., & Apffel-Marglin, F. (Eds.). (2005). *Re-thinking Freire: Globalization and the environmental crisis.* Mahwah, NJ: Lawrence Erlbaum.
Brizuela, B. M., & Soler-Gallart, M. (1998). Cultural action for freedom: Editors' introduction. *Harvard Educational Review, 68*(4), 471–475.
Bruner, J. (1990). *Acts of meaning.* Cambridge, MA: Harvard University Press.
Buber, M. (1959). *I and thou.* Edinburgh, Scotland: Clark.
Buber, M. (2002). *Between man and man* (R. Gregor-Smith, Trans.). New York, NY: Routledge Classics.
Butler, J. (1898). *The works of Joseph Butler* (W. E. Gladstone, Ed.). Oxford, UK: Clarendon Press.
Camus, A. (2006). *The fall* (R. Buss, Trans). London, UK: Penguin Books.
Carr, E. H. (1931). *Dostoevsky (1821–1881): A new biography.* London, UK: G. Allen & Unwin.
Cicero, M. T. (1991). *On duties* (M. T. Griffin & E. M. Atkins, Eds.). New York, NY: Cambridge University Press.
Clothier, H. M. N. (2000). *WHAKAPUTA KORERO "TELLING STORIES" Maori women, education and the mainstream* (Unpublished doctoral dissertation). Canterbury University, Christchurch, New Zealand.
Coleridge, S. T. (1906). *The friend: A series of essays to aid in the formation of fixed principles in politics, morals and religion, with literary amusements interspersed.* London, UK: G. Bell.
Coleridge, S. T. (1969). *The collected work of Samuel Taylor Coleridge* (B. E. Rooke, Ed.). Princeton, NJ: Princeton University Press.
Conrad, J. (1995). *Heart of darkness.* New York, NY: Broadview Press.
Cowling, M. (1994). One-and-a-half cheers for Arnold. In M. Arnold (Ed.), *Culture and anarchy* (pp. 202–212). New Haven, CT: Yale University Press.

Cunliffe, C. (1992). *Joseph Butler's moral and religious thought: Tercentenary essays.* Oxford, UK: Clarendon Press.
Damasio, A. R. (1994). *Descartes' error: Emotion, reason, and the human brain.* New York, NY: G. P. Putnam's Sons.
Darder, A. (2002). *Reinventing Paulo Freire: A pedagogy of love.* Boulder, CO: Westview Press.
Darwin, C. (1871). *The descent of man.* London, UK: John Murray.
Davies, C. G. (1990). *Conscience as consciousness: The idea of self awareness in French philosophical writing from Descartes to Diderot.* Oxford, UK: The Voltaire Foundation.
De Mello, A. (1990). *Awareness: The perils and opportunities of reality.* New York, NY: Image Books.
Descartes, R. (1995). *The philosophical works of Descartes* (E. S. Haldane et al., Trans.). New York, NY: Dover.
Descartes, R. (1996). *Meditations on first philosophy* (J. Cottingham, Trans. & Ed.). Cambridge, UK: Cambridge University Press.
Despland, M. (1987). Conscience. In M. Eliade (Ed.), *The encyclopaedia of religion* (pp. 45–52). New York, NY: Macmillan.
Dewey, J. (1916). *Democracy and education.* New York, NY: Macmillan.
Dostoevsky, F. (1866). *Crime and punishment: A Russian realistic novel.* London, UK: Vizetelly.
Elias, J. L. (1994). *Paulo Freire: Pedagogy of liberation.* Malabar, FL: Krieger.
Ellsworth, E. (1989). Why doesn't this feel empowering? Working through the repressive myths of critical pedagogy. *Harvard Educational Review, 59*(3), 297–324.
Engelberg, E. (1972). *The unknown distance: From consciousness to conscience, Goethe to Camus.* Cambridge, MA: Harvard University Press.
Feng, Y. L. (1960). *A short history of Chinese philosophy* (D. Bodde, Ed.). New York, NY: Macmillan.
Feuerbach, L. (1957). *The essence of Christianity* (G. Eliot, Trans.). New York, NY: Harper.
Flinders, D. J. (2001). Nel Noddings. In J. A. Palmer (Ed.), *Fifty modern thinkers on education, from Piaget to the present* (pp. 210–215). London, UK: Routledge.
Foucault, M. (1980). *Power/Knowledge: Selected interviews and other writings* (C. Gordon, Trans.). Brighton, Sussex, UK: Harvester Press.
Foucault, M. (1982). The subject and power. *Critical Inquiry, 8*(4), 777–795. Retrieved from http://links.jstor.org/sici?sici=00931896%28198222%298%3A4%3C777%3ATSAP%3E2.0.CO%3B2-S
Foucault, M. (2000). The ethics of care for self as a practice of freedom. In P. Rabinow (Ed.), *Ethics, essential works of Foucault 1954–1984*, Vol. 1 (R. Hurley & others Trans.; pp. 281–301). London, UK: Penguin Books.
Foucault, M. (2002). *The order of things.* New York, NY: Routledge Classics.
Frase, P., & O'Sullivan, B. (2005, April 18). The future of education under the WTO. Retrieved from http://www.campusdemocracy.org/wtoed.html [or on October 22, 2013 from http://www.corporations.org/campusdemocracy/wtoedu.html, 180-Movement for Democracy and Education.]

Freedman, R. (1979). *Hermann Hesse, pilgrim of crisis*. London, UK: Jonathan Cape.
Freire, P. (1970b). Cultural action and conscientization. *Harvard Educational Review, 40*(3), 452–477.
Freire, P. (1970a). Cultural action for freedom. *Harvard Educational Review, 40*(2), 205–225.
Freire, P. (1972b). *Cultural action for freedom*. Harmondsworth, Middlesex, UK: Penguin Education.
Freire, P. (1972a). *Pedagogy of the oppressed* (M. B. Ramos, Trans.). Harmondsworth, Middlesex, UK: Penguin Education.
Freire, P. (1973). *Education for critical consciousness*. New York, NY: Seabury Press.
Freire, P. (1976). *Education, the practice of freedom*. London, UK: Writers and Readers Publishing Cooperative.
Freire, P. (1978). *Pedagogy in Process: The Letters to Guinea-Bissau*. New York, NY: Continuum.
Freire, P. (1985). *The politics of education* (D. Macedo, Trans.). London, UK: Macmillan.
Freire, P. (1993a). Foreword. In P. McLaren & P. Leonard (Eds.), *Paulo Freire: A critical encounter* (pp. ix–xii). New York, NY: Routledge.
Freire, P. (1993b). *Pedagogy of the city* (D. Macedo, Trans.). New York, NY: Continuum.
Freire, P. (1994a). *Education for critical consciousness*. New York, NY: Continuum.
Freire, P. (1994b). *Pedagogy of hope* (R. R. Barr, Trans.). New York, NY: Continuum.
Freire, P. (1996). *Letters to Cristina* (D. Macedo, Q. Macedo, & A. Oliveira, Trans.). New York, NY: Routledge.
Freire, P. (1997). *Pedagogy of the heart* (D. Macedo & A. Oliveira, Trans). New York, NY: Continuum.
Freire, P. (1998a). *Pedagogy of freedom* (P. Clark, Trans.). Lanham, MD: Rowman & Littlefield.
Freire, P. (1998b). *Teachers as cultural workers: Letters to those who dare teach* (D. Macedo, D. Koike, & A. Oliveira, Trans.). Boulder, CO: Westview Press.
Freire, P. (1998c). *Politics and education* (P. L. Wong, Trans). Los Angeles, CA: UCLA Latin American Centre Publications.
Freire, P. (1998d). Cultural action for freedom. *Harvard Educational Review, 68*(4), 476-522.
Freire, P. (2004). *Pedagogy of indignation*. Boulder, CO: Paradigm Publishers.
Freire, P. (2007). *Daring to dream: Toward pedagogy of the unfinished* (A. K. Oliveira, Trans.). Boulder, CO: Paradigm Publishers.
Freire, P. (2012, February 8). Liberation theology and Marx [Video file]. Retrieved from http://www.youtube.com/watch?v=1Wz5y2V1af0
Freire, P., & Macedo, D. (1987). *Literacy: Reading the word and the world*. South Hadley, MA: Bergin & Garvey.
Freire, P., & Shor, I. (1987). *A pedagogy for liberation*. London, UK: Macmillan.
Friedman, M. (2002). Introduction. In M. Buber (Ed.), *Between man and man* (pp. xi–xx). New York, NY: Routledge Classics.
Fromm, E. (1957). *The art of loving*. London, UK: Unwin Books.
Fromm, E. (1964). *The heart of man: Its genius for good & evil*. New York, NY: Harper & Row.
Giroux, H. A. (1985). Introduction. In P. Freire (Ed.), *The politics of education* (pp. xi–xxv). London, UK: Macmillan.

Giroux, H. (1992). *Border crossings: Cultural workers and the politics of education*. New York, NY: Routledge.
Goethe, J. W. (1989). *The sorrows of young Werther* (M. Hulse, Trans.). New York, NY: Penguin Books.
Goonetilleke, D. C. R. A. (1995). Introduction. In J. Conrad (Ed.), *Heart of darkness* (pp. 9–47). New York, NY: Broadview Press.
Glass, R. D. (2001). On Paulo Freire's philosophy of praxis and the foundations of liberation education. *Educational Researcher, 30*(2), 15–25.
Gramsci, A. (1971). *Selections from the prison notebooks*. London, UK: Lawrence & Wishart.
Hamilton, C. (2008). *The freedom paradox: Towards a post-secular ethics*. Crows Nest, New South Wales, Australia: Allen & Unwin.
Harris, K. (1979). *Education and knowledge*. London, UK: Routledge & Kegan Paul.
Hayek, F. A. (2001). *The road to serfdom*. New York, NY: Routledge Classics.
Hegel, G. W. F. (1971). *The phenomenology of mind* (J. B. Baillie, Trans.). London, UK: Allen & Unwin.
Hegel, G. W. F. (1974). *Hegel's lectures on the history of philosophy* (E. S. Haldane & Frances H. Simson, Trans.). New York, NY: Humanities Press.
Heidegger, M. (1968). *What is called thinking?* (W. H. Denken, Trans.). New York, NY: Harper & Row.
Heidegger, M. (1996). *Being and time* (J. Stambaugh, Trans.). New York, NY: State University of New York.
Hesse, H. (2008). *Siddhartha* (H. Rosner, Trans.). London, UK: Penguin Books.
Higgins, K. M. (1987). *Nietzsche's Zarathustra*. Philadelphia, PA: Temple University Press.
Hill, D. (2001). More free or less constrained? Freire and Foucault on the problem of human submissiveness. *New Zealand Journal of Educational Studies, 37*(1), 15–26.
Hobbes, T. (1996). *Leviathan* (J. C. A. Gaskin, Ed.). Oxford, UK: Oxford University Press.
Hooks, B. (1994). *Teaching to transgress: Education as the practice of freedom*. New York, NY: Routledge.
Horton, M., & Freire, P. (1990). *We make the road by walking: Conversations on education and social change* (B. Bell, J. Gaventa, & J. Peters, Eds.). Philadelphia, PA: Temple University Press.
Howard, A. (2005). Lessons of poverty: Towards a literacy of survival. *Journal of Curriculum Theorizing, 21*(4), 73–82.
Hume, D. (1992). *Treatise of human nature*. New York, NY: Prometheus Books.
Hurka, T. (2011). *The best things in life*. Oxford, UK: Oxford University Press.
Jackson, S. (2007). Freire re-viewed. *Educational Theory, 57*(2), 199–213.
Kant, I. (1873). *Kant's critique of practical reason and other works on theory of ethics* (T. K. Abbott, Trans.). New York, NY: Longmans, Green & Company.
Kant, I. (1956). *Critique of practical reason* (L. W. Beck, Trans.). New York, NY: The Bobbs-Merrill Company.
Kant, I. (1963). The groundwork of the metaphysics of morals. In H. J. Paton (Ed.), *The moral law: Kant's groundwork of the metaphysic of morals, a new translation with analysis and notes*. London, UK: Hutchinson University Library.

Kant, I. (1991). *The metaphysics of morals* (M. Gregor, Trans.). New York, NY: Cambridge University Press.

Kant, I. (1998) *Critique of pure reason* (P. Guyer & A. W. Wood, Trans). New York, NY: Cambridge University Press.

Kaye, K. (1982). *The mental and social life of babies.* Chicago, IL: The University of Chicago Press.

Kierkegaard, S. (1954). *Fear and trembling and the sickness unto death* (W. Lowrie, Trans.). New York, NY: Doubleday Anchor.

Kierkegaard, S. (2009). *Works of love* (H. Hong & E. Hong, Trans.). New York, NY: Harper Perennial Modern Thought.

Kurath, H., & Kuhn, S. M. (Eds.). (1952–2001). *Middle English dictionary.* Ann Arbor, MI: University of Michigan Press.

Lackey, M. (1999). Killing God, liberating the 'subject': Nietzsche and post-God freedom. *Journal of the History of Ideas, 60*(4), 737–754.

Langston, D. (2006). Medieval theories of conscience. In Edward N. Zalta (Ed.), *Stanford encyclopedia of philosophy.* Retrieved from http://plato.stanford.edu/entries/conscience-medieval

Lankshear, C. (1993). Functional literacy from a Freirean point of view. In P. McLaren & P. Leonard (Eds.), *Paulo Freire: A critical encounter* (pp. 90–118). New York, NY: Routledge.

Levinas, E. (1969). *Totality and infinity* (A. Lingis, Trans.). Pittsburgh, PA: Duquesne University Press.

Lipman, S. (1994). Why should we read *Culture and Anarchy.* In M. Arnold (Ed.), *Culture and anarchy* (pp. 213–227). New Haven, CT: Yale University Press.

Locke, J. (1959). *An essay concerning human understanding.* New York, NY: Dover.

Locke, J. (1996). *An essay concerning human understanding* (K. P. Winkler, Ed.). Indianapolis, IN: Hackett Publishing.

Locke, J. (1997). *An essay concerning human understanding* (R. Woolhouse, Ed.). New York, NY: Penguin Books.

Lu, Xun. (1972). *The true story of Ah Q* (Hsien-yi & Gladys Yang, Trans.). Peking, China: Foreign Languages Press.

Lyotard, J. F. (1984). *The postmodern condition: A report on knowledge* (G. Bennington & B. Massumi, Trans.). Minneapolis, MN: University of Minnesota Press.

Lyotard, J. F. (1988). *The differend: Phrases in dispute* (G. V. D. Abbeele, Trans.). Minneapolis, MN: University of Minnesota Press.

Lyotard, J. F. (1994). *Lessons on the analytic of the sublime: Kant's critique of judgment, [sections] 23–29* (E. Rottenberg, Trans.). Stanford, CA: Stanford University Press.

Mackie, R. (Ed.). (1981). *Literacy and revolution: The pedagogy of Paulo Freire.* New York, NY: Continuum.

Mao, Tse-tung. (2009, October 16). The foolish old man who removed the mountains. Retrieved from http://www.marxists.org/reference/archive/mao/selected-works/volume-3/mswv3_26.htm

Marshall, J. (1997). The new vocationalism. In M. Olssen & K. M. Matthews (Eds.), *Education policy in New Zealand: The 1990s and beyond* (pp. 304–326). Palmerston North, New Zealand: Dunmore Press.

Marshall, J. D. (1996). *Michel Foucault: Personal autonomy and education.* London, UK: Kluwer Academic.

Martyn, J. R. C. (Ed.). (1972). *Cicero and Virgil: Studies in honour of Harold Hunt.* Amsterdam, the Netherlands: Hakkert.

Marx, K. (1964). *The economic and philosophical manuscripts of 1844.* New York, NY: International Publishers.

Marx, K. (1973). *Marx's Grundrisse* (D. McLellan, Ed. & Trans.). St Albans, Herts, UK: Paladin.

Marx, K. (1976). *Capital: A critique of political economy* (B. Fowkes, Trans.) Harmondsworth, Middlesex, UK: Penguin Books, in association with New Left Review.

Marx, K. (1977). *Selected writings* (D. McLellan, Ed.). Oxford, UK: Oxford University Press.

Marx, K., & Engels, F. (1972). *The German ideology* (C. J. Arthur, Ed.). New York, NY: International Publishers.

Mason, M. (2007). Critical thinking and learning. *Educational Philosophy and Theory, 39*(4), 339–349.

May, L. (1983). On conscience. *American Philosophical Quarterly, 20*(1), 57–67.

Mayo, P. (1997). Tribute to Paulo Freire (1921–1997). *International Journal of Lifelong Education, 16*(5), 365–370.

Mayo, P. (1999). *Gramsci, Freire & adult education.* New York, NY: Zed Books.

McLaren, P. (2000a). *Che Guevara, Paulo Freire, and the pedagogy of revolution.* Boulder, CO: Rowman & Littlefield.

McLaren, P. (2000b). Paulo Freire's pedagogy of possibility. In Stanley F. Steiner, H. Mark Krank, Peter McLaren, & Robert E. Bahruth (Eds.), *Freirean pedagogy, praxis and possibilities* (pp. 1–22). New York, NY: Falmer Press.

McLaren, P., & Leonard P. (Eds.). (1993). *Paulo Freire: A critical encounter.* New York, NY: Routledge.

Mencius. (2003). *Mencius* (D. C. Lau, Trans.). New York, NY: Penguin Books.

Mill, J. S. (1998). *Utilitarianism.* Oxford, UK: Oxford University Press.

Montaigne, M. (1958). *Essays* (J. M. Cohen, Trans.). New York, NY: Penguin Books.

Murdoch, I. (2001). *The sovereignty of food.* New York, NY: Routledge Classics.

Murphy, J. (2004). Postmodernism and space. In S. Connor (Ed.), *The Cambridge companion to postmodernism* (pp. 116–135). Cambridge, UK: Cambridge University Press.

Nelson, B. (1981). *On the roads to modernity.* Boulder, CO: Rowman & Littlefield.

Nietzsche, F. (1966). *Beyond good & evil* (W. Kaufmann, Trans.). New York, NY: Random House.

Nietzsche, F. (1968). *On the genealogy of morals* (W. Kaufmann & R. J. Hollingdale, Trans.). New York, NY: Vintage Books.

Nietzsche, F. (1999). *The birth of tragedy and other writings* (R. Speirs, Trans). New York, NY: Cambridge University Press.

Nietzsche, F. (2000). *Basic writings of Nietzsche* (W. Kaufmann, Trans.). New York, NY: The Modern Library.

Ollman, B. (1971). *Alienation: Marx's conception of man in capitalist society*. Cambridge, UK: Cambridge University Press.

Osborne, P. (2005). *How to read Marx*. London, UK: Granta Books.

Paton, H. J. (Trans. & Ed.). (1963). *The moral law: Kant's groundwork of the metaphysic of morals*. London, UK: Hutchinson University Library.

Peters, M. A. (2007). Kinds of thinking, styles of reasoning. *Educational Philosophy and Theory, 39*(4), 350–363.

Peters, M. A., & Ghiraldelli, P. Jr. (Eds.). (1999). Neoliberalism. In *The Encyclopedia of Philosophy of Education*. Retrieved from http://www.ffst.hr/ENCYCLOPAEDIA /doku.php?id/

Peters, R. S. (1966). *Ethics and education*. London, UK: Allen & Unwin.

Plato. (1955). *The republic* (D. Lee, Trans.). New York, NY: Penguin Books.

Plato. (1993a). *Phaedo* (C. J. Rowe, Ed.). New York, NY: Cambridge University Press.

Plato. (1993b). *The republic* (R. Waterfield, Trans.). Oxford, UK: Oxford University Press.

Potts, T. C. (1980). *Conscience in medieval philosophy*. Cambridge, UK: Cambridge University Press.

Roberts, P. (1996). Rethinking conscientization. *Journal of Philosophy of Education, 30*(2), 179–196.

Roberts, P. (2000). *Education, literacy and humanization: Exploring the work of Paulo Freire*. Westport, CT: Bergin & Garvey.

Roberts, P. (2005). Pedagogy, politics and intellectual life: Freire in the age of the market. *Policy Futures in Education, 3*(4), 446–458.

Roberts, P. (2007). Conscientization in Castalia: A Freirean reading of Hermann Hesse's *The glass bead game*. *Studies in Philosophy and Education, 26,* 509–523.

Roberts, P. (2010). *Paulo Freire in the 21st century*. Boulder, CO: Paradigm Publishers.

Rossatto, Cesar A. (2005). *Engaging Paulo Freire's pedagogy of possibility: From blind to transformative optimism*. Lanham, MD: Rowman & Littlefield.

Rousseau, J. J. (1911). *Emile* (B. Foxley, Trans.). London, UK: Dent.

Rousseau, J. J. (1979). *Emile: Or, on education* (A. Bloom, Trans.). New York, NY: Basic Books.

Safranski, R. (1990). *Schopenhauer and the wild years of philosophy* (E. Osers, Trans.). Cambridge, MA: Harvard University Press.

Sartre, J. (1994). *Being and nothingness* (H. E. Barnes, Trans.). New York, NY: Gramercy Books.

Saussure, F. de (1966). *Course in general linguistics* (W. Baskin, Trans.). New York, NY: McGraw-Hill.

Schopenhauer, A. (1966). *The world as will and presentation, vol. 1* (E. F. J. Payne, Trans.). New York, NY: Dover.

Schopenhauer, A. (2009). *The two fundamental problems of ethics* (C. Janaway, Trans.). New York, NY: Cambridge University Press.

Schopenhauer, A. (2010). *The two fundamental problems of ethics* (D. E. Cartwright & E. E. Erdmann, Trans.). Oxford, UK: Oxford University Press.

Sen, A. K. (1987). *On ethics and economics*. New York, NY: Blackwell.

Shor, I. (1993). Education is politics. In P. McLaren & P. Leonard (Eds.), *Paulo Freire: A critical encounter* (pp. 25–35). New York, NY: Routledge.

Simpson, J. A., & Weiner, E. S. C. (Eds.). (1989). *Oxford English dictionary* (2nd ed.). Oxford, UK: Clarendon Press.

Singer, P. (Ed.). (1994). *Ethics.* Oxford, UK: Oxford University Press.

Singer, P. (2010). *Marx.* New York, NY: Sterling.

Smith, G. H. (1999). Paulo Freire: Lessons in transformative praxis. In P. Roberts (Ed.), *Paulo Freire, politics and pedagogy* (pp. 35–41). Palmerston North, New Zealand: Dunmore Press.

Smith, W. (1976). *The meaning of conscientization: The goal of Paulo Freire's pedagogy.* Amherst, MA: Centre for International Education.

Taylor, C. (1989). *Sources of the self: The making of the modern identity.* New York, NY: Cambridge University Press.

Taylor, P. V. (1993). *The texts of Paulo Freire.* Maindenhead, UK: Open University Press.

The Ma Jia-jue Incident. (2009, October, 16). (My own translation based on the Chinese version). Retrieved from http://baike.baidu.com/view/4136.htm

Tolstoy, L. (1993). *War and peace* (L. Maude & A. Maude, Trans.). Kent, UK: Wordsworth Classics.

Torres, C. A. (1994). Education and archaeology of consciousness: Freire and Hegel. *Educational Theory, 44*(4), 429–445.

Torres, C. A. (1998a). Introduction: The political-pedagogy of Paulo Freire. In P. Freire (Ed.), *Politics and education* (pp. 1–21). Los Angeles, CA: UCLA Latin American Centre Publications.

Torres, C. A. (Ed.). (1998b). *Education, power, and personal biography.* New York, NY: Routledge.

Vygotsky, L. S. (1962). *Thought and language* (E. Hanfmann & G. Vakar, Eds. & Trans.). Cambridge, MA: The MIT Press.

Vygotsky, L. S. (1978). *Mind in society* (M. Cole, V. John-Steiner, S. Scribner, & E. Souberman, Eds.). Cambridge, MA: Harvard University Press.

Walker, J. (1980). The end of dialogue: Paulo Freire on politics and education. In R. Mackie (Ed.), *Literacy and revolution: The pedagogy of Paulo Freire* (pp. 120–150). London, UK: Pluto Press.

Weil, S. (2002a). *The need for roots* (A. Wills, Trans.). New York, NY: Routledge Classics.

Weil, S. (2002b). *Gravity and grace* (E. Crawford & M. von der Ruhr, Trans.). New York, NY: Routledge Classics.

Weiler, K. (1991). Paulo Freire and a feminist pedagogy of difference. *Harvard Educational Review, 61*(4), 449–474.

West, C. (1993). Preface. In P. McLaren & P. Leonard (Eds.), *Paulo Freire: A critical encounter* (pp. xiii–xiv). New York, NY: Routledge.

Westrheim, K. (2009). *Education in a political context: A study of knowledge processes and learning sites in the PKK.* Allkopi, Bergen, Norway: University of Bergen.

Wild, J. (1969). Introduction. In E. Levinas (Ed.), *Totality and infinity* (pp. 11–20). Pittsburgh, PA: Duquesne University Press.

Wilkinson, R., & Pickett, K. (2009). *The spirit level: Why equality is better for everyone.* London, UK: Penguin Books.

Wogaman, J. P. (1994). *Christian ethics: A historical introduction.* Louisville, KY: Westminster/John Knox Press.

Wordsworth, W. (1970). *The prelude: The 1805 text.* Oxford, UK: Oxford University Press.

Yang, B. J. (1960). *Mengzi Yi Zhu* [Mencius, translation and annotation]. Beijing, China: Zhonghua Book Company.

Yang, B. J. (1980). *Lun Yu Yi Zhu* [Confucius's analects, translation, and annotation]. Beijing, China: Zhonghua Book Company.

Zhu, Xi. (1983). *Si Shu Zhang Ju Ji Zhu* (Notes on the chapters and sentences of The Four Great Books, the editorial department of Zhonghua Book Company, Ed.). Beijing, China: Zhonghua Book Company.

Zimbardo, P. (2007). *The Lucifer effect: Understanding how good people turn evil.* New York, NY: Random House.

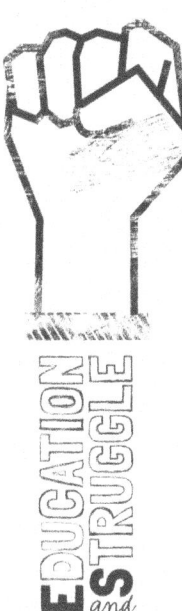

**Narrative, Dialogue and the Political Production of Meaning**

Michael A. Peters
Peter McLaren
Series Editors

To submit a manuscript or proposal for editorial consideration, please contact:

Dr. Peter McLaren
UCLA Los Angeles
School of Education &
Information Studies
Moore Hall 3022C
Los Angeles, CA 90095

Dr. Michael Peters
University of Waikato
P.O. Box 3105
Faculty of Education
Hamilton 3240
New Zealand

WE ARE THE STORIES WE TELL. The book series Education and Struggle focuses on conflict as a discursive process where people struggle for legitimacy and the narrative process becomes a political struggle for meaning. But this series will also include the voices of authors and activists who are involved in conflicts over material necessities in their communities, schools, places of worship, and public squares as part of an ongoing search for dignity, self-determination, and autonomy. This series focuses on conflict and struggle within the realm of educational politics based around a series of interrelated themes: indigenous struggles; Western-Islamic conflicts; globalization and the clash of worldviews; neo-liberalism as the war within; colonization and neocolonization; the coloniality of power and decolonial pedagogy; war and conflict; and the struggle for liberation. It publishes narrative accounts of specific struggles as well as theorizing "conflict narratives" and the political production of meaning in educational studies. During this time of global conflict and the crisis of capitalism, Education and Struggle promises to be on the cutting edge of social, cultural, educational, and political transformation.

Central to the series is the idea that language is a process of social, cultural, and class conflict. The aim is to focus on key semiotic, literary, and political concepts as a basis for a philosophy of language and culture where the underlying materialist philosophy of language and culture serves as the basis for the larger project that we might call dialogism (after Bakhtin's usage). As the late V.N. Volosinov suggests "Without signs there is no ideology," "Everything ideological possesses semiotic value," and "individual consciousness is a socio-ideological fact." It is a small step to claim, therefore, "consciousness itself can arise and become a viable fact only in the material embodiment of signs." This series is a vehicle for materialist semiotics in the narrative and dialogue of education and struggle.

---

To order other books in this series, please contact our Customer Service Department:

    (800) 770-LANG (within the U.S.)
    (212) 647-7706 (outside the U.S.)
    (212) 647-7707 FAX

Or browse online by series:

    www.peterlang.com

www.ingramcontent.com/pod-product-compliance
Ingram Content Group UK Ltd.
Pitfield, Milton Keynes, MK11 3LW, UK
UKHW022239230426
12048UKWH00018BA/1352